T0190105

.P Flexible Real Estate Management: Guide for Implementing and Optimizing SAP Flexible Real Estate Management Solution

ayant Daithankar
A-303 Walia Apartment, Goregaon East, Mumbai
India

ISBN-13 (pbk): 978-1-4842-1483-1   ISBN-13 (electronic): 978-1-4842-1482-4
DOI 10.1007/978-1-4842-1482-4

Library of Congress Control Number: 2016951309

Managing Director: Welmoed Spahr
Lead Editor: Celestin Suresh John
Technical Reviewer: Siddharth Khandelwal
Editorial Board: Steve Anglin, Pramila Balan, Laura Berendson, Aaron Black, Louise Corrigan, Jonathan Gennick, Robert Hutchinson, Celestin Suresh John, Nikhil Karkal, James Markham, Susan McDermott, Matthew Moodie, Natalie Pao, Gwenan Spearing
Coordinating Editor: Prachi Mehta
Copy Editor: April Rondeau
Compositor: SPi Global
Indexer: SPi Global
Artist: SPi Global

Distributed to the book trade worldwide by Springer Science+Business Media New York, 233 Spring Street, 6th Floor, New York, NY 10013. Phone 1-800-SPRINGER, fax (201) 348-4505, e-mail orders-ny@springer-sbm.com, or visit www.springeronline.com. Apress Media, LLC is a California LLC and the sole member (owner) is Springer Science + Business Media Finance Inc (SSBM Finance Inc). SSBM Finance Inc is a Delaware corporation.

For information on translations, please e-mail rights@apress.com, or visit www.apress.com.

Apress and friends of ED books may be purchased in bulk for academic, corporate, or promotional use. eBook versions and licenses are also available for most titles. For more information, reference our Special Bulk Sales–eBook Licensing web page at www.apress.com/bulk-sales.

Any source code or other supplementary materials referenced by the author in this text are available to readers at www.apress.com. For detailed information about how to locate your book's source code, go to www.apress.com/source-code/. Readers can also access source code at SpringerLink in the Supplementary Material section for each chapter.

Printed on acid-free paper

SAP Flexible Real Estate Management

Guide for Implementing and Optimizing SAP Flexible Real Estate Management Solution

Jayant Daithankar

Apress®

I dedicate this book to Krishnan Ramanujam,
who is an inspiration to me and many of us,
and to all my wonderful colleagues in SAP Practice for the support they provided.

Contents at a Glance

Contents

About the Author

Jayant Daithankar has more than 26 years of industry and SAP experience with multiple implementations, upgrades, and consultancy engagements for global clients. He is a certified SAP consultant for finance and controlling with strong domain experience in the financial arena; he has multiple professional qualifications at his credit. He has senior-level industry experience in finance, business process re-engineering (BPR), and in the delivery of BPR in large ERP projects. Experiences include domestic and international business development, system integration, change management, strategic planning, RFPs, proof-of-concept management, governance process and system analysis, and application design of SAP processes for customer-specific requirements. He had done multiple implementations of SAP REFX for Fortune 500 oil companies, international airports, and retail companies. He is currently working as SAP Centre of Excellence head for business applications in global IT major.

About the Technical Reviewer

Siddharth Khandelwal is an experienced SAP REFX/FICO consultant from India. Siddharth holds an honors degree in electrical engineering from Rajasthan Technical University, Kota.

He is currently working with Infosys-Pune as a senior associate consultant. Prior to Infosys, he served IBM as an application consultant for the SAP REFX module. Siddharth is also an active contributor in SCN (SAP Community Network) and in the leaderboard of the SAP REFX thread.

You can follow Siddharth on SCN (http://scn.sap.com/people/siddharth_khandelwal) or find out more about him through his LinkedIn profile (in.linkedin.com/in/sidk13)

About the Technical Reviewer

Acknowledgments

I would like to express my gratitude to the many people who provided support and guided me throughout my journey.

I would like to thank Mr. U. Sundararajan (Ex C&MD of BPCL) and Mr. S.K. Joshi (Ex Director Finance of BPCL) for providing me with an opportunity in the amazing world of SAP–my journey continues today.

I would like to thank Shreekant Shiralkar for motivating and guiding me in writing my first SAP book.

I would like to thank Apress for enabling me to publish this book. Thanks to Laura, Prachi, and Suresh of Apress, and Siddhartha and Punit–without you, this book would not have been possible.

Above all I want to thank my wife, and son, who supported and encouraged me in spite of all the time it took me away from them.

Last, but not least, I thank the entire SAP ecosystem, of which I am proud to be a part.

Introduction

To succeed in today's global and highly competitive economy, asset optimization in real estate management has become a strategic task. Organizations need to ensure full visibility into their property portfolio, make informed decisions, improve portfolio performance, and reduce compliance costs. Increased global competition has elevated the need for sophisticated solutions for handling changing consumer demands, global workforce management, information management, compliance adherence, leasing management, and property management more effectively. SAP Flexible Real Estate Management (SAP REFX) is a full-featured and integrated solution enabling the effective management of real estate and greater insight into one's real estate portfolio. The application addresses all phases of the real estate life cycle, including real estate acquisition or disposal, portfolio management, and property and technical management.

This book provides insights intended to make the SAP REFX journey more relevant and fruitful. Furthermore, it can help decision makers, such as chief intelligence officers (CIOs) and chief experience officers (CXOs), with the important tasks of creating a business case for management approval and designing a roadmap for the organization. It also provides a comprehensive understanding of what SAP REFX is and is useful for ensuring the preparedness of teams involved in REFX implementation and rollouts. The book explains end-to-end real estate configurations, functional system landscapes, implementation challenges, and post go-live precautions important for optimizing one's investment in SAP REFX.

This book is structured as follows:

Overview of the Real Estate Industry: Evolution and Trends

Master Data Objects

Real Estate Contracts

Accounting

Business Integration

Service Charge Settlement

Sales-Based Contracts

Industry Best Practices

Transformation Impact of SAP REFX Implementation

Step-by-Step Guide for Configuring and Implementing SAP REFX

CHAPTER 1

Overview of the Real Estate Industry: Evolution and Trends

This chapter will provide an overview of the real estate business, its information technology (IT) challenges, and the need for a strong and integrated business solution. The chapter will further provide details on why a real estate business needs a comprehensive IT solution, and on the benefits of implementing Real Estate Flexible Management (REFX). The chapter is divided into the following topics:

- Overview and evolution of the real estate industry

- Need for IT solutions

- Challenges with existing available solutions

- Need for an integrated Enterprise Resource Planning (ERP) solution

Overview and Evolution of the Real Estate Industry

Real estate is defined as "property consisting of land and the buildings on it, along with its natural resources such as crops, minerals, or water." The business of real estate includes the buying, selling, or renting of land or buildings.

The real estate sector assumed greater prominence with the liberalization of the global economy, and the increase in business opportunities and labor migration led to a greater need for commercial and housing space. Demand for real estate is driven by population growth, employment opportunities, income levels, interest rates, and access to capital. The real estate landscape is changing because of urbanization, demographic changes, sustainability, technological changes, and the changed financial system. These changes have major implications for the real estate industry, increasing the size of the real estate asset base via huge investments. The profitability of individual companies depends on property values and demand, which are both impacted by general economic conditions.

The real estate industry has been instrumental in the overall growth of core infrastructure in last few years, and the trend shows a continuance of development globally in all geographies. The conventionally residential housing sector was first to grow, but now development in retail, hospitality, and commercial sectors is occurring at a much faster speed. The growth in the hospitality and retail sector (hotels, resorts, shopping malls, and so on) is also the result of the growing middle class, the changing habits of society, and rapid urbanization. Governments worldwide are focusing more on the development of tourism, resulting in more investment in the construction of hotels, malls, multiplexes, and so forth. Cross-country travel to obtain cheaper medical services has grown medical tourism and has resulted in the construction of hospitals and medical centers. Educational institutions are established to attract students from global markets. The information technology boom and outsourcing to provide low-cost services resulted in a huge investment in call centers.

© Jayant Daithankar 2016
J. Daithankar, *SAP Flexible Real Estate Management*, DOI 10.1007/978-1-4842-1482-4_1

The real estate sector in developing countries is at a crucial juncture of its evolution. A significantly large portion of the industry is still influenced by unorganized retail players, but there has been a consistent rise in the share of organized players, with the number of companies growing in recent years. The global spread of many industries and the foreign direct investment in the real estate sector have contributed to a fast transformation of this sector over the past decade. Dynamic entrepreneurs have moved out from their traditional cities to major cities across the globe to expand business and capture global markets. This has resulted in a huge demand for real estate and the exponential growth of the sector.

Over the past few years, the real estate industry's strong growth has resulted in an increased demand for real estate consulting and advisory services. This includes brokerage services to enable the leasing of property, research, analysis and valuation support for real estate investors and developers, and relocation services. Real estate companies may provide expertise in either residential or commercial properties. However, many of them deal in both to expand their business sphere.

Real estate is riding on massive growth, and more and more players are entering into the market to reap the benefits. With this boom, a lot of real estate solution providers are emerging into the market. CIOs of real estate companies are on the hunt for the right technology solution, which can increase productivity, reduce costs, and enhance efficiency. The success of today's real estate organization depends on accurate information that provides deep visibility into past and future performance so as to improve decision making. Without accurate data, there is a strong risk of experiencing a reduction in operating income and return.

Need for an IT Solution

The main requirements of any real estate solution would be as follows:

Management of Real Estate

The key objective of any real estate player would be to manage the real estate efficiently and in a cost-effective and optimal way. The real estate solution should help in achieving this objective. A complete view of master data–from location and size to value and usage–has to be provided so as to manage and maintain it. The SAP REFX solution provides a dual view of master data (both architectural view and usage view) to enable the management of all types of real estate objects, like a business entity, land, building, or rental object; i.e., pooled space, rental space, or rental unit. The assignment of various real estate objects to REFX master data is simple in nature.

Contract Management

The management of contracts with different stakeholders is an essential activity from a legal and statutory perspective. Real estate players deal with different vendors from whom they take a property on lease, and various customers to whom property is leased out. An IT solution should enable the effective management of these contracts to ensure legal, accounting, and statutory requirements are met. SAP REFX covers multiple business scenarios where contracts such as lease-in, lease-out, security deposit, vendor/customer contract, or GL contract are required, and such contracts can be configured in the system easily.

Space Management

Space management forms a key part of any real estate business. The real estate player should have complete details of architectural hierarchies and structures, usage considerations, and technical facilities before planning to rent out property. The IT solution must have the capability to capture and provide these details. SAP REFX provide options to capture the complete details of the property, which ensures the optimum utilization of the space.

Lease-in/Lease-out

The lease-in/lease-out process is one of the key processes in any real estate business. When a real estate player takes land on rent from a landlord for a specific period of time, the process it is called a lease-in. The lease-out process is when the real estate player rents out the space to their customer. The lease-in process enables a cash payment to the landlord and the accounting of expenses to the appropriate account, whereas the lease-out process lets you deal with cash flow from a tenant and the posting of income. The solution should be able to support both of these processes.

Reporting

Another requirement of any real estate player is that of reporting. The reporting needs to be in categories such as operational, accounting, legal, and statutory reporting, including occupancy report, valuation report, report related to tax, days outstanding report, and so on. The solution should be able to cater to all such reporting requirements. For example, it should be able to generate an occupancy report that provides details of properties that are vacant as well as the vacancy duration so as to find reasons for the vacancy and take corrective action to avoid notional loss. SAP REFX caters to multiple business requirements by providing an exhaustive reporting system.

Challenges with Existing Solutions

The real estate industry may be bifurcated into different sectors, like commercial, residential, retail, and hospitality. Each of these business types has different business models, requirements, and challenges. A solution provider must understand the business dynamics and critical business requirements of each type of business. Real estate solution implementation is not merely a technical initiative driven by the information technology department, but rather is a complete transformation initiative to be owned and driven by the entire organization.

As major real estate players are aggressive in tapping the market, most of them handle several projects across the city and nation. Hence, it is impossible for them to keep track of the properties purchased and sold and the management or development of on-going projects in all locations. Today, IT has transformed the way property business is done, and technology has provided tools to keep a check on all of their needs. Real estate solution providers have helped them to enhance the whole process through their innovative solutions. Also, there are several other solution providers that assist the real estate sector with their end-to-end support products. Such software helps their clients to automate business workflows, building strong and everlasting relationships with existing and prospective customers.

However, a major concern for real estate players is the sustainability of IT systems, which are expected to meet business demands over a reasonable period of time. The challenge of higher IT infrastructure spends amid decreased budgets hampers enterprises from effectively responding to an evolving IT infrastructure. Currently, real estate companies rely on various internal IT systems and product vendors to create new offerings and successfully run the business. This leads to maintenance overheads and an increased dependency on third-party products.

Need for an Integrated ERP Solution

Currently, solutions are available in the market that address multiple requirements of the real estate industry, like accounts receivable, billing and invoicing, planning, reporting, expense management, and Customer Relationship Management (CRM). But a single integrated solution addressing all the requirements of the industry is a must. There is a need for scalable ERP solutions with functionality designed to solve real estate industry–specific business challenges, with solutions tailored to every real estate market and

3

meeting the complex requirements for retail (shopping malls and strip malls), franchises, commercial, and real estate investment trusts. Existing SAP modules like Financial (FI), Project Systems (PS), and Sales and Distribution (SD) are able to take care of real estate requirements, but they are not able to specifically meet the needs of real estate businesses. SAP Asset Accounting captures details of assets owned by a company but does not specifically focus on real estate assets; i.e., land and buildings. Businesses require detailed master data regarding land and buildings, with details like quality of land, value, architectural details, and measurements, which are provided in minute detail by SAP REFX. Containing not only the appropriate master data, but also contract processing, accruals/deferrals, rent adjustment, sales based settlement, and so forth, the SAP REFX module is the perfect solution for the real estate industry. Real estate assets constitute a major component of the asset value of an organization and need to be monitored effectively. SAP REFX provides this with strong integration with the financial module.

Summary

This chapter provided an overview of the real estate sector, its evolution, and the key requirements that any IT solution needs to provide to manage a real estate business effectively. We also discussed the challenges with current IT solutions and the need for an integrated ERP solution to meet the expectations of a growing real estate business. Also, we saw how SAP REFX meets these requirements and is the suggested solution for any real estate business.

CHAPTER 2

■ ■ ■

Master Data Objects

This chapter will elaborate upon master data concepts and the different real estate views available in the Flexible Real Estate Management module. In this chapter, we will discuss the following:

- Architectural view

- Usage view

- Business entity

- Land/Building

- Rental object

- Business partners and their roles

The Flexible Real Estate Management (REFX) module is robust in managing real estate properties for activities and processes like leasing, property maintenance, and so on. The main master data in SAP REFX are business entity, property, buildings, and rental units, which are controlling objects and are called *RE-Objects*.

In order to understand the master data concepts, let us consider the following business scenario.

Vistala Reality Limited, a renowned real estate builder in Mumbai, India, has taken a plot of land on lease for 25 years from Puna Multinational Retail. Vistala Reality Limited has constructed a shopping mall on that plot of land. The shopping mall, Vistala Shopping Mall, consists of three floors and an open parking lot. The entire first floor is let out to a multinational retail store. The second floor is divided into multiple shops, which are let out to different stores and a bank ATM. It also consists of a lobby, which is commonplace. The third floor has a common lobby, a multiplex, a cafeteria, and a bank ATM. As shown in Figure 2-1, the mall is constructed on a piece of land, and some part of the land is converted into parking spaces.

© Jayant Daithankar 2016
J. Daithankar, *SAP Flexible Real Estate Management*, DOI 10.1007/978-1-4842-1482-4_2

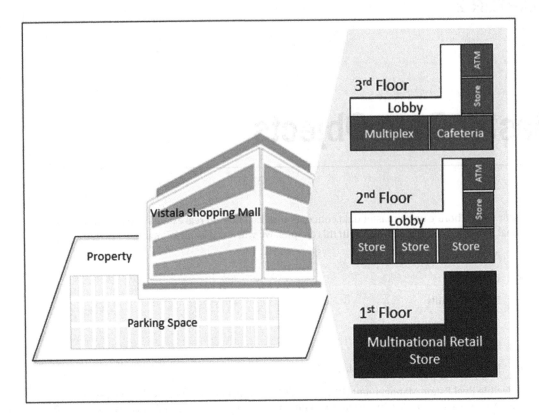

Figure 2-1. *Concept of master data in SAP REFX using example*

■ **Note**   The preceding example will be used throughout the book to explain different concepts.

The master data in SAP REFX, in which users can process real estate objects, is divided into two views:

- Architectural view
- Usage view

Architectural View

T-Code: REBDAO

Architectural views represent the overall architecture that is meaningful and can be represented from a variety of viewpoints, all of which can be combined to create a holistic view of the system. The architectural view represents the actual architectural framework of a real estate object, taking into account all of the chronological changes relevant to its usage. This is an informative view that is used to integrate with external designing software like Computer Aided Design (CAD) and also defines the space measurements, which then flow to the usage view.

It is not mandatory to maintain the architectural view, but it has to be defined before you can create the usage view. We can implement the architectural view in the following situations:

- Detailed information about the architectural structure of the real estate object is required to be maintained in the system.

- The usage of the objects changes frequently. In this case, the architectural view remains constant and new usage objects are created as needed. In our scenario, the second floor of Vistala Mall has four shops that have been leased out to four different stores. In the future, the Vistala Mall management may combine two shops and lease it as one. In this case, the architectural object would not change but the number of shops that could be leased out would be three instead of four.

- Graphical systems such as CAD are required to be mapped to the real estate system.

The architectural view is a technical view of your real estate. Using SAP REFX customizing, the following master data can be defined for the architectural view:

- Locality

- Land

- Building

- Floor

- Part of building

- Space (such as parking space, storage space, office space, and so on)

- Area

Referring to our scenario, the different master data that constitute the architectural object are locality, building, property, floor, area, and space. Figure 2-2 depicts the architectural objects related to our scenario.

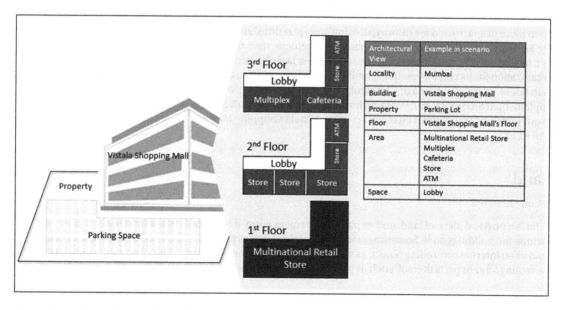

Figure 2-2. *Master data in the architectual view*

Usage View

This is the accounting view in which the actual postings will happen in SAP. The usage view forms the basis for all object-related information used to represent real estate objects in the system. The following master data can be created for the usage view:

- Business entity
- Property
- Building
- Rental object
- Pooled space
- Rental space
- Rental unit

Now that you have a high-level understanding of the master data elements of the usage view, let us review them in more detail.

Business Entity

T-Code REBDBE

The highest element in the hierarchy of the usage view is the business entity. The business entity is usually made up of a group of buildings and properties sharing the same utilities and subject to the same tax regulations. The business entity is assigned uniquely to one company code and is the starting point for creating the usage view structure. It can contain any number of buildings and properties, which are unique within the business.

Let us take an international airport as an example, which consists of multiple buildings and areas, like terminal buildings, commercial buildings with duty free shops, parking spaces, control tower, fuel depot, open piece of space used for runway, di-icing area, pre-threshold area, and so on. If we are implementing the SAP REFX solution for rental and space management, then the international airport will be defined as a business entity. Let's look at another example–a large housing complex that was constructed by an organization for its employees. It has multiple buildings, roads, a community center, swimming pool, and club house. In order to manage allotment, maintenance, and capacity utilization, the organization has implemented SAP REFX, and the large housing complex will be defined as a business entity. Coming back to our previously mentioned business scenario, Vistala Shopping Mall will be defined as a business entity in SAP REFX.

Land

T-Code REBDPR

Land is a physical piece of land, and as part of a business entity it refers only to the land itself; it does not include the buildings on it. Sometimes land is also referred to as property. The system automatically creates land as an internal controlling object, as they are account assignment object. This object forms the basis for renting land or parts thereof, such as parking spaces or storage spaces. SAP REFX land master data is detailed and intensive. It provides various screens to capture data related to general data/building law and usage/economic balance/values/posting parameters, quality of the land, land values, and municipality and topographical location, as well as data on building and usage rights. These fields are used for capturing land details only. In our scenario, the parking area will be defined as land/property.

Building

T-Code REBDBU

A building is part of a business entity. The system automatically creates a building as an internal controlling object, as they are account assignment objects. Buildings, or their parts, are the basis for renting spatial units, such as apartments, warehouses, and stores. SAP REFX building master data is detailed and intensive. It provides various screens to capture general data/additional data/fixtures and fittings characteristics/posting parameters, and so on. We categorize the building according to its type and condition; describe its fixtures and fittings, characteristics, and area usage; and enter important dates (such as construction year, start and end of construction, date of modernization, etc.). You can also assign a building to a profit center or a business area.

Rental Objects

T-code (REBDRO)

Rental objects comprise three objects:

- Rental unit: A rental unit is created when one unit is to be leased out in totality and is treated as one complete piece. In our scenario, the entire first floor of Vistala Shopping Mall is leased out to a multinational retail store and hence we will define it as a rental unit.

- Pooled space: This is the total space available from which we can take rental spaces for lease-out. We can have a proper regulation in the space that can be leased out as pooled space and will allow the exact rental spaces to be rented out. In our scenario, the pooled space will be defined to represent the complete floor area.

- Rental space: A space extracted from a pooled space for lease-out. In our scenario, the second and third floors of Vistala Shopping Mall are divided into multiple smaller spaces and rented out to multiple stores, a bank for an ATM, a multiplex, and a cafeteria. We will define rental spaces to represent the multiple smaller spaces. For example, we have pooled space (PS1) of 1000 square feet, out of which one rental space (RS1) of 400 square feet is extracted. Now the system will only allow the creation of rental spaces that will have an area of 600 square feet total.

The data elements of the usage view applicable in our scenario are business entity, building, property, pooled space, rental space, and rental unit. The same is depicted in Figure 2-3.

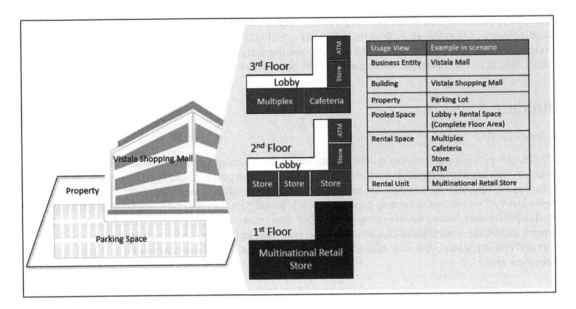

Figure 2-3. *Master data in usage view*

The master data in SAP REFX is defined in a hierarchical manner. Each object at the lower level is linked to a corresponding object at a higher level. The hierarchy is maintained as shown in Figure 2-4.

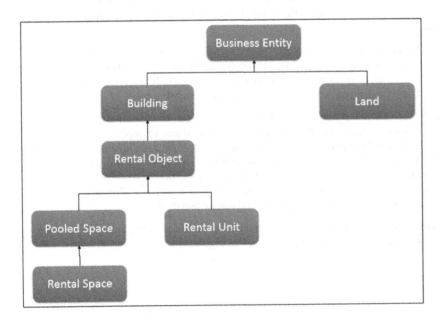

Figure 2-4. *Master data hierarchy maintained in SAP REFX*

The differences between the architecture view and the usage view are shown in Figure 2-5.

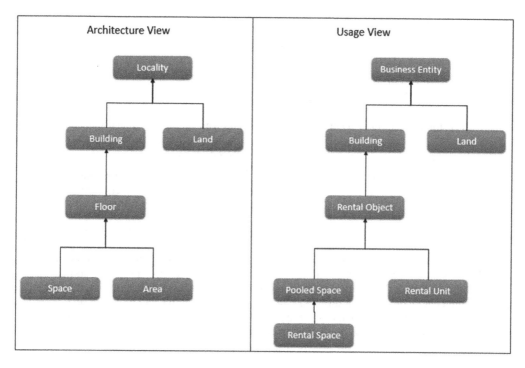

Figure 2-5. *Master data hierarchy maintained in SAP REFX*

Business Partners and Their Roles

A business partner in SAP REFX is a person or an organization with whom a business interest exists. Vital data such as name, addresses, bank details, and data related to persons, organizations, or groups is maintained as part of business partner data. Different real estate management processes require different business partner data.

The business partner can assume multiple business partner roles depending on the business process involved, such as lease-in, lease-out, or real estate services. You do not need to create the general data–which is independent of a business partner's function or of application-specific extensions–again in each case for each business partner. This prevents data from being created and stored redundantly. Each business partner role also brings additional application-specific attributes to the business partner. In effect, a role is a certain view of the business partner that is dependent on the business context.

The functions of the business partner are defined in financial transactions via business partner roles, such as counterparty, issuer, payment bank, or depository bank. The rights and obligations of the business partner are defined at the time of assigning the role category.

In SAP REFX, all customers or vendors must be defined as a business partner (T-Code: BP) in order to generate FI postings. We can also create a business partner from existing customers or vendors by using T-Codes FLBPD1 and FLBPC1 respectively. Also, the linkage of an existing customer or vendor to a business partner can be done via T-Codes FLBPD2 and FLBPC2 respectively. We can also automate the creation of a customer or vendor when the business partner is created.

SAP Financial Accounting has accounts receivable (AR) and accounts payable (AP) subledgers to manage accounting data for all customers and vendors, by using customer/vendor master records. Customer and vendor integration with the business partner is required for SAP REFX to use Financial Accounting (FI). For example, say you have business partner XYZ, who is also a customer. In SAP REFX, for XYZ the business partner number is 8781 and the customer master number is 2456. Now, in order to ensure the sanity of data and one single source of truth, the business partner and customer master records of XYZ need to be integrated so that any data change made in one master record is reflected in another.

There are multiple business roles available in SAP REFX, but we will consider two main roles–those of vendor and customer–to support the lease-in and lease-out processes. Table 2-1 explains these two main business partner roles.

Table 2-1. *Two Main Business Partner Roles*

Technical Name	Business Meaning
Master tenant with customer account (TR0600)	A standard tenant who concludes a real estate contract. The tenant's customer account is used to handle the rent receivables and credit memos.
Landlord with vendor account (TR0602)	Landlord of an object (leased-in by the company code). The landlord is assigned to a contract. The rent to be paid is handled on the vendor account assigned to the landlord.

Let us try to understand business partners using our business scenario. Vistala Reality Limited has taken a plot of land on lease for 25 years from Puna Multinational Retail, to whom monthly rent is paid. Landlord with vendor account is the business partner role that is taking care of this business relationship. Vistala Reality Limited has let out different shops, such as stores, ATM, cafeteria, and multiplex, to different customers for monthly rent. They are all tenants of the mall owner, and thus their role is that of a master tenant with customer account. Figure 2-6 showcases these two main business partner roles.

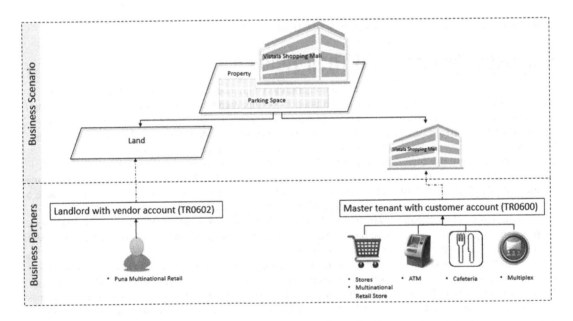

Figure 2-6. *Two main business partner roles*

Summary

In this chapter, we explained the two real estate views available in SAP REFX–architectural view and usage view–with a business case as an example. We also discussed various master data elements like business entity, land, building, and rental objects. These elements are used to create a real estate structure and to control and monitor real estate assets effectively. Lastly, we also explained the concept of business partners and two main roles that can be used for capturing vendor and customer transactions for lease-in and lease-out processes.

Summary

CHAPTER 3

■ ■ ■

Real Estate Contracts

This chapter will explain different types of real estate contracts carried out as well as contract management. In this chapter, we will discuss the following:

- Lease-in contracts

- Lease-out contracts

- Terms and security deposit agreements

- Critical dates with reason

- Condition amounts

- Steps in contract management

A real estate contract is a contract between two parties, the lessor and the lessee. The lessor is the legal owner of the asset who provides the lessee the right to use the asset for consideration, which is a rental payment. A formal document called an *agreement* contains details like property, term, rental amount, and also detailed terms and conditions. SAP REFX has provisions to capture these details. It also updates accounting data once periodic postings are carried out.

Some of the key aspects related to contracts are mentioned next.

Lease-in Contracts

A lease-in contract would be created in cases where we are renting land or building premises from a third party. Take the example of a gasoline company with large gasoline stations across country. Each station is constructed on land that is taken on lease from a local landlord. This is a lease-in contract for the gasoline company. In SAP REFX, this contract is supported by the general contract, which enables accounts payable postings to be made on the lease-in contract.

Lease-out Contracts

Lease-out contracts can be of residential or commercial properties. This is determined based on the usage type of the assigned rental unit. Lease-outs may be segregated according to company-specific criteria using freely defined contract types like garage agreements or residential or commercial agreements.

The gasoline company uses the land taken on lease for a gasoline station and lets out the balance of the area to different tenants for a fast food restaurant, bank ATM, tire shop, and so forth, which are all lease-out contracts. In SAP REFX, this contract type is supported by the general contract, which enables accounts receivable postings to be made on the lease-out contracts.

© Jayant Daithankar 2016
J. Daithankar, *SAP Flexible Real Estate Management*, DOI 10.1007/978-1-4842-1482-4_3

Terms and Security Deposit Agreements

All real estate contracts need terms information, such as the start and end dates of the contract, duration, termination notice rules, renewal option rules if applicable, and so on. In SAP REFX, rental objects are assigned to lease-out or lease-in contracts, and those that are not assigned to any contract type are considered as being vacant and available for rent. SAP REFX also provides information on contracts that are expiring and will serve notices until they are renewed.

The security deposit contracts are those where the tenant pays a deposit, which is refundable after the end of the contractual duration. The security deposit can be due on various dates and be subject to adjustment when conditions are changed, like an increase in rent. Besides contractually fixed security deposits, the agreed upon security deposit can also be calculated based on the contract conditions.

Critical Dates with Reason

Critical dates are those dates that are important from a contractual and statutory perspective. SAP REFX contracts provide the functionality to capture critical dates of the contract, like start date, end date, and notice period, and can provide alerts to ensure timely action. The contract term stipulates start and end dates, which ensures that overlapping rental periods are not created for the rental object. You can specify critical dates on each contract, and the system will provide you with a periodic critical-dates report for your entire real estate (RE) portfolio. Automatic reminders can be set in the system to ensure no critical contract date goes unnoticed and that timely actions are initiated. You can manually enter critical dates, renewal option dates, and notices, and the system will automatically generate reminders based on these dates.

Condition Amounts

The condition amounts are rents to be charged for use of property and are freely definable in an SAP REFX contract. This means that the basic rent, service charges, advance payments, flat rates, and surcharges can be structured as required and assigned time-dependently to the lease-outs. Condition amounts are derived from condition types and are mapped to a condition group and then assigned to a contract type. Let us take the example of "Basic rent," which is created as condition type and mapped to condition group "Customer contract," which in turn is assigned to contract type "customer contract-commercial."

When the lease-out is created, the conditions in the rental unit are proposed and can be modified as required. You can also determine time-dependent rent reductions for each condition of a lease-out. This is also available for lease-in contracts.

Steps in Contract Management

Let us see how to create a commercial lease-out contract for a department store that is let on monthly fixed charges. We have captured key tabs from the SAP REFX contract-creation process.

In order to post receivables to the customer account in case any space has been leased out to alliance partners, a commercial lease-out contract needs to be created in SAP REFX.

The creation of a contract in SAP REFX should only be done after the agreement has been signed between the organization and the alliance partner and all necessary approvals have been obtained by the respective role holders.

Before the contract can be created, necessary master data objects should have been created in the system, such as the business entity, pooled space, and rental space. The business partner entry also needs to be created for the customer with whom the alliance has been made.

To define a process contract in SAP Easy Access, choose Accounting ➤ Flexible Real Estate Management ➤ Contract ➤ Process Contract, or use transaction code RECN (Figure 3-1).

The procedure is as follows:

1. Start the transaction using the menu path or transaction code as just described.

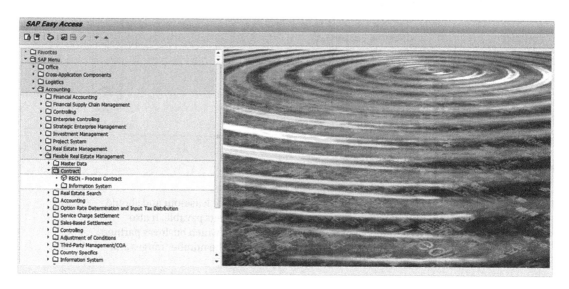

Figure 3-1. *SAP Easy Access*

2. Click 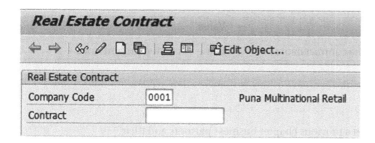 .

    With this, the contract creation starts and the user is presented with the screen seen in Figure 3-2.

Real Estate Contract

Real Estate Contract		
Company Code	0001	Puna Multinational Retail
Contract		

Figure 3-2. *Real Estate Contract window*

3. Click ▢.

    The user is presented with a screen that provides different contract types, as shown in Figure 3-3. There are multiple options for lease-in and lease-out contracts. For our example, we select the "Commercial lease-out" contract option.

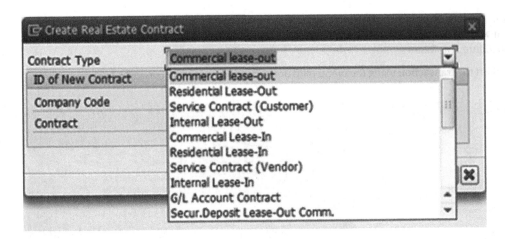

Figure 3-3. *Create Real Estate Contract window*

The contract type specifies whether contract is lease-in or lease-out and should integrate the contract with accounts receivable or accounts payable. It also specifies if it is a commercial or residential contract and which business partners, such as tenants or landlords, are allowed on the lease. The number ranges and display screens are defined at the contract-type level.

4. Click ✅.

We get to a screen with multiple tabs, and it is required that details are entered in relevant tabs wherever applicable.

As required, enter the data in the General Data with Fast Entry tab, as mentioned in Table 3-1 and shown in Figure 3-4.

Table 3-1. *General Data with Fast Entry Tab*

Field Name	Description	Value
Contract name	Description of the contract name	Lease out of department store

5. Click Partners.

We have already discussed in a previous chapter business partners and their roles, and now we will see how they are assigned in a contract (Figure 3-5).

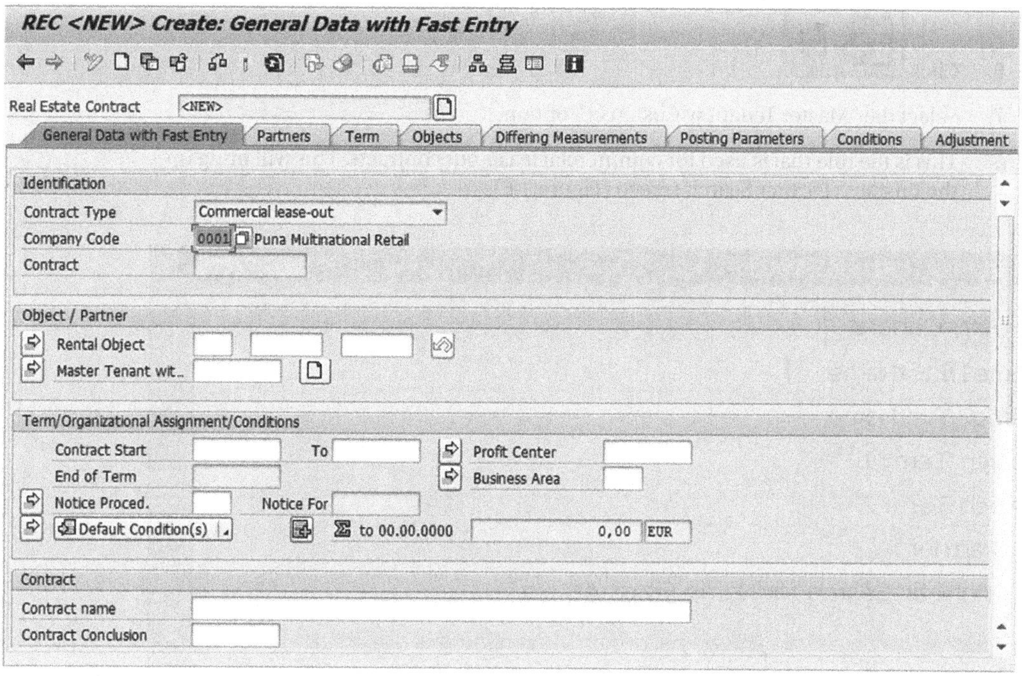

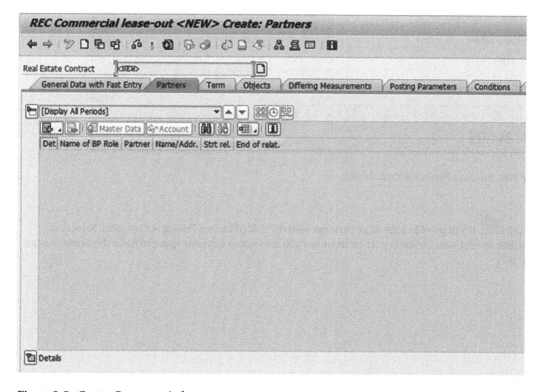

Figure 3-4. *Create: General Data with Fast Entry window*

Figure 3-5. *Create: Partners window*

6. Click .

7. Select the "Master Tenant w.Cust.Acct." option.

    This is the role that is used for commercial lease-out contracts. This will bring up the Business Partner Search screen (Figure 3-6).

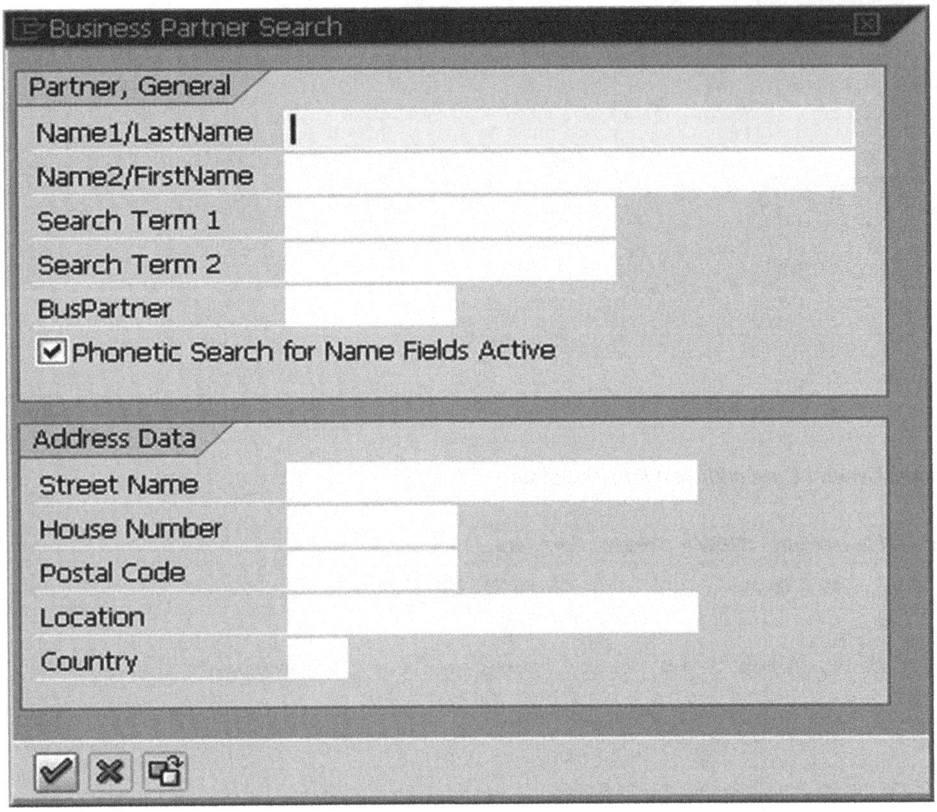

Business Partner Search

Partner, General

Name1/LastName	
Name2/FirstName	
Search Term 1	
Search Term 2	
BusPartner	

☑ Phonetic Search for Name Fields Active

Address Data

Street Name	
House Number	
Postal Code	
Location	
Country	

Figure 3-6. Business Partner Search screen

Click ✔. It will provide a list of all partners with the role of Master Tenant w.Cust.Acct. Select the appropriate one for your business partner to whom you are leasing out your space to run a department store (Figure 3-7).

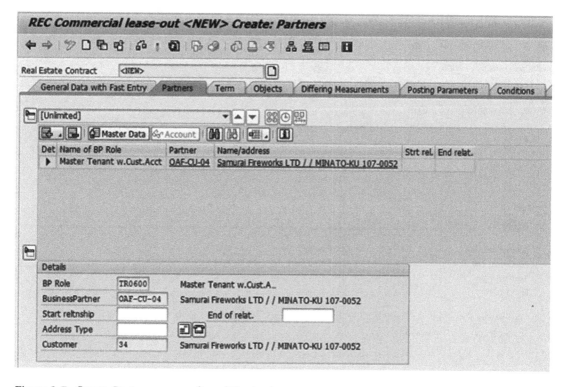

Figure 3-7. *Create: Partners screen after adding business partner*

8. Click **Term** .

Enter the data in the Term tab as mentioned in Table 3-2 and shown in Figure 3-8.

Table 3-2. *Term Tab*

Field Name	Description	Value
Contract start date	Start date of contract	01.01.2015
1st Contract End	End date of 1st contract	31.12.2015

Real Estate Contract Commercial lease-out <NEW> Create: Term

Real Estate Contract   <NEW>

General Data with Fast Entry | Partners | Term | Objects | Differing Measurements | Posting Parameters | Conditions | Adjustment

Det	TermCateg.	No.	Name of Term	Memo
▶	Term			☐
	Notice		<No Period of Notice>	☐

Term

Term | ○ Memo

Contract start date	01.01.2015	Cash Flow From	01.01.2015
1st Contract End	31.12.2015	First Posting From	01.01.2015
Term in months	12		
End of Term			

Term Information

Current Status	Undefined

Figure 3-8. *Create: Term screen*

9. Click Objects .

The contract needs to be assigned to a rental object (Figure 3-9). This specifies which real estate property, like land, building, spaces, or other items, are let out as per the agreement. Rental objects are assigned for a specific time duration or period as agreed upon by both parties. When multiple properties are included in the same contract or with similar conditions, they can be grouped to simplify processing.

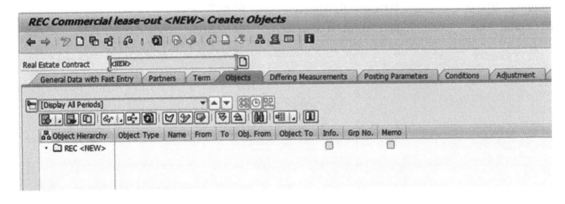

REC Commercial lease-out <NEW> Create: Objects

Real Estate Contract   <NEW>

General Data with Fast Entry | Partners | Term | Objects | Differing Measurements | Posting Parameters | Conditions | Adjustment

[Display All Periods]

Object Hierarchy	Object Type	Name	From	To	Obj. From	Object To	Info.	Grp No.	Memo
• ☐ REC <NEW>							☐		☐

Figure 3-9. *Create: Object screen*

10. Click 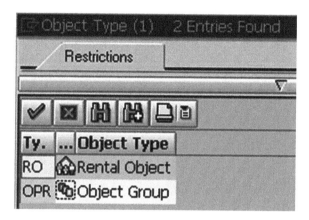. This will show a list of object types (Figure 3-10).

Figure 3-10. *Select rental object type*

11. Double-clicking **🏠Rental Object** will bring up the Rental Object Search screen (Figure 3-11).

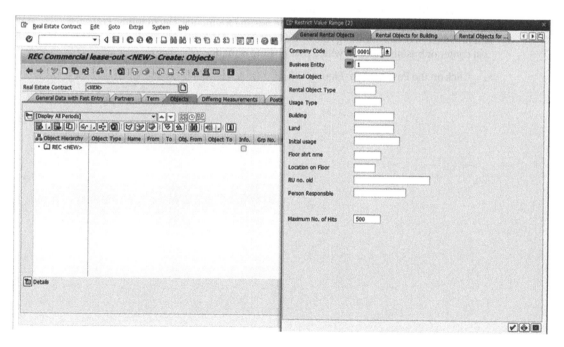

Figure 3-11. *Search Rental Object screen*

12. Click ✔. This will show a list of rental objects fitting your criteria (Figure 3-12).

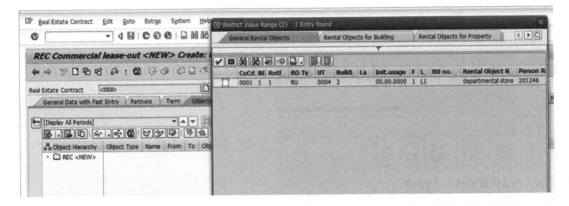

Figure 3-12. *Result of rental object search*

13. Click .

    You will find the department store that is a rental object and has been let in its entirety.

14. Click **Posting Parameters**.

    Posting parameters determine what financial and controlling postings are used in the books of the company. Details include posting frequency, calculations, tax and jurisdiction codes, dunning rules, and controlling information relating the cost center or business area in which that posting is made.

    a. Click on the Postings tab (Figure 3-13).

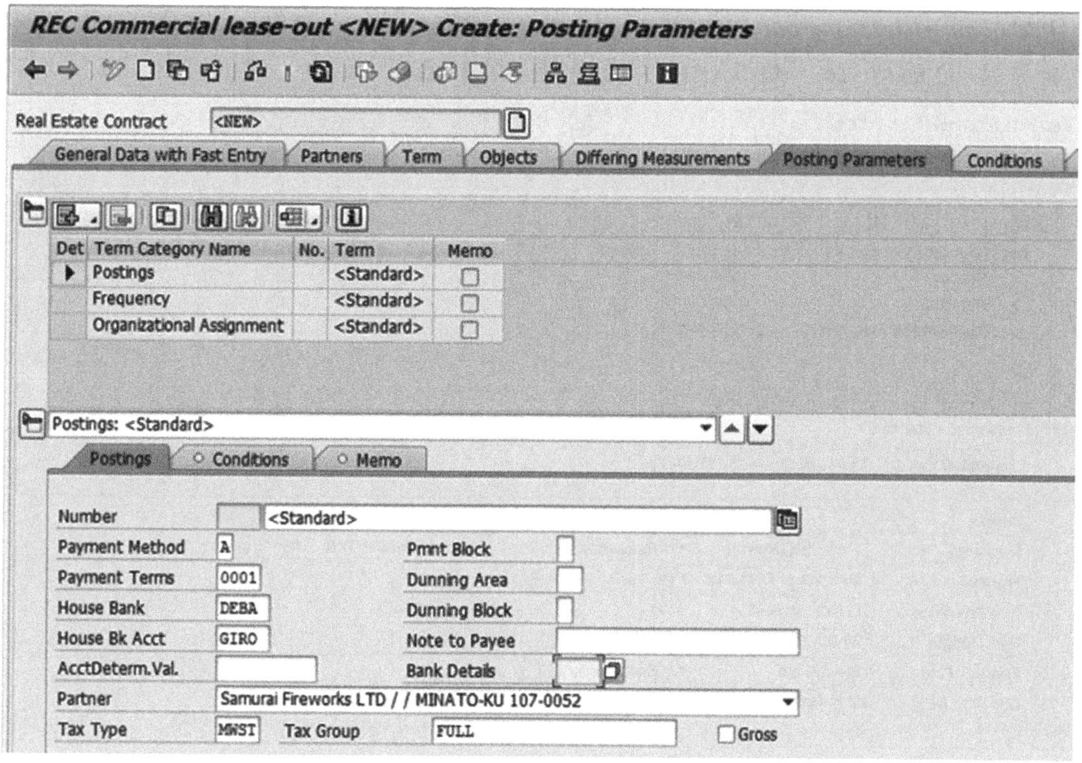

REC Commercial lease-out <NEW> Create: Posting Parameters

Real Estate Contract   <NEW>

| General Data with Fast Entry | Partners | Term | Objects | Differing Measurements | Posting Parameters | Conditions |

Det	Term Category Name	No.	Term	Memo
▶	Postings		<Standard>	☐
	Frequency		<Standard>	☐
	Organizational Assignment		<Standard>	☐

Postings: <Standard>

| Postings | ○ Conditions | ○ Memo |

Number	<Standard>
Payment Method	A
Payment Terms	0001
House Bank	DEBA
House Bk Acct	GIRO
AcctDeterm.Val.	
Partner	Samurai Fireworks LTD / / MINATO-KU 107-0052
Tax Type	MWST Tax Group FULL ☐ Gross

Pmnt Block
Dunning Area
Dunning Block
Note to Payee
Bank Details

Figure 3-13.   *Create: Posting Parameters screen, with Postings tab selected*

    b.   Select "Frequency" in the Term Category Name column (Figure3-14).

           Key aspects to note are as follows:

           Frequency: If the frequency of payable is monthly, choose the option as "1 Month" in the Frequency field drop-down menu. Depending upon the frequency agreed upon, the same needs to be selected from the option available in the dropdown.

           FrequencyStart: Choose the appropriate frequency start from the options available in the drop-down. In cases of monthly frequency, you can choose the option "Start of condition," in which case the frequency of payments will start from the date of the start of condition.

           Prorated: In case the agreement starts from any date within the month–say, the 16th or so–and the agreement says to make the first payment for the first 14 days in the current month and then pay on a monthly basis, the Prorated option "Contract or Rental Object Start of End Date" needs to be chosen.

           Amt Reference: Choose the option from the drop-down entries as to whether the amount is paid monthly, yearly, or cyclical, as the case may be.

           Calc. Method: Whether the calculation of the amount due is based on an exact number of days in a month or a fixed 30 days in a month. Choose the appropriate option as the case may be.

           Payment Form: Whether the payment is received at the beginning of the month for the month ahead or at the end of the month for the previous month. Choose the options "In Advance" or "In Arrears" respectively as the case may be.

25

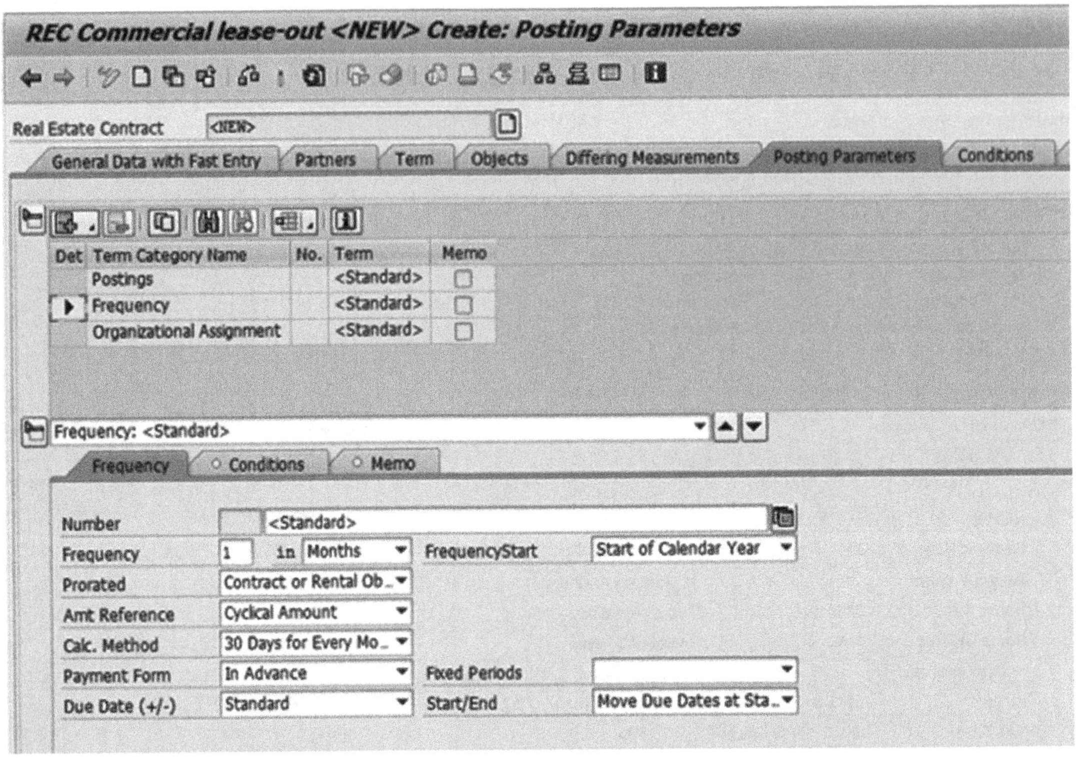

Figure 3-14. *Create: Posting Parameters, with Frequency tab selected*

15. Click **Conditions** .

We use the Conditions tab to indicate the type of rental amount agreed upon by the parties. It can be a fixed rate charged on a periodic basis, or that is to be calculated based on the measurements of the individual rental objects assigned to the contract. All rental charges are time specific. Based on the conditions specified, we can capture advanced payments or prepayments that are reconciled at a later date. You can use the Conditions tab to initiate a controlling or financial posting action. When you enter conditions in a contract, the system automatically creates a cash-flow projection of planned income or expenses, which is posted to the Financials module, and planned income or expense data is converted into open items.

We also have sales-based rent, where rentals are charged based on sales revenue or volume of sales. When a contract is sales based, the system captures all conditions, calculations, and relevant information for the sales-based rent settlement process. Take an example of a duty-free shop in an airport lounge, where airport authorities have rented out a space and rent is determined based on the volume of sales at the shop. SAP REFX provides functionality to capture detailed information on the types of eligible products, number of products sold, product schedule or grading, and any effective sales caps. Once you enter this information in the contract, the system tracks reported tenant sales, processes rent calculations at specified intervals, and posts open items in the financials. This process is supported by the SAP Interactive Forms software by Adobe. The tenant enters sales data using the SAP Interactive Forms software, which compiles sales reports and correspondence. The sales-based lease functionality can also be used for expense leases; for example, when a retailer leases a shop from a shopping mall operator.

Click 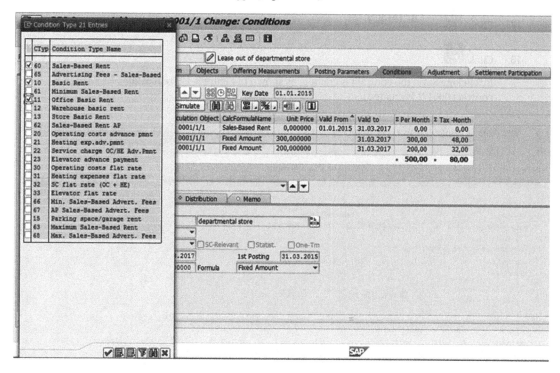 to add the condition type (Figure 3-15).

Figure 3-15. *Conditions: Condition Type screen*

Clicking ☑ will add the selected condition type, as shown in Figure 3-16. Enter the relevant condition amount for the condition type.

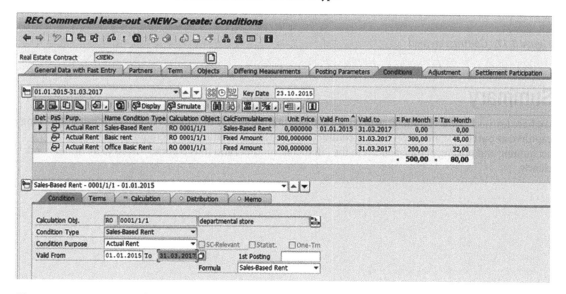

Figure 3-16. *Create: Conditions screen*

16. Click **General Data with Fast Entry**.

17. Click ✔ **Activate**.

18. Click 🖫.

By clicking Save, the contract is created, as shown in Figure 3-17 (real estate contract 0001/1 is created).

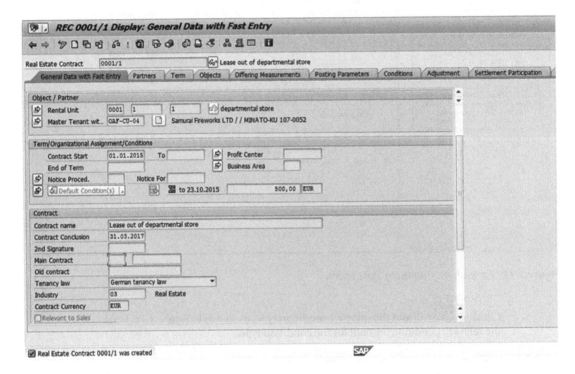

Figure 3-17. Contract created

Summary

We have learned in this chapter how to create real estate contracts, with different business information being captured as part of a standard SAP REFX contract. An SAP REFX contract is a prerequisite to having the accounting and posting of transactions in the Financials module, and thus contracts need to be understood clearly.

CHAPTER 4

■ ■ ■

Accounting

In this chapter we will talk about how to configure accounting in an REFX implementation. In this chapter, we will discuss the following:

- Periodic posting of lease-out contracts

- Reversal of periodic posting of contracts

- Verification of posting document after periodic posting

- Vacancy for rental objects

- Account determination

- One-time posting

- Accrual/deferral postings

We saw in an earlier chapter that real estate contracts are formed between two parties, where the lessor is the legal owner of the asset and provides the lessee the right to use the asset for consideration, which is a rental payment. The contract is an agreement entered into by both parties and covers details like property, term, rental amount, terms, and conditions. The SAP REFX module provides various tabs in which to capture these details at the time of contract creation. It also updates accounting data once periodic postings are carried out.

The periodic processing program generates payments and receivables based on the conditions assigned to the SAP real estate contract. The program also automatically creates follow-up postings based on changes made to conditions for back-dated changes. These postings are automatically recorded in the general ledger and within the controlling module. The periodic processing program is run for any contract type and within both simulation and update modes. Reversal of entries may also be generated through the periodic processing reversal program. Entries created using the periodic processing program must be reversed using the periodic processing reversal program. However, it is not necessary to reverse periodic postings when changes are made to a condition after the periodic posting run, since any changes made to the condition will be recorded during the next periodic posting run. Besides generating financial postings for accounts payable and receivable, it also distributes contract costs among the real estate objects assigned to the contract.

Let us take for an example a company that leased commercial spaces to tenants and invoices them on a yearly basis using Flexible Real Estate Management (REFX), where the real estate contract contains payment terms and conditions. The company is required to invoice the customers on due dates by posting the Financials (FI) document periodically, updating both the customer account and the revenue General Ledger (GL) account.

There is seamless integration between REFX and the accounting modules (Finance and Controlling), and these postings are automated.

SAP REFX's lease accounting is fully integrated into SAP Financials and SAP Controlling.

© Jayant Daithankar 2016
J. Daithankar, *SAP Flexible Real Estate Management*, DOI 10.1007/978-1-4842-1482-4_4

- Period postings of all payable, receivable, and GL transactions are based on the cash flow of the real estate contract conditions.

- Open items are managed through accounts payable and accounts receivable

- One-time posting transactions may be generated through the real estate module.

- Periodic postings of all vacant rental objects, where the vacancy cost centers are billed

Real estate invoices are created and printed from within the REFX module based on postings made to the vendor account. The periodic postings will identify all plan items within the defined due date and generate a debit and a credit posting for each one of the plan items. There is also a CO posting against the real estate contract (for a payable lease, this is a cost posting, whereas the receivable lease will have a revenue cost element). The transfer posting then allows these costs/revenues on the lease to be distributed to the RE objects or other CO objects. The vacancy posting creates either lost revenue or vacancy cost postings against the identified cost center. The periodic posting run can first be simulated to enable review and modifications, if required. All changes should be made in the contract to generate the right cash-flow adjustment, resulting in the proper postings.

One-time posting transactions allow for a pre-configuration of RE-specific posting transactions (based on transaction FB50) and can be posted to accounts payable, receivable, a GL account, or a combination of these.

Let us see how periodic posting for lease-out contracts is carried out.

Periodic Posting for Lease-out Contracts

You use the periodic posting run (creation of debits on customers) to generate open items in a customer account, which can be cleared by receipt of money from customer against these debits.

Trigger

Perform this procedure when periodic posting is due. In a real estate contract for lease-out, it will be specified whether it is a monthly, quarterly, or yearly contract. The periodic posting run has to be carried out as per that criteria.

Prerequisites

Following are the prerequisites for using real estate accounting for posting of transactions:

- Creation of contract

- Release of contract

Menu Path

SAP Easy Access Menu ➤ Accounting ➤ Flexible Real Estate Management ➤ Accounting ➤ Periodic posting ➤ Periodic posting

Transaction Code

RERAPP

Procedure

Follow these steps to carry out Periodic posting process:

1. Start the transaction using the menu path or transaction code.

   The Periodic posting process: Contracts screen, as shown in Figure 4-1, will be displayed.

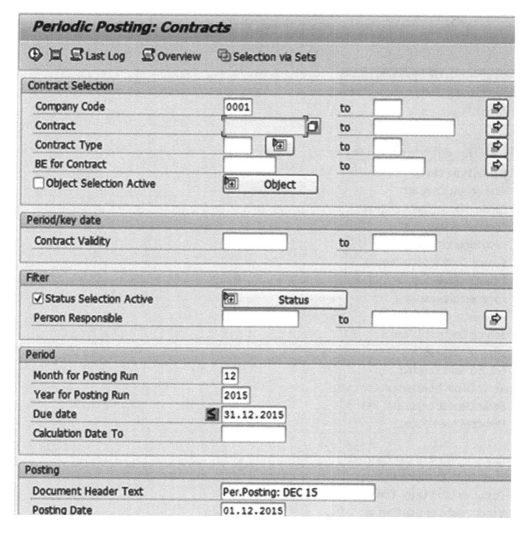

Figure 4-1. *Periodic posting process: Contracts screen*

2. As required, complete or review the necessary fields, as shown in Table 4-1.

Table 4-1. Periodic posting process: Contracts–Contract Selection Section

Field Name	Description	Value
Contract Number	Description of the contract number	3
Contract Type	Description of the contract type	CO01

3. Click 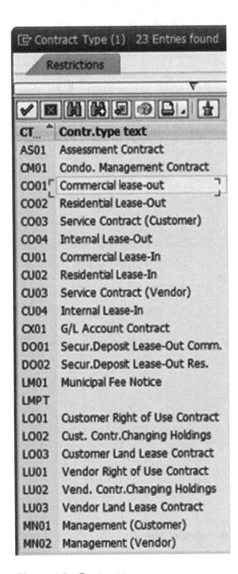. This will show the list of contract types (Figure 4-2).

Figure 4-2. Contract types

4. Double-clicking "Commercial lease-out" will populate the contract type field (Figure 4-3).

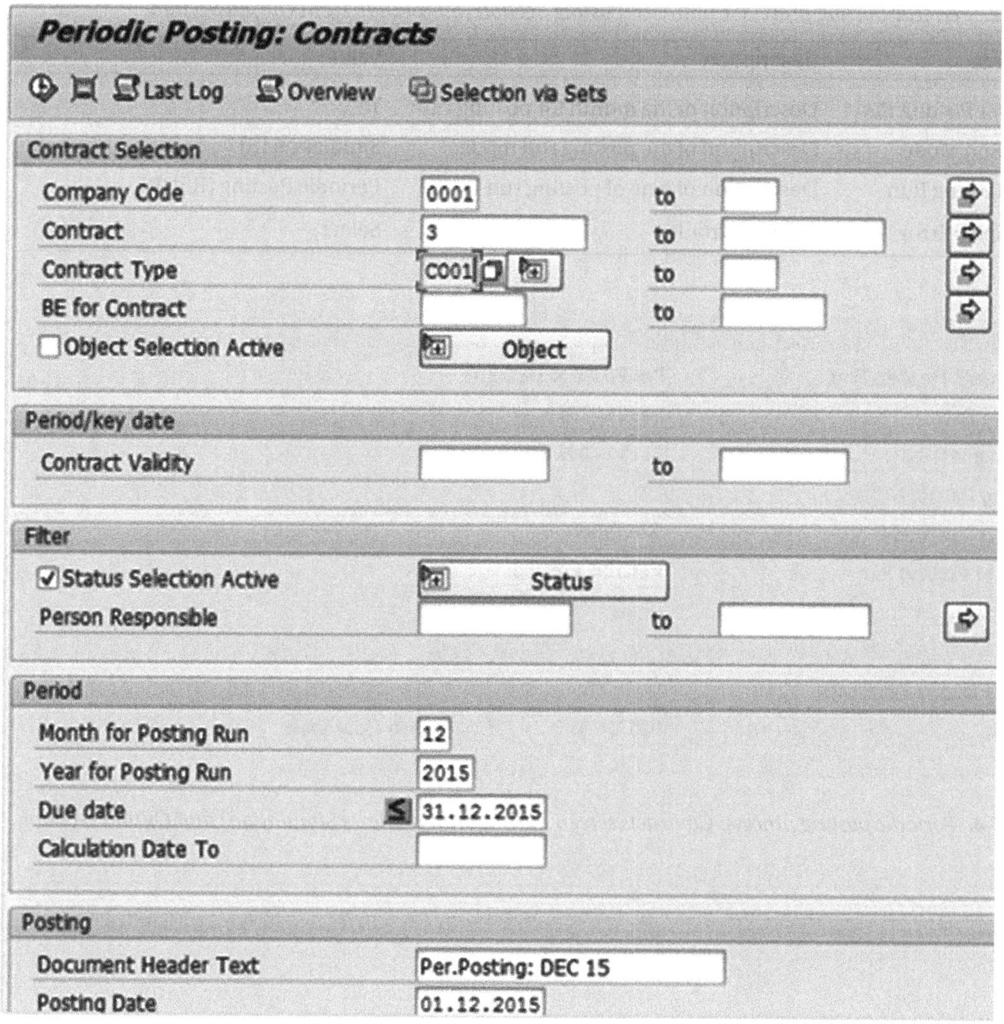

Figure 4-3. Periodic posting process: Contracts screen after selecting contract type

5. As required, complete and review the following fields, as shown in Table 4-2 and Figure 4-4.

Table 4-2. *Periodic posting process: Contracts–Posting Section (Simulation) and Output Section*

Field Name	Description	Value
Month For Posting Run	Description of the month for posting run	12
Posting Run Mode	Description of the posting run mode	Simulation (S)
Type of Posting Run	Description of type of posting run	Periodic Posting (REDP)
Only Display Error Log	Display error log	Select

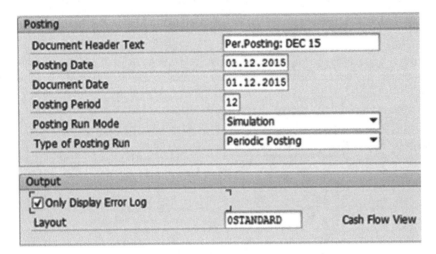

Figure 4-4. *Periodic posting process: Contracts screen Posting (run mode as Simulation) and Output sections*

6. Clicking 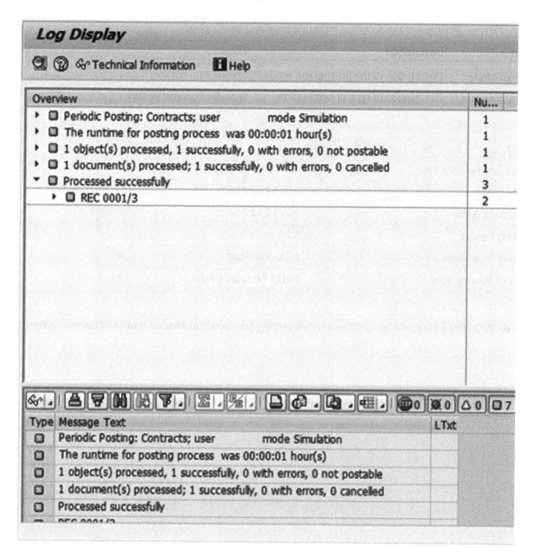 will display the log (Figure 4-5).

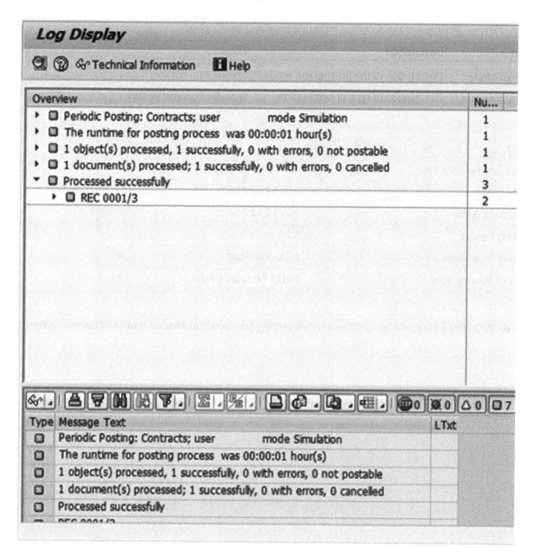

Figure 4-5. *Posting log for simulation*

7. As required, complete and review the following fields, as shown in Table 4-3 and Figure 4-6.

Table 4-3. *Periodic posting process: Contracts–Posting Section (Update Run)*

Field Name	Description	Value
Posting Run Mode	Description of the posting run mode	Update Run (E)
Type of Posting Run	Description of type of posting run	Periodic Posting (REDP)

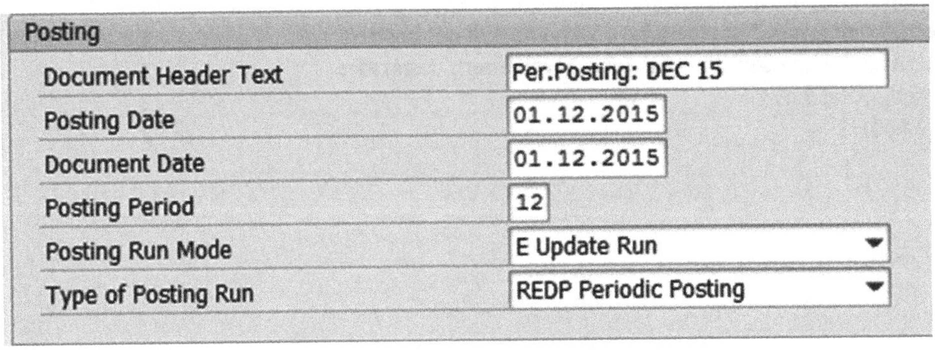

Posting	
Document Header Text	Per.Posting: DEC 15
Posting Date	01.12.2015
Document Date	01.12.2015
Posting Period	12
Posting Run Mode	E Update Run
Type of Posting Run	REDP Periodic Posting

Figure 4-6. *Periodic posting process: Contracts screen Posting (run mode as Update Run) and Output sections*

8. Clicking 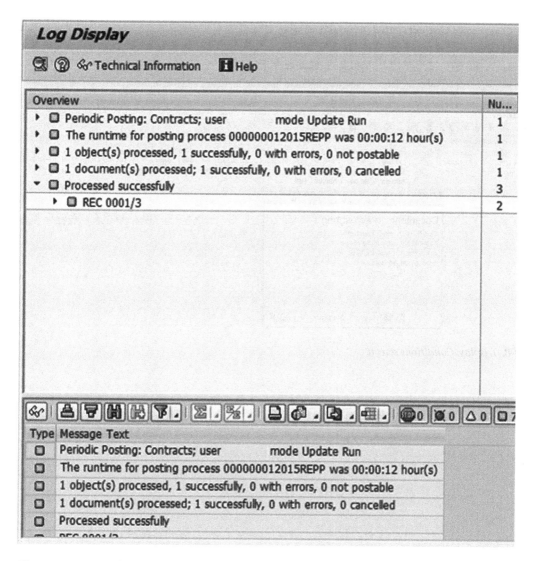 will display the log (Figure 4-7).

Figure 4-7. Posting log for update run

You can verify accounting, controlling, and real estate documents by displaying the contract and selecting the Conditions tab and click on status field (Figure 4-8).

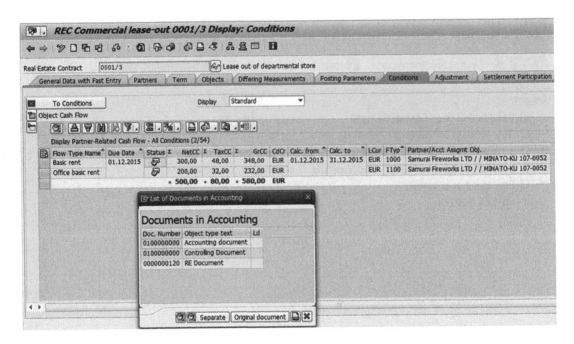

Figure 4-8. *Display: Conditions screen*

Double-clicking on "Accounting document" will display the document posted and its accounting entry (Figure 4-9)

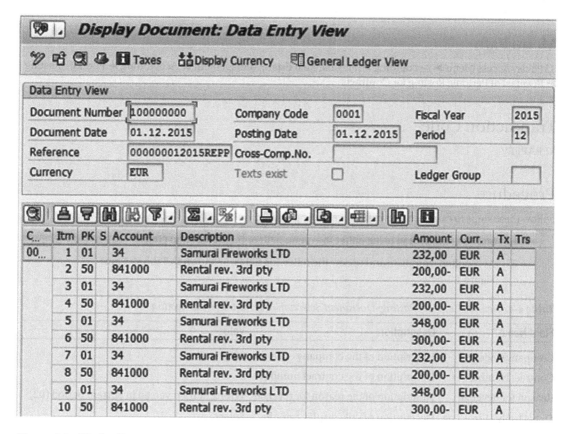

Figure 4-9. *Display Document screen*

9.   The transaction is complete.

Result

Periodic posting run was successful.

Reversal of Periodic Posting

You will use this procedure to reverse a periodic posting run just carried out.

Trigger

Perform this procedure in cases where you want to reverse periodic posting carried out for any contract.

Prerequisites

Periodic posting run has been carried out.

Menu Path

SAP Easy Access Menu ➤ Accounting ➤ Flexible Real Estate Management ➤ Accounting ➤ Periodic Posting ➤ Reversal of Periodic Posting for Contracts

Transaction Code

RERAPPRV

Procedure

Follow these steps to carry out a reversal of Periodic posting process:

1. Start the transaction using either the menu path or the transaction code.

2. As required, complete and review the following fields, as shown in Table 4-4 and Figure 4-10.

Table 4-4. Reverse Contract Posting: Document Selection and Posting Data Section

Field Name	Description	Value
Company Code	Description of the company code	0001
Contract Number	Description of the contract number	3
Reason for Reversal	Description of the reason for reversal	Wrong entry reversed in current period (02)
Only Display Error Log	Description of only display error log	Select

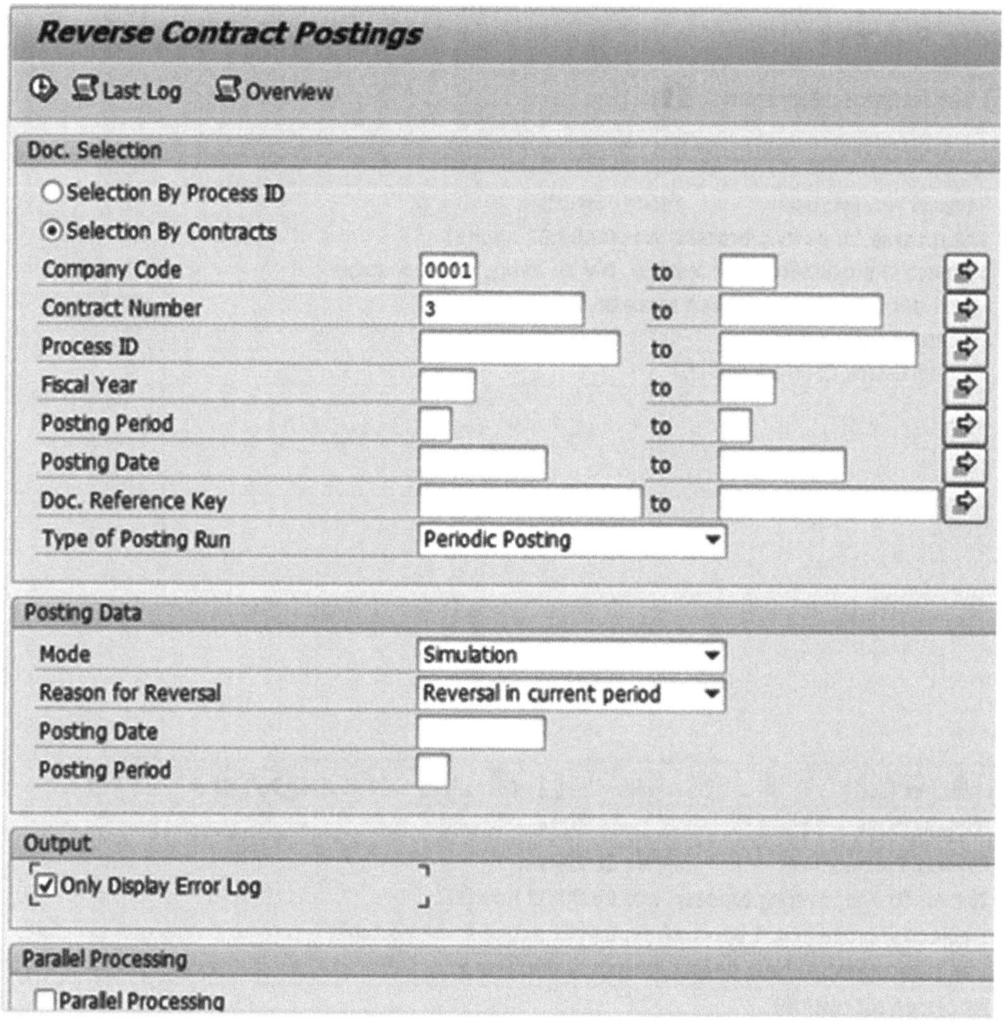

Reverse Contract Postings

⊕ ⊟ Last Log ⊟ Overview

Doc. Selection

○ Selection By Process ID
● Selection By Contracts

Company Code	0001	to	⇨
Contract Number	3	to	⇨
Process ID		to	⇨
Fiscal Year		to	⇨
Posting Period		to	⇨
Posting Date		to	⇨
Doc. Reference Key		to	⇨
Type of Posting Run	Periodic Posting ▼		

Posting Data

Mode	Simulation ▼
Reason for Reversal	Reversal in current period ▼
Posting Date	
Posting Period	

Output

☑ Only Display Error Log

Parallel Processing

☐ Parallel Processing

Figure 4-10. *Reverse Contract Postings screen*

3. Clicking ⊕ will display the log (Figure 4-11).

41

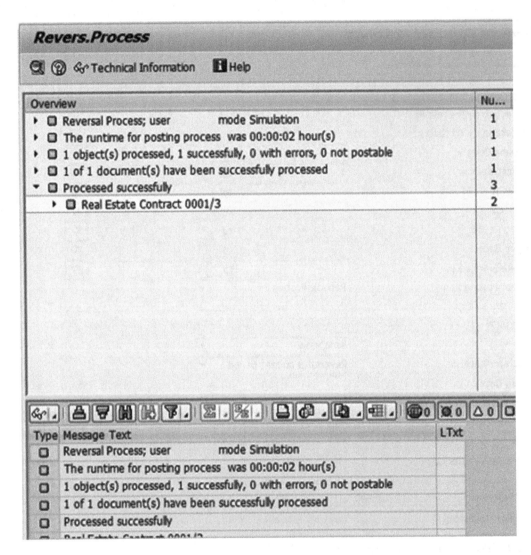

Figure 4-11. *Revers.Process screen*

4. Click .

5. As required, complete and review the following fields, as shown in Table 4-5 and Figure 4-12.

Table 4-5. *Reverse Contract Posting: Posting Data Section*

Field Name	Description	Value
Mode	Description of mode	Update Run (E)

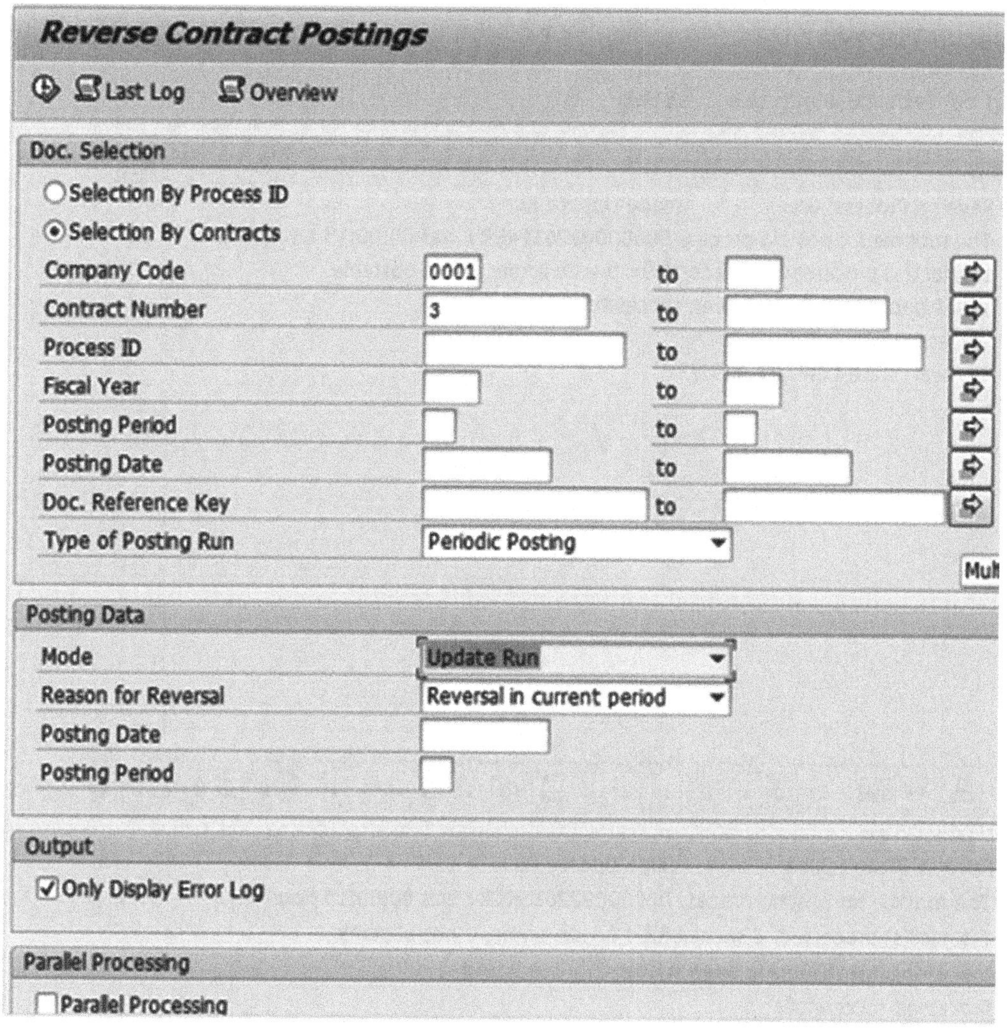

Figure 4-12. *Reverse Contract Postings screen*

6. Click ⊕.

7. You have completed this transaction (Figure 4-13).

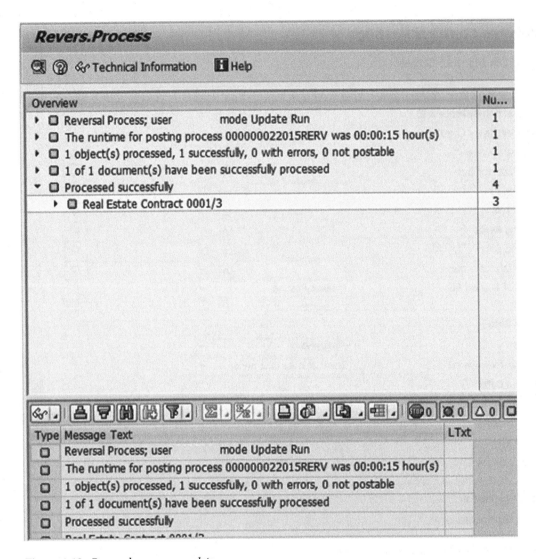

Figure 4-13. *Reversal process complete*

Result

You have reversed the periodic posting.

Verification of Posting Document after Periodic Posting

Use this procedure to verify the documents have been posted and the accounting entry passed.

Trigger

Perform this procedure after periodic posting is over.

Prerequisites

Periodic posting run has been carried out.

Menu Path

SAP Easy Access Menu ➤ Accounting ➤ Flexible Real Estate Management -> Contract

Transaction Code

RECN

Procedure

Follow these steps to carry out the verification of a posting document:

1. Start the transaction using either the menu path or the transaction code.

2. As required, complete and review the following fields, as shown in Table 4-6 and Figure 4-14.

Table 4-6. *Real Estate Contract*

Field Name	Description	Value
Contract Number	Description of the contract number	3

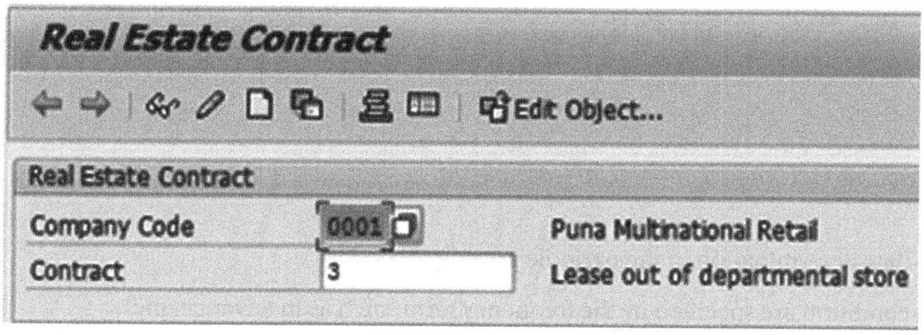

Figure 4-14. *Real Estate Contract screen*

3. Click ⚭ to display the contract (Figure 4-15).

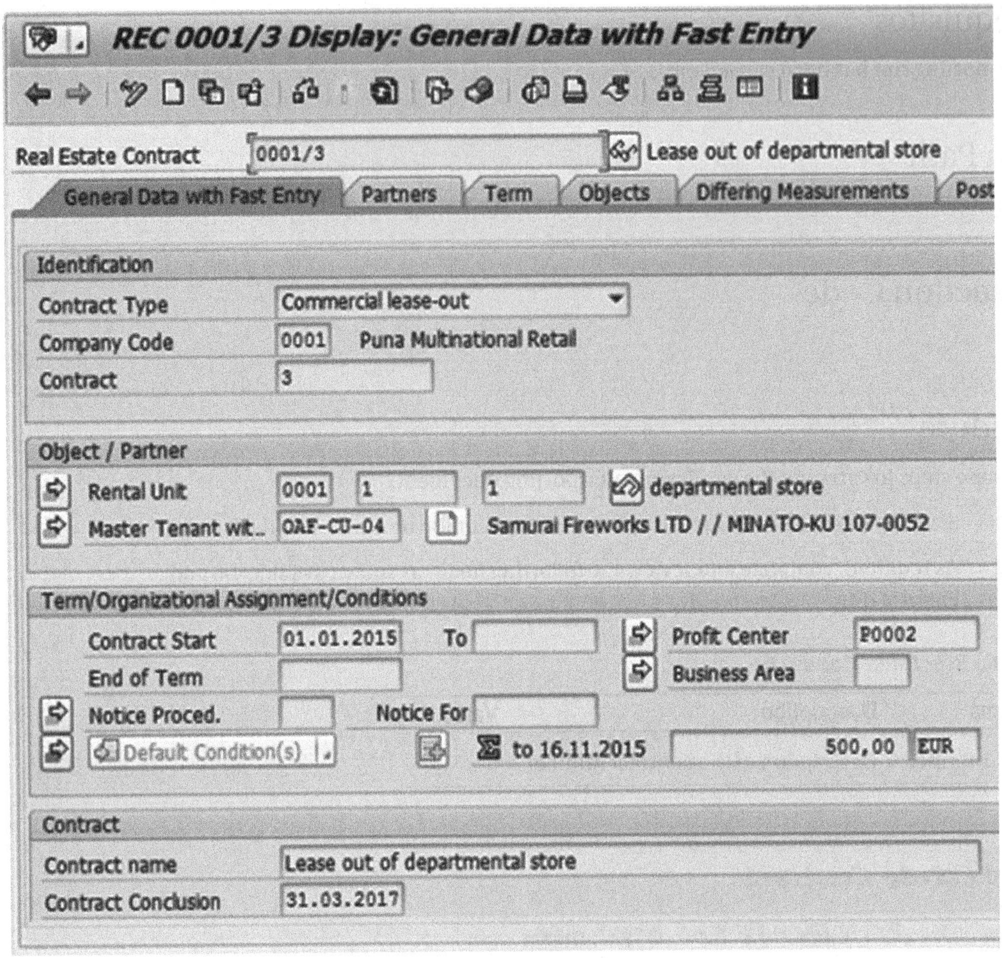

Figure 4-15. Display: General Data screen for commercial lease-out

4. Regarding due-date determination in the periodic posting process:

Due dates for a condition are specified by the frequency term, such as in advance, mid-month, or in arrears. For more complex payment requirements, a correction rule is defined for determining the due date. The correction rule is also assigned to the frequency term. An organization may have a business process in place to make rent payments 7 days in advance of the next month's rental payment. Additionally, the rent expense should be recorded in the same month in which the check was issued, not the month for which the payment was due. The periodic processing program selects rent payments based on their due dates and posts those rents to the period specified within the posting program. For example, if a company processes July's rent payments on 06/23, then on 06/24 the periodic processing program is executed for period 9 with a due date of <= 06/30 and a posting date of 06/24, in period 8. A seven-day correction rule will be configured with the name and will by default applied to the contract.

5. Click the **Conditions** tab (Figure 4-16).

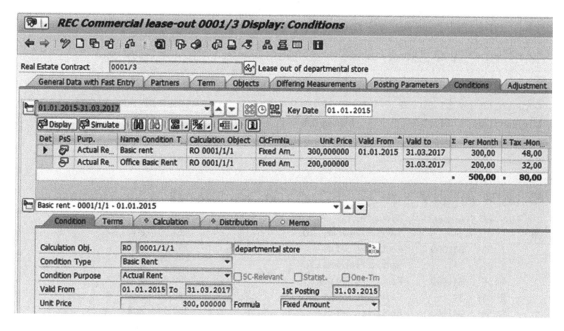

Figure 4-16. *Display: Conditions screen for commercial lease-out*

6. Click ![Display].

7. Click ![icon] to display the list of documents in accounting (Figure 4-17).

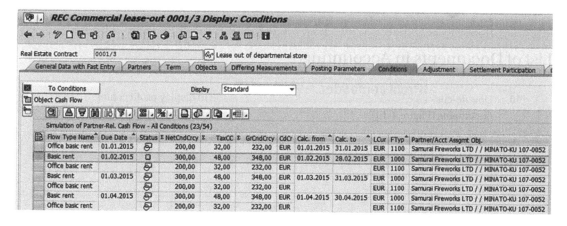

Figure 4-17. *List of documents in accounting*

8. Double-click **Accounting document** to view accounting document (Figure 4-18).

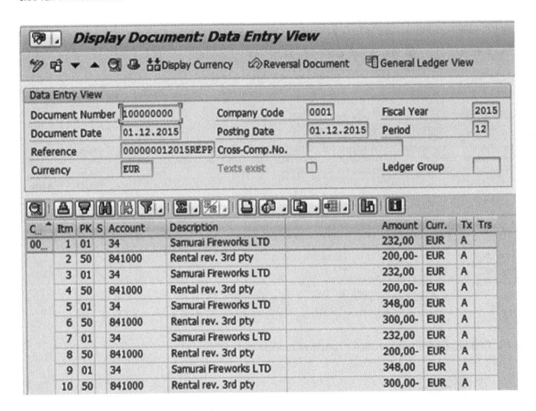

Figure 4-18. *Document overview display*

9. Click ⬤ _____ .

List of Documents in Accounting

10. Double-click [Profit center doc.] to display profit center documents (Figure 4-19).

Figure 4-19. *Profit center's actual line items*

11. Click _____.

12. Double-click on RE Document to display real estate documents (Figure 4-20).

Display RE Document

Proc Item	Proc IC	Accounting D/C	ID Amount	Crcy	Pstng Date Calc. from	Doc. Date Calc. to	Rev Object ID	Entered Ref. Date	SouIntEntr Partner	CoCd	DocumentNo FTyp BusA	Revs. Profit Ctr	Doc. Year PMeth
REPF	REDF	000000032015REPF			01.12.2015	01.12.2015			RERAPP		0001 100000002		2015
1	OI D		232,00	EUR	01.01.2015	31.01.2015	REC 0001/3		OAF-CU-04	1100		P0002	A
2	C		200,00	EUR	01.01.2015	31.01.2015	REC 0001/3		OAF-CU-04	1100		P0002	A
3	OI D		232,00	EUR	01.02.2015	28.02.2015	REC 0001/3		OAF-CU-04	1100		P0002	A
4	C		200,00	EUR	01.02.2015	28.02.2015	REC 0001/3		OAF-CU-04	1100		P0002	A
5	OI D		348,00	EUR	01.03.2015	31.03.2015	REC 0001/3		OAF-CU-04	1000		P0002	A
6	C		300,00	EUR	01.03.2015	31.03.2015	REC 0001/3		OAF-CU-04	1000		P0002	A
7	OI D		232,00	EUR	01.03.2015	31.03.2015	REC 0001/3		OAF-CU-04	1100		P0002	A
8	C		200,00	EUR	01.03.2015	31.03.2015	REC 0001/3		OAF-CU-04	1100		P0002	A
9	OI D		348,00	EUR	01.04.2015	30.04.2015	REC 0001/3		OAF-CU-04	1000		P0002	A
10	C		300,00	EUR	01.04.2015	30.04.2015	REC 0001/3		OAF-CU-04	1000		P0002	A

Figure 4-20. *Display RE documents*

13. You have completed this transaction.

Result

You have verified that the accounting, profit center, and controlling documents have posted.

Vacancy for Rental Objects

We can post notional costs (or revenue) resulting from the conditions of the rental objects to vacancy cost centers. We use this function to analyze vacancy costs. Let us take an example of a rental object that is let out for part of the year and vacant for the remaining period. This needs to be analyzed as to what is the notional cost of failure to rent out property or building on said rental.

Periodic postings are made for a company code or codes. You can simulate and reverse posting runs as previously discussed. Posting and error logs display current information about the posting status. If you define conditions on the rental object, and the rental object is vacant, the system updates the cash flow based on the conditions defined for the case of vacancy (vacancy cash flow). With every subsequent periodic posting for the vacancy, the system generates a cash flow and posts the receivables according to the conditions defined.

Retroactive changes (such as the subsequent activation of a contract) could result in follow-up postings. If the notional cost is to be posted to a cost center in your organization, you have to assign the cost center to the rental object (in the Posting Data tab). The posting can also be made across company codes; in other words, the posting is made to a cost center belonging to another company code in the same controlling area. If the rental object is not assigned to a cost center, you post the expense to the rental object itself.

Let us take the example of a department store situated in building 1 of a mall that has been vacant since 01/01/2016. As per the market rate, the store can be leased out for monthly rent of EUR 16,000. We can carry out the posting to arrive at a vacancy cost resulting from the non-letting of the store. This cost is attributable to the non-occupancy of the premises and the notional loss thereby incurred. Follow the steps mentioned next to carry out a vacancy posting for this example.

Menu Path

SAP Easy Access Menu ➤ Accounting ➤ Flexible Real Estate Management ➤ Accounting ➤ Periodic Postings ➤ Periodic posting process: Vacancy for Rental Objects

Transaction Code

RERAVP

Procedure

Follow these steps to carry out a vacancy posting.

1. Start the transaction using either the menu path or the transaction code. Enter the relevant details, like business entity, rental object, posting period, due date, posting date, etc. (Figure 4-21).

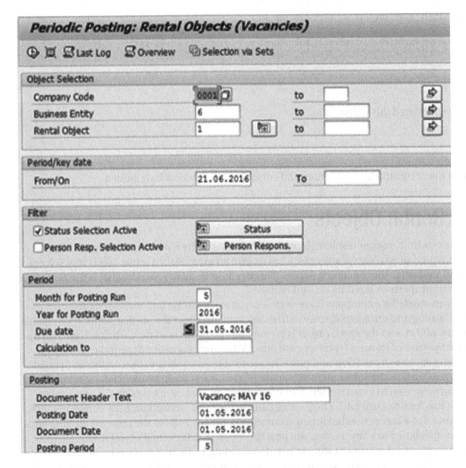

Figure 4-21. *Periodic posting process: Rental Objects (Vacancies) screen*

2. Clicking ⊕ will execute the vacancy posting (Figure 4-22).

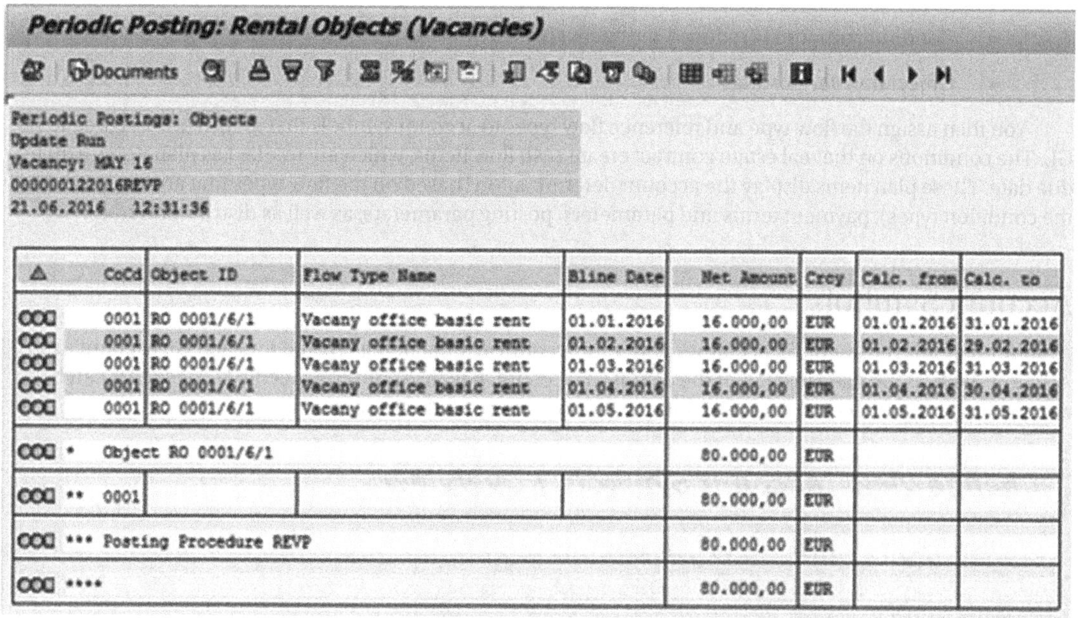

Figure 4-22. *Periodic posting process: Rental Objects (Vacancies) result screen*

3. Click 🗋 Documents to display the posting documents (Figure 4-23).

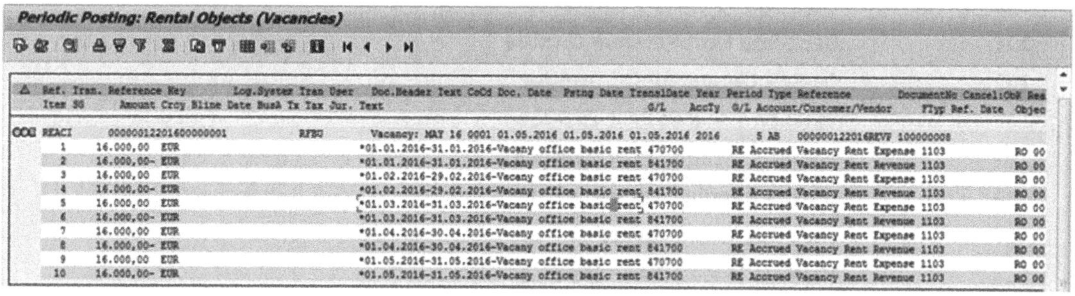

Figure 4-23. *Periodic posting process: Rental Objects (Vacancies) documents screen*

Account Determination

All the master data in REFX (for example, business entity, building, and rental objects) falls under a company code, which is created in FI. Automatic account determination is the process whereby the system finds the relevant GL accounts to be posted to. The system debits the customer account specified in the real estate contract and credits the income account in the case of lease-out contracts. These settings are mandatory, and without them you cannot execute the periodic postings for real estate contracts.

In REFX, the accounting flow type depends on the condition type. We need to assign the condition type to a flow type, which you then link to reference flow types for three different scenarios:

- Condition amount is increased retroactively

- Condition amount is reduced retroactively

- Object transfer postings

You then assign the flow type and reference flow types to account symbols that in turn are assigned to the GL. The conditions on the real estate contract create cash flow items, which are marked as plan items with a due date. These plan items display the account determination (based on the flow types that are assigned to the condition types), payment terms and parameters, posting parameters, as well as distribution rules.

Account Symbols

Account symbols represent GL accounts, with one account symbol being created for each GL account used. Account symbols are used instead of the actual GL account, because country-specific GL accounts can be assigned to just one account symbol. Examples of account symbols are shown in Figure 4-24.

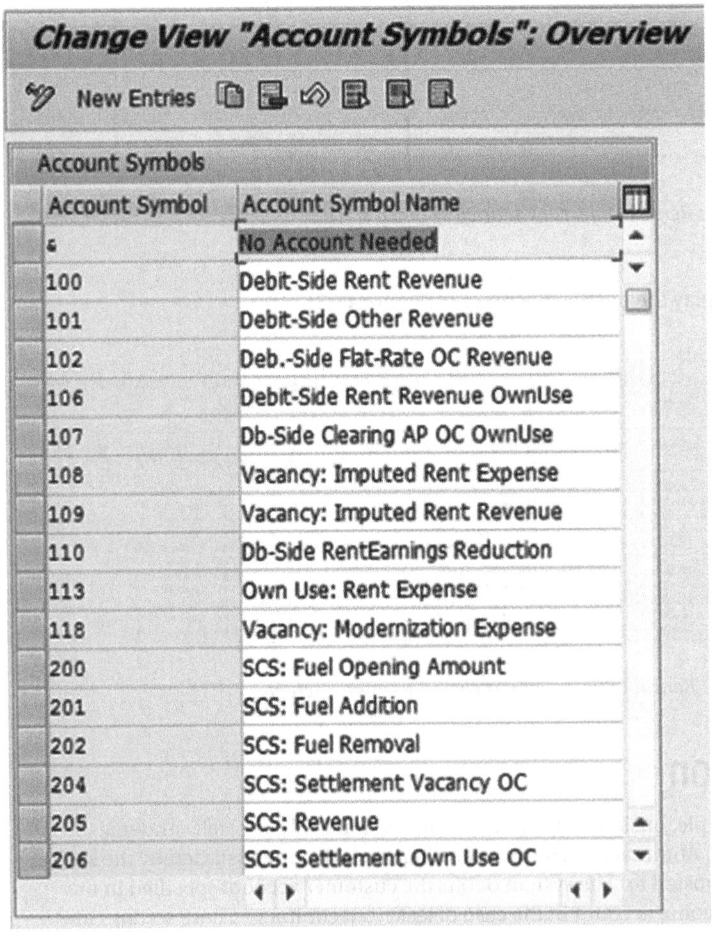

Change View "Account Symbols": Overview

Account Symbol	Account Symbol Name
&	No Account Needed
100	Debit-Side Rent Revenue
101	Debit-Side Other Revenue
102	Deb.-Side Flat-Rate OC Revenue
106	Debit-Side Rent Revenue OwnUse
107	Db-Side Clearing AP OC OwnUse
108	Vacancy: Imputed Rent Expense
109	Vacancy: Imputed Rent Revenue
110	Db-Side RentEarnings Reduction
113	Own Use: Rent Expense
118	Vacancy: Modernization Expense
200	SCS: Fuel Opening Amount
201	SCS: Fuel Addition
202	SCS: Fuel Removal
204	SCS: Settlement Vacancy OC
205	SCS: Revenue
206	SCS: Settlement Own Use OC

Figure 4-24. *Account symbols*

Account Symbols to Flow Types

The final step in configuring the account determination is the assignment of account symbols to flow types (Figures 4-25 and 4-26). This ensures the correct GL assignment for each condition based on the posting requirements.

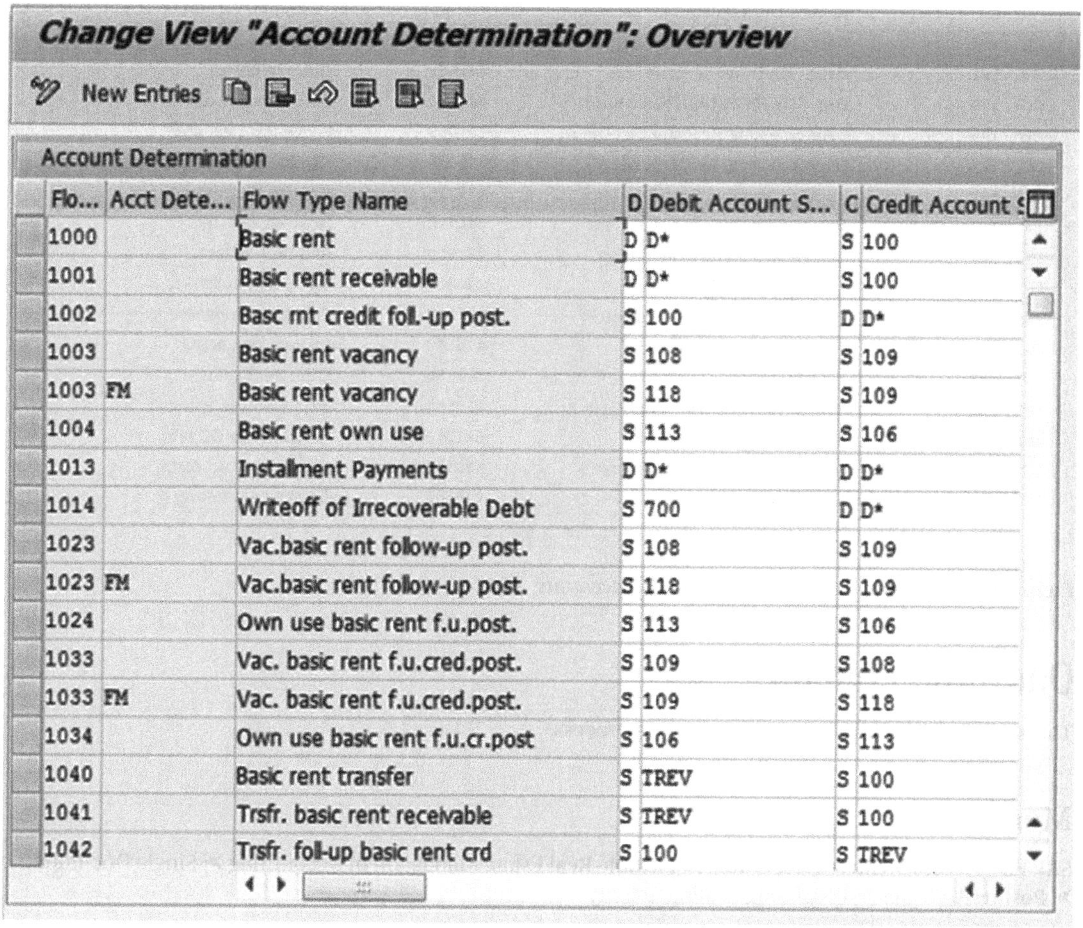

Change View "Account Determination": Overview

New Entries

Account Determination

Flo...	Acct Dete...	Flow Type Name	D	Debit Account S...	C	Credit Account S
1000		Basic rent	D	D*	S	100
1001		Basic rent receivable	D	D*	S	100
1002		Basc rnt credit foll.-up post.	S	100	D	D*
1003		Basic rent vacancy	S	108	S	109
1003	FM	Basic rent vacancy	S	118	S	109
1004		Basic rent own use	S	113	S	106
1013		Installment Payments	D	D*	D	D*
1014		Writeoff of Irrecoverable Debt	S	700	D	D*
1023		Vac.basic rent follow-up post.	S	108	S	109
1023	FM	Vac.basic rent follow-up post.	S	118	S	109
1024		Own use basic rent f.u.post.	S	113	S	106
1033		Vac. basic rent f.u.cred.post.	S	109	S	108
1033	FM	Vac. basic rent f.u.cred.post.	S	109	S	118
1034		Own use basic rent f.u.cr.post	S	106	S	113
1040		Basic rent transfer	S	TREV	S	100
1041		Trsfr. basic rent receivable	S	TREV	S	100
1042		Trsfr. foll-up basic rent crd	S	100	S	TREV

Figure 4-25. Assignment of account symbols to flow types

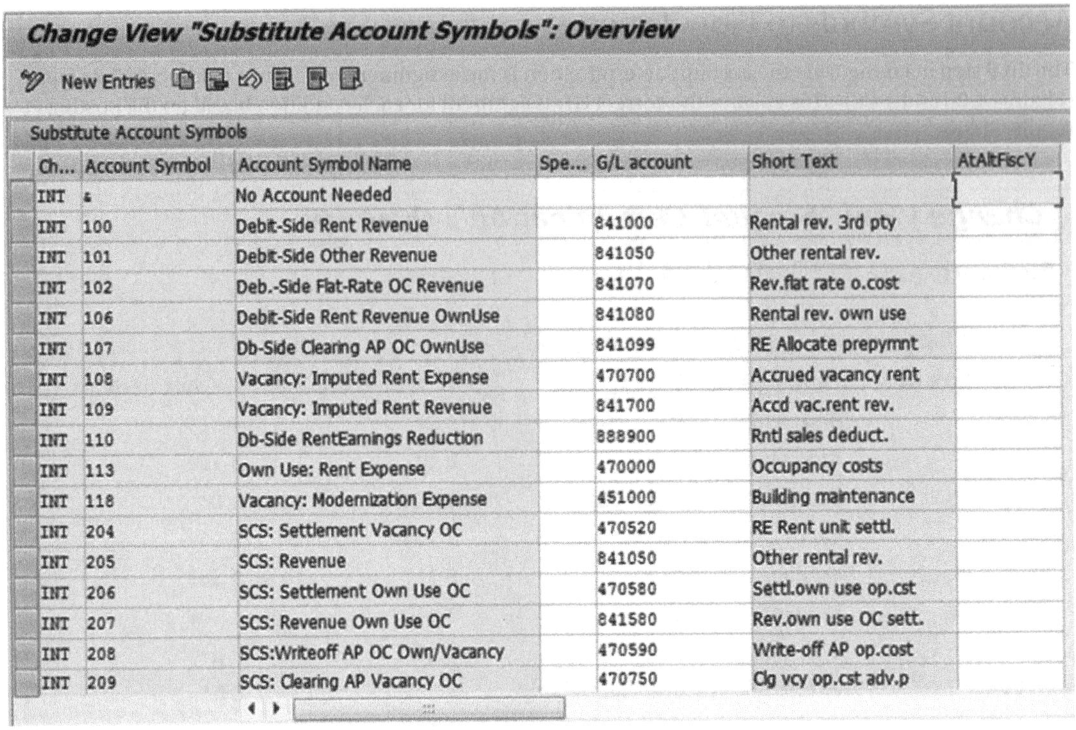

Ch...	Account Symbol	Account Symbol Name	Spe...	G/L account	Short Text	AtAltFiscY
INT	&	No Account Needed				
INT	100	Debit-Side Rent Revenue		841000	Rental rev. 3rd pty	
INT	101	Debit-Side Other Revenue		841050	Other rental rev.	
INT	102	Deb.-Side Flat-Rate OC Revenue		841070	Rev.flat rate o.cost	
INT	106	Debit-Side Rent Revenue OwnUse		841080	Rental rev. own use	
INT	107	Db-Side Clearing AP OC OwnUse		841099	RE Allocate prepymnt	
INT	108	Vacancy: Imputed Rent Expense		470700	Accrued vacancy rent	
INT	109	Vacancy: Imputed Rent Revenue		841700	Accd vac.rent rev.	
INT	110	Db-Side RentEarnings Reduction		888900	Rntl sales deduct.	
INT	113	Own Use: Rent Expense		470000	Occupancy costs	
INT	118	Vacancy: Modernization Expense		451000	Building maintenance	
INT	204	SCS: Settlement Vacancy OC		470520	RE Rent unit settl.	
INT	205	SCS: Revenue		841050	Other rental rev.	
INT	206	SCS: Settlement Own Use OC		470580	Settl.own use op.cst	
INT	207	SCS: Revenue Own Use OC		841580	Rev.own use OC sett.	
INT	208	SCS:Writeoff AP OC Own/Vacancy		470590	Write-off AP op.cost	
INT	209	SCS: Clearing AP Vacancy OC		470750	Clg vcy op.cst adv.p	

Figure 4-26. *Replace account symbol with GL accounts*

One-time Posting

This section will look at the one-time posting process.

Menu Path

SAP Easy Access Menu ➤ Accounting ➤ Flexible Real Estate Management Accounting ➤ Single Documents ➤ Posting Activities ➤ Post Using Posting Activity

Transaction Code

RERAOP

Procedure

Follow these steps to carry out a one-time posting:

1. Start the transaction using either the menu path or the transaction code (Figure 4-27)

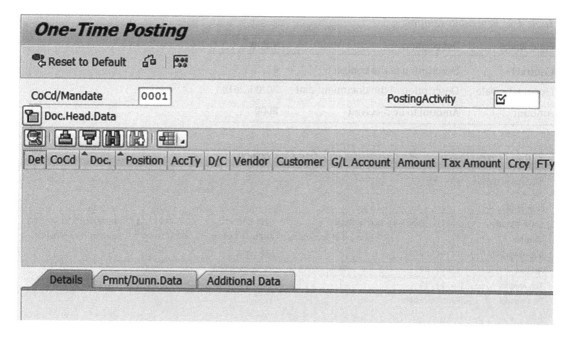

Figure 4-27. *One-Time Posting screen*

2. Press F4 to get the list of posting activities from the drop-down menu (Figure 4-28)

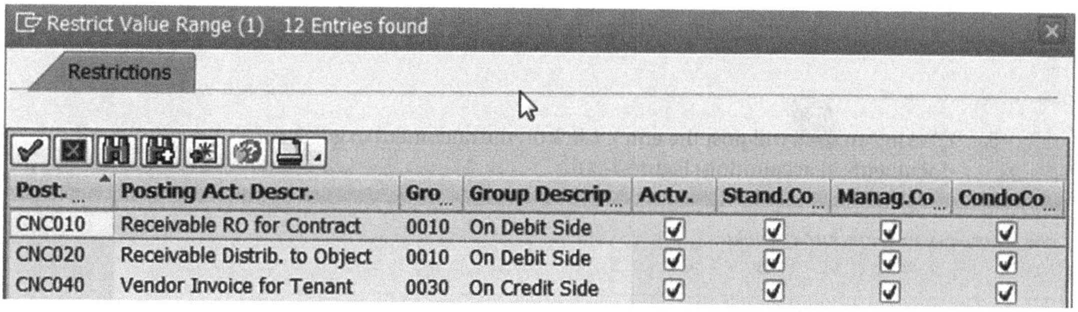

Post.	Posting Act. Descr.	Gro...	Group Descrip...	Actv.	Stand.Co...	Manag.Co...	CondoCo...
CNC010	Receivable RO for Contract	0010	On Debit Side	✔	✔	✔	✔
CNC020	Receivable Distrib. to Object	0010	On Debit Side	✔	✔	✔	✔
CNC040	Vendor Invoice for Tenant	0030	On Credit Side	✔	✔	✔	✔

Figure 4-28. *Posting activity list*

3. Double-click on the "Receivable RO for Contract" activity.

4. As required, complete and review the following fields, as shown in Table 4-7, and click on ✅ (Figure 4-29).

Table 4-7. *Real Estate Contract*

Field Name	Description	Value
Contract	Description of the contract	4
Document Date	Description of the document date	20/06/2016
Amount	Amount to be received	8000

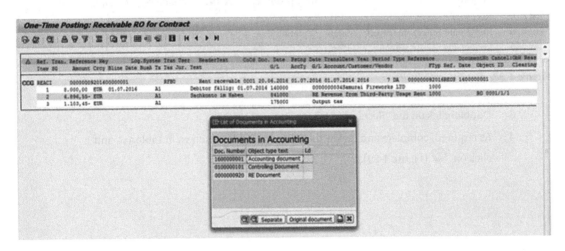

Figure 4-29. *One-Time Posting: Receivable RO for Contract screen*

> 5. Clicking on ⊞ will post the entry. Click on the document to get list of documents in accounting (Figure 4-30).

Figure 4-30. *One-Time Posting: Receivable RO for Contract screen and List of Documents in Accounting popup*

6. Double-click on accounting document number 1600000001 (Figure 4-31).

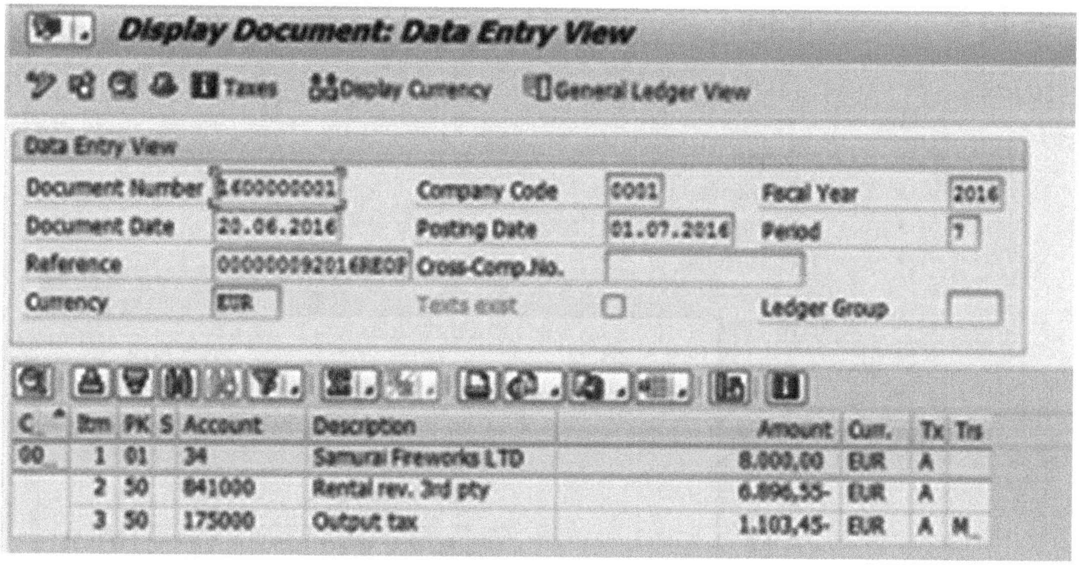

Figure 4-31. *Display Document: Data Entry View screen*

Accrual/Deferral Postings

An accrual of an expense refers to the reporting of an expense and the related liability in the period in which it occurs, and that period is prior to the period in which the payment is made. An example of an accrual for an expense is when the electricity consumed in December, but the payment will not be made until January.

A deferral of an expense refers to a payment that was made in one period, but will be reported as an expense in a later period. An example is the payment in December for the six-month insurance premium that will be reported as an expense in the months of January through June.

An accrual of revenues refers to the reporting of revenues and the related receivables in the period in which they are earned, and that period is prior to the period of the cash receipt. An example of the accrual of revenues is the interest earned in December on an investment in fixed deposit, but the interest will not be received until January.

The system can calculate accruals and deferrals to the day or month. The system differentiates between accruals and deferrals, and Accrual Engine is used for posting accruals and deferrals in REFX. Standard settings make it so that data is transferred from REFX to Accrual Engine, and at the same time accrual postings are made.

Settings for Accrual/Deferrals

Copy the settings for the REFX application component that are provided by SAP in the standard system, and then modify your enterprise structure (company codes, accounting principles, and so on) as required. Change your settings in the following IMG activities:

1. Create accrual types for the REFX component by clicking Define Accrual Types and filling in the Applic. Component field (Figure 4-32), which takes you to a screen where you (Figure 4-33).

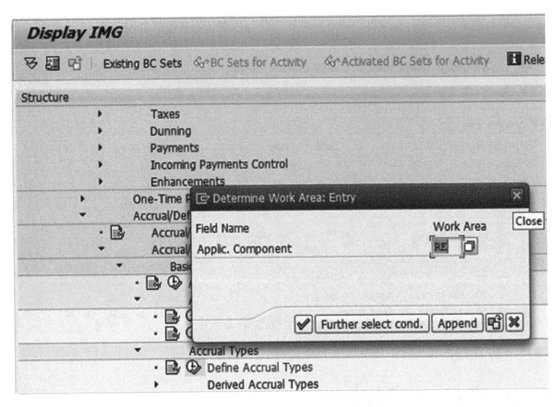

Figure 4-32. *Determine Work Area: Entry screen*

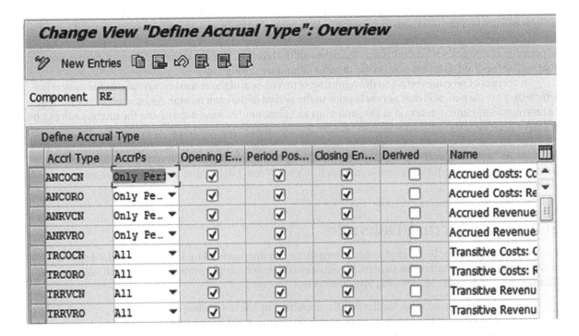

Figure 4-33. *Define accrual types*

2. You need to enter an accounting principle for the REFX component in Define Customer Settings for Components (Figure 4-34 and Figure 4-35)

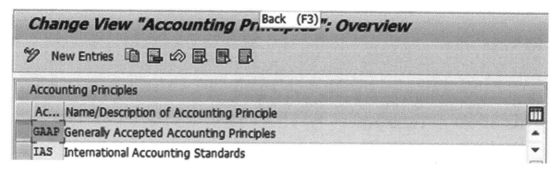

Figure 4-34. *Define customer settings for components*

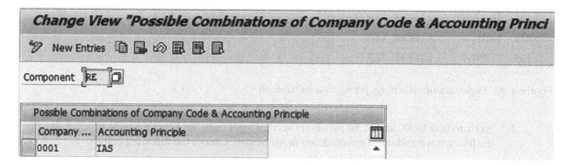

Figure 4-35. *Assign accounting principle to company code*

3. Enter a standard accrual method in Define Standard Settings for Accrual Calculation (Figure 4-36)

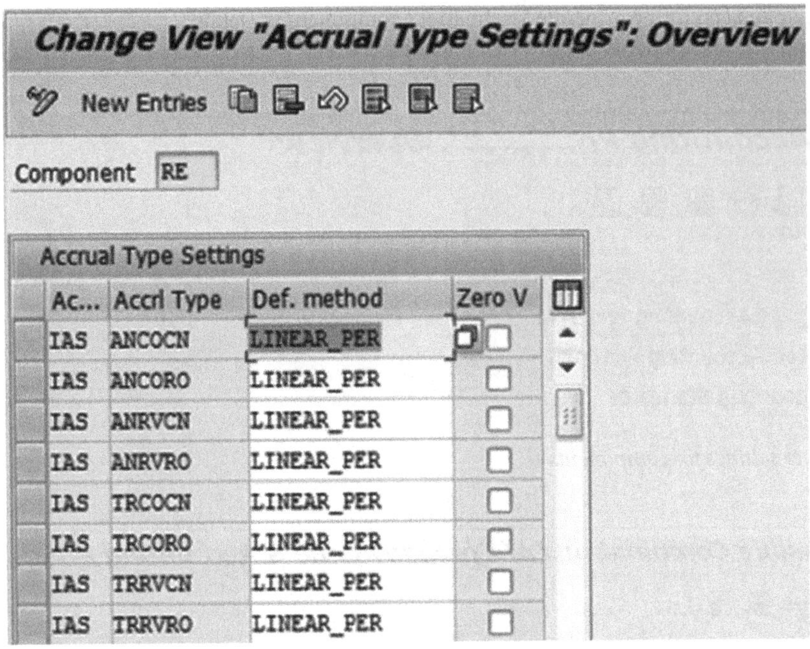

Figure 4-36. *Define standard settings for accrual calculation*

4. To customize REFX, assign the necessary accrual types from the Accrual Engine to the flow types for which accruals/deferrals are posted. Choose the following path:

   SAP Customizing Implementation Guide ➤ Flexible Real Estate Management (Enterprise Extension) ➤ Conditions and Flows ➤ Flow Types ➤ Define Flow Types (Figure 4-37).

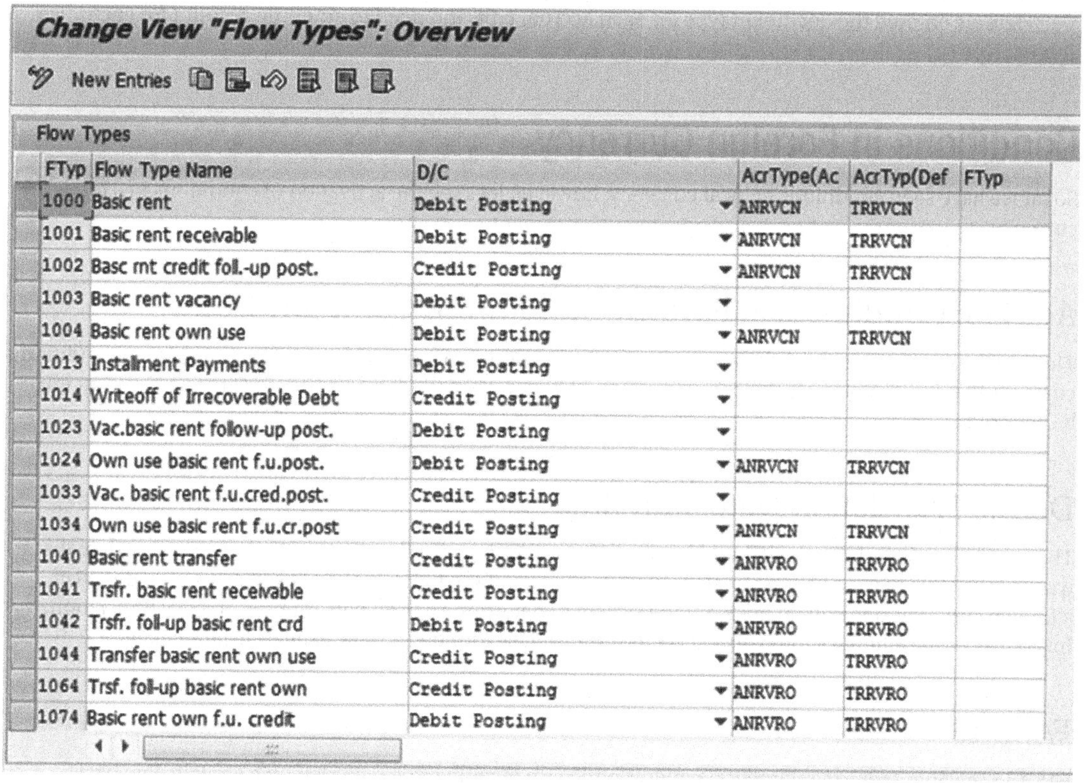

Change View "Flow Types": Overview

⚙ New Entries 🗈🗐⤶🖩🖩🖩

Flow Types

FTyp	Flow Type Name	D/C		AcrType(Ac	AcrTyp(Def	FTyp
1000	Basic rent	Debit Posting	▼	ANRVCN	TRRVCN	
1001	Basic rent receivable	Debit Posting	▼	ANRVCN	TRRVCN	
1002	Basc rnt credit foll.-up post.	Credit Posting	▼	ANRVCN	TRRVCN	
1003	Basic rent vacancy	Debit Posting	▼			
1004	Basic rent own use	Debit Posting	▼	ANRVCN	TRRVCN	
1013	Instalment Payments	Debit Posting	▼			
1014	Writeoff of Irrecoverable Debt	Credit Posting	▼			
1023	Vac.basic rent follow-up post.	Debit Posting	▼			
1024	Own use basic rent f.u.post.	Debit Posting	▼	ANRVCN	TRRVCN	
1033	Vac. basic rent f.u.cred.post.	Credit Posting	▼			
1034	Own use basic rent f.u.cr.post	Credit Posting	▼	ANRVCN	TRRVCN	
1040	Basic rent transfer	Credit Posting	▼	ANRVRO	TRRVRO	
1041	Trsfr. basic rent receivable	Credit Posting	▼	ANRVRO	TRRVRO	
1042	Trsfr. foll-up basic rent crd	Debit Posting	▼	ANRVRO	TRRVRO	
1044	Transfer basic rent own use	Credit Posting	▼	ANRVRO	TRRVRO	
1064	Trsf. foll-up basic rent own	Credit Posting	▼	ANRVRO	TRRVRO	
1074	Basic rent own f.u. credit	Debit Posting	▼	ANRVRO	TRRVRO	

◀ ▶

Figure 4-37. *Define flow types*

5. We create the accrual types for accruals and deferrals for the REFX component as follows:

SAP Customizing Implementation Guide ➤ Flexible Real Estate Management (Enterprise Extension) ➤ Accounting ➤ Accrual/Deferral ➤ Accrual/Deferral ➤ Accrual/Deferral Posting ➤ Account Determination ➤ Simple Account Determination ➤ Define Set of Rules (Figure 4-38).

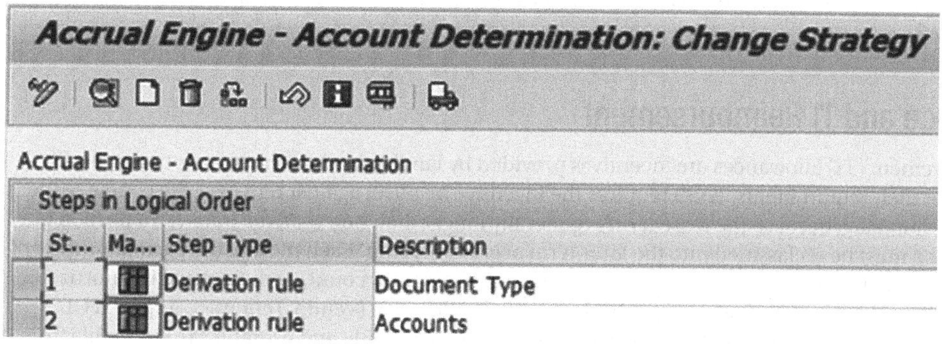

Accrual Engine - Account Determination: Change Strategy

⚙ 🗐🗋 🗑🗐 ⤶🖩🖳 🖶

Accrual Engine - Account Determination

Steps in Logical Order

St...	Ma...	Step Type	Description
1	🎟	Derivation rule	Document Type
2	🎟	Derivation rule	Accounts

Figure 4-38. *Define set of rules*

61

Here we entered the document type for each accrual type and need to enter the account for each given accrual type.

Conditions in Foreign Currency

So far we have seen conditions in local currency; however, let's see the activation of conditions in a foreign currency.

Activate Conditions in Foreign Currency in Company Code

The first step is to define the default currency for each company code. If the company is to allow a condition currency that is different from the company code currency, then the "Diff Condition Currency" option must be selected.

Define Translation Date Shift Rule

The translation date shift rule defines how the system determines a date on the basis of a starting date that was entered. You have to define translation date shift rules if the following applies: You use conditions in a foreign currency, and you do not want the system to determine a fixed date for the currency translation. Instead, the date entered should only serve as a starting date for determining the translation date.

FASB 13

FASB 13 specifies that irregular rent payments and lease incentives be recorded on a straight-line basis. Based on US GAAP, the company needs to record the following entries into the general ledger:

Straight-Line Requirements

SAP has provided a FAS13 sample BAdI. This BAdI may be implemented in order to automate the straight-lining of entries associated with irregular rent payments and lease incentives. At the time of Go live , FAS13 functional specification document containing detailed requirements and developments may be prepared. Existing leases may be excluded from the FAS13 calculation, because the values being amortized may not match the system-calculated values due to the timing of the conditions and recognition of all one-time payments that are FAS13 relevant. In order to exclude leases from this calculation, a custom table with company code, contract number, and an exclusion indicator can be created listing all existing leases at the time of "go-live."

TI Allowance and TI Reimbursement

Tenant improvement (TI) allowances are incentives provided by landlords with which tenants can modify a space to meet their requirements. FASB requires the incentive be offset against rent over the course of the lease term. Additionally, because the lease term is generally longer than one year, the long-term portion of the TI allowance must be reclassified into the long-term accrual account. Each month, the current portion of the long-term accrual should be reclassified to the short-term accrual account, as the accrual is amortized. Because a TI allowance requires that a receivable be set up on a lease-in (vendor) contract, a special GL indicator will need to be configured to appropriately classify the receivable and prohibit the receivable from being offset against rent expenses.

Key Aspects

Key aspects to be considered in RE accounting are as follows:

- When SAP Real Estate is activated, real estate–specific fields are made available for use within the various finance modules. To use these fields, the field status group should be changed to allow an "Optional" entry. The real estate cost object may then be used just like any other SAP cost object.

- Generally, vendor master records will be created by the accounts payable department, and the corresponding landlord with vendor account is created automatically. This automation should only create business partners with the role "Landlord w/ Vendor Account" if the vendor is specifically for real estate. However, all invoices related to real estate should be posted directly to a real estate object. The real estate object will eventually settle the expenses with the real estate cost center. It is critical that all costs are posted to the real estate object to enable full cost allocation to all tenants.

- With the activation of real estate accounting, the real estate cost objects become available for use within FI postings, but the field status for group "Real Estate Management" must be marked as an optional entry. The following field status groups should be modified to allow postings to real estate object.

- You can post conditions for withholding tax using RE posting processes. You can use this function, for example, in the United States to deal with sales tax on lease payments. When a contract is created, the tax indicator is assigned to the posting parameter. During periodic processing, the tax payment is reduced from or added to the payment amount based on the tax configuration. The tax amount is paid directly to the appropriate tax authorities.

- A consistent issue most organizations encounter is the lack of ability to link fixed assets to a building or property. To alleviate this issue, the real estate key (IM Key) will be displayed on the asset master record for assignment to a real estate object. Additionally, users may assign fixed assets to a building or property object through the architectural view.

- The "Define Screen Layout for Asset Master Data" asset classes must be identified who must have the real estate indicator.

- In order to receive depreciation postings to a real estate object, the account assignment object's IM Key must be activated for both expense and balance sheet postings. The account assignment is then assigned to each company code and depreciation area that has real estate assets.

Service Tax

In India, companies leasing buildings or properties for commercial purposes are required to pay service tax to the corresponding federal tax office. Real estate contracts are considered to be contracts for services and not for goods, and therefore, from a business point of view, in India no value-added tax (VAT) needs to be maintained in the contracts, only service tax. From a technical point of view, the service tax is handled like VAT. It is levied on the services rendered and is applied on the total price of the service. For lease-out contracts, it is a deferred tax that is levied at the time of the incoming payment.

In cases of commercial contracts, the owner of the real estate object reports and pays the service tax to the corresponding tax authorities. The geographical location of the real estate object determines which local tax authority the service tax should be reported to. The owner of the real estate object enters the tax office information in the real estate object master data. Residential contracts are not subject to service tax.

The business place represents the organizational unit responsible for collecting service tax. You maintain business places in the following master data of Flexible Real Estate Management (REFX):

- Business entities (Sites)

- Buildings

- Properties (Land)

You fill in the required customization settings. You might maintain business entities, buildings, properties, and rental objects. You assign the objects to your commercial contract and create conditions for your contract with tax types and tax groups that correspond to the service tax. Each month, you make a periodic posting of your commercial contract. Whenever the tenant pays the rent for the real estate object, you post the incoming (partial) payments with the Incoming Payments program and account for the service tax in the GL tax accounts, and then you make a payment to the tax authorities.

Summary

We have seen how accounting is managed in SAP REFX, including different types of postings, how to do a reversal, and how REFX updates accounting data in RE object. Periodic postings create accounting, controlling, and RE documents that are updated within real estate contracts. We have also discussed some of the key aspects of real estate contracts from an accounting perspective.

CHAPTER 5

Business Integration

This chapter will explain how SAP REFX integrates with the SAP Asset Accounting (AA), SAP Plant and Maintenance (PM), SAP Project Systems (PS), SAP Customer Relationship Management (CRM), and SAP Document Management Systems (DMS) modules. The chapter is divided into the following topics:

- Integration with Asset Accounting

- Integration with PM, PS, and CRM

- Integration with DMS

- Integration of CAD and GIS

The SAP Flexible Real Estate Management solution is used by organizations in various sectors, such as retail, technology, banking, heavy industry, airports, oil and energy, utility energy, and many others. All of these industries have multiple production sites, gasoline stations, warehouses, and ports located in owned or rented property. SAP REFX helps these companies to manage the real estate assets, such as for property maintenance, and to assess the profitability of individual branches and outlets. SAP REFX has strong integration capabilities and can be used by organizations with an SAP backend and also by companies operating other ERP systems. It naturally integrates with other SAP modules, industry solutions, and SAP business objects. It is capable of integrating with third-party solutions and enables operational efficiency and attainment of business objectives for different sectors using the solution.

REFX provides seamless integration with other SAP modules that cover things like Fixed Assets, Finance and Controlling, Sales and Distribution, Project Management, Investment Management, Plant Maintenance, and HR. The ability to integrate with the Microsoft Office software package helps the solution's users to communicate with vendors, customers, and business partners who are associated with a property. In such a case, it is possible to use SAP REFX for lease agreements, to send invoices to tenants, and to order additional maintenance work. You can generate dynamic reports, which can then be uploaded to Excel.

Integration with Asset Accounting

The Asset Accounting (FI-AA) module is used for managing fixed assets and providing detailed information on transactions regarding fixed assets. The R/3 Asset Accounting module transfers data directly to and from other SAP modules via its integration capabilities. When you purchase an asset, you can post an entry from the Materials Management (MM) module directly to FI-AA, or when it is constructed in house, all the costs—like material, labor, and services—can be posted to a "Work in progress" account within the work breakdown structure (WBS), which can then be settled to an asset account.

The link between real estate objects and an asset is established by entering details of the real estate objects in the asset master under the time-dependent tab, and it is used as an account assignment object. Correspondingly, we need to assign the relevant asset number in the Assignment tab of the Rental Objects screen. A real estate object can be used as a depreciation account assignment after following certain steps.

We need to release the real estate object from the RE master data dialog for account assignment and then manually maintain the real estate account assignment in the Time-dependent tab of the asset master record. The use of the real estate object as an account assignment for depreciation is only possible if the corresponding settings are made in the Customization screen of the Asset Accounting module.

Customization in Asset Accounting

The following are the activities to be carried out for the integration of Asset Accounting with REFX.

Master Data Screen Layout

We have to change the configuration settings for Asset Accounting in the Master Data screen, defining a screen layout rule. In the screen layout rule, under time-dependant data section, we have to select the "field group rule" option for a real estate object.

Integration with GL

Now, we have to define the field status variant and select "Real Estate Management" under that.

Additional Account Assignment Objects

In this step we will handle settings for additional account assignment objects—settings like cost center, investment order, and real estate object. We need to activate additional account assignment objects (IMKEY) so that transactions can be posted to the general ledger. Real estate objects like business entity, land, building, and rental object can be set as account assignment objects.

The standard reports are available in REFX for object assignments in Buildings/Rental Objects (ROs), and depreciation values can be checked in asset reports.

Let us take, for example, a building structure at a mall that is partially used for internal purposes by a company while the remaining space is let out to different tenants, such as shops, bank, commercial establishments. etc. In SAP FI-AA, you capitalize the building as one structure, and depreciation and maintenance costs are captured for the building as a whole. This is as per statutory and accounting requirements of the respective country. You do not capitalize each unit of the building separately in Asset Accounting, as shown in the following screenshots (Figure 5-1). The asset master record for the building is created in FI-AA, and under the Time-dependent tab you can see that the real estate object is assigned (Figure 5-2).

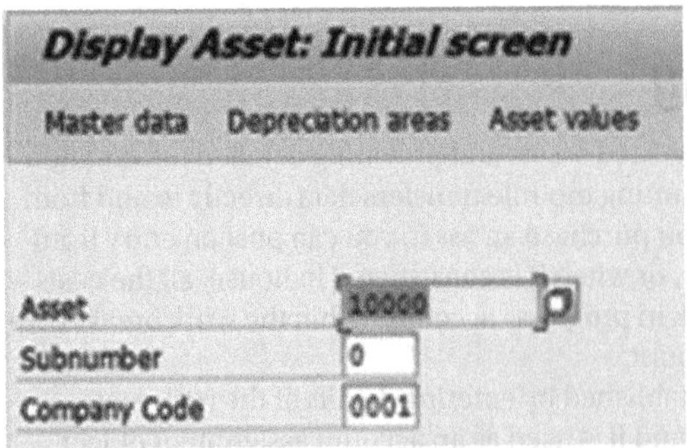

Figure 5-1. *Asset master record's Initial screen*

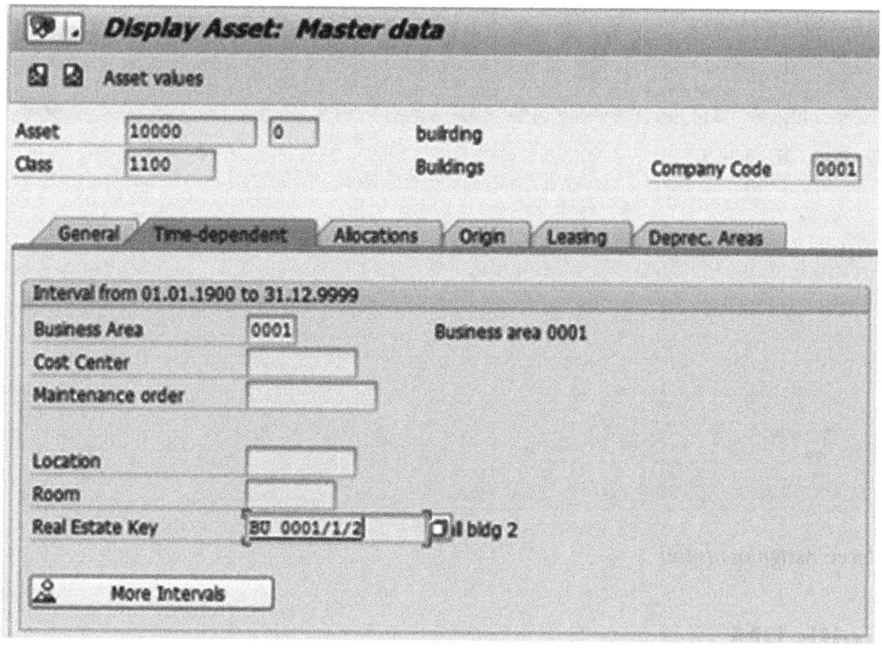

Figure 5-2. *Asset master record: Time-dependent tab*

However, all of the sub-units in the one building are captured as separate real estate objects by SAP REFX. You need to enter these objects in the asset's master screen in FI-AA and enter the asset number generated in FI-AA in the Assignments tab of the rental object (Figure 5-3 and Figure 5-4). You may also enter the business entity in the asset's master record.

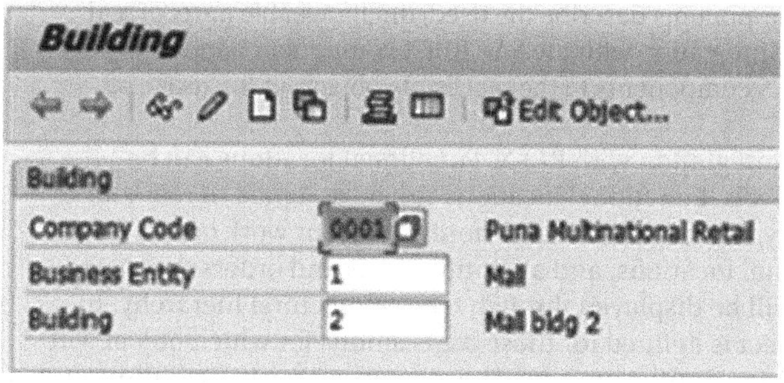

Figure 5-3. *Rental object: Initial screen*

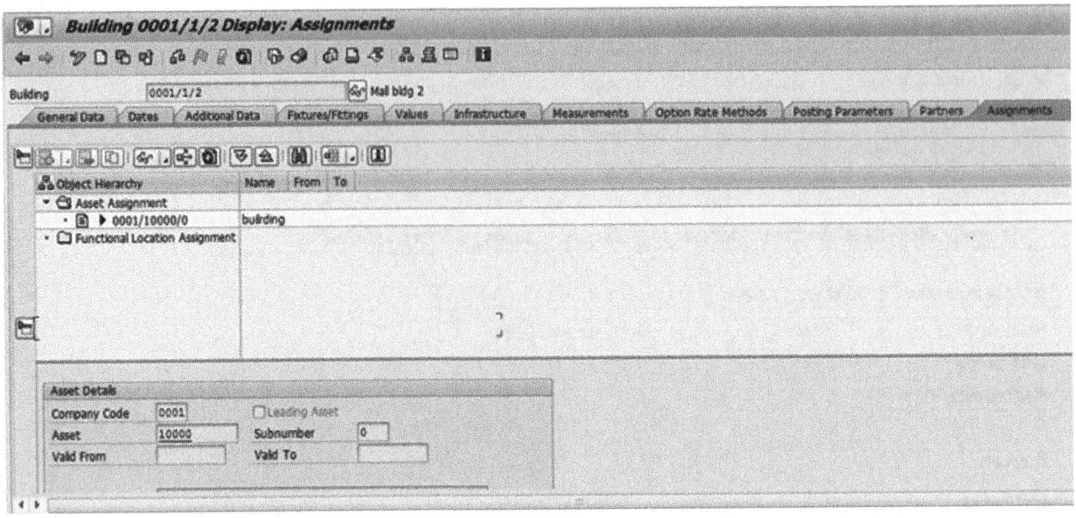

Figure 5-4. Rental object: Assignments tab

Integration with PM

SAP PM module provides a comprehensive solution for all maintenance activities performed within the organization. Let us take an example of an airport building. Various real estate objects that are part of the building need maintenance. You may have a plant in the same structure, and it may be necessary to ensure regular and preventive maintenance tasks. Some examples of maintenance are cleaning of premises, repairing various systems, preventative maintenance of elevators and air conditioning systems, and many other such services. Airport authorities can use the Plant Maintenance module to manage their real estate objects. We can use the Customer Services module for real estate objects used by tenants, customers, or other companies within group. The master data objects of both components are same.

Functional locations in the PM and CS components describe the fixed, unchangeable parts of real estate, such as maintenance groups or rooms. Integration with the SAP REFX component happens by assigning functional locations of the PM and CS components to the real estate objects in the usage or architectural views.

The architectural view controls the PM integration with REFX. Functional locations can be maintained at the plant, building, and site levels. Functional locations can be assigned to real estate master data either manually or automatically. The user can create notifications or work orders from the architectural hierarchy for these functional locations, and all notifications and orders that have been linked to a building, property, or site will be displayed through the architectural hierarchy. In this configuration step, the architectural object is defined for those transactions for which object will be used to create notifications and work orders. Notifications may be created at the site, building, and property levels.

You may use functionality for the automatic creation of functional locations from the architectural hierarchy. However, there has to be a business requirement to drive functional locations to lower levels, such as part of building or room.

Integration with PS

SAP PS is an integrated project management tool used for planning, managing, and controlling projects; it supports the entire project lifecycle from planning to invoicing. Project System is used for new project and development work like construction projects that have a certain time cycle for completion. Let us take the previous example of an airport where we have to construct a runway with other facilities around it. You may have to start with design, drawing, consultancy expenses, and so on. You have to procure materials and incur labor costs, and after completion of construction, you must transfer all costs to create and capitalize assets. You need to capture these costs until completion in a separate account assignment object—or work breakdown structure (WBS)—and settle it with the asset master data created in FI-AA, where the cost value is posted and then linked with a real estate object.

You can assign a complete project (project definition with several WBS elements) or parts of a project (one or more WBS elements). In the application, you maintain the assignment in the Assignments tab of the relevant data object. However, you must have already enabled the assignment in Customizing before you can do this.

The PS component does not have an attribute that you can use to maintain the assignment. You may use other ways, like configuring the project number in such a way that part of the number contains the relevant information to represent the assignment.

Integration with CRM

The integration point between CRM and REFX is the real estate master data. SAP CRM integration is available to cater the service/complaint management needs of SAP REFX. We can define the product or service that is the subject of the complaint by entering a reference object for an item. You can enter a reference to products, installed base components, or objects (e.g., rental objects, buildings, land, business entities). Let us take the same example of an airport where space is allotted to a customer for duty-free shops, cafeteria, and so on. Any complaint about maintenance or other issues related to space allotted or a specific service request is sent with a reference to the rental object that is the property created in REFX. Besides this, we can also automatically create functional locations upon REFX object creation, which can be updated as an installed base in SAP CRM. We can use this functionality of SAP CRM while having objects linked to the SAP REFX object.

SAP provides a business role called Real Estate Professional (/CRMRE/PRO) that provides a user interface that enables you to manage campaigns, leads, and opportunities for your real estate.

SAP also provides a business adapter object called Real Estate Rental Object (/CRMRE/ROBJ) and a customizing adapter object called Rental Object Customizing Table (/CRMRE/CUST_RO) to enable replication of data for real estate objects like entity, RO, land, and building from SAP ECC. These real estate objects exist in SAP CRM as objects, but replication of the real estate objects is one-way only, and we cannot do it reverse.

Campaign Management for Real Estate

We can create campaign types using the Real Estate Campaign (CCM_RCPG) UI scenario. When we create a campaign using one of these campaign types, a new assignment block of rental objects is made available. In this assignment block, you can enter the rental objects that you want to market. Let us take the example of the airport where we have vacant places to be given for commercial purposes; we can create a campaign for letting them out and can also perform availability checks for the same places.

Lead Management for Real Estate

A new transaction type called Real Estate Lead (LDRE) provided by SAP helps in lead management for real estate. When we create a lead using this transaction type, a new assignment block of rental objects and a new date type of "Expected Contract Period" are made available. We can enter the rental objects that are available for lease-out in the rental objects assignment block. The expected contract period date type enables system checks to verify the occupancy of a rental object during the specified period.

Opportunity Management for Real Estate

A new transaction type called Real Estate Opportunity (OPRE) helps in opportunity management for real estate. When you create an opportunity using this transaction type, a new assignment block of rental objects and a new date type of "Expected Contract Period" are made available. We can enter the rental objects that we want to rent in the rental objects assignment block. The expected contract period date type enables system checks to verify the occupancy of a rental object during the specified period.

Integration with DMS

Document Management System in SAP REFX enables you to store the documents involved in the rental management process (such as agreements, legal documents, land records, tenant ID proofs, any legal documents, master data summaries, letters, contract forms, presentations, structural drawings, or photos of buildings/properties, etc.) The SAP REFX system is data intensive and is used for maintaining complex land records. Let us take for an example an oil and gas company that has a refinery as its production unit and retail outlets spread across regions distributing gas to vehicle owners. These retail outlets, or gas pumps, are constructed on either purchased land or leased land. Each piece of land has different records, agreements, designs, and so forth that need to be referred to for lease payment or at the time of legal disputes. DMS is used by organizations to maintain complete data against real estate objects—which is land in this case. It improves business value greatly, as companies do not have complete visibility as to area of land or lease terms disputes, if any, and integration of real estate with DMS helps to address these painful areas. We can select the DMS of our choice; SAP DMS is also available along with third-party DMS. We can also manage the SAP REFX workflow through DMS. SAP DMS, when used with REFX, will require the creation of a dedicated document type, which then will be used for uploading the soft copies of documents(s).

We can follow this path for configuring DMS for SAP REFX:

SPRO ➤ Flexible Real Estate Management (REFX) ➤ General Settings for Master Data and Contract ➤ Document Management ➤ Document Management System.

There is also an integration process for SAP REFX and DMS; SAP note 860779 is available to explain that.

Integration with CAD/GIS

Organizations have been striving to optimize their processes and improve efficiency by using SAP. GIS is used for location-based information management, and SAP is used for other business requirements at an overarching level. Both systems have strong points, and integrating both adds tremendous value to a business. However, in spite of many attempts, no direct integration has been accomplished due to the complexity involved in handling both systems. Integration of both is a win-win situation, as SAP can leverage the spatial analysis capabilities of GIS and GIS can use the integrated business functionalities of SAP. Most business data have a geographic or spatial component that can be geo-referenced on a GIS map to visualize, understand, and interpret data, which is not possible through a spreadsheet or table. By visualizing relationships, connections, and patterns in business data, GIS helps in making appropriate decisions and increasing efficiency. The strength of SAP is its responsiveness to market changes and customer requirements, which could be further enhanced with the integration of GIS applications into business workflows. Development in digital technology and service-oriented architecture concepts made it possible to embed GIS applications with different systems such as SCADA and SAP.

Let us take, for example, the utility and energy sector, where geographical mapping is a key element for having an efficient decision-making processes for site selection, routing, resource allocation, planning, and asset management. GIS gives businesses the geographic advantage to become more responsive to daily business needs, such as land management, site selection, facility maintenance, emergency response, construction activities, fleet management and tracking, equipment mobilization, pipelines routing, and many others.

Integrating SAP REFX with CAD/GIS systems enables a visual interface for the architectural view. Master data of a land register or business entity or building can be attached real estate object to view the (CAD) design or (GIS) map of the property. We can make this assignment from either the usage view or the architectural view. However, the system always copies the measurements from the architectural object to the usage object.

The unique ability of GIS to model complex spatial relationships is challenging in hierarchical SAP structures, such as networks. GIS is also well suited to creating accurate SAP master data for attributes such as distance or area for use in such activities. We need to check that for every SAP business object where a graphic representation is desired, there is a corresponding feature in the GIS database. For example, a gas company may wish to capture information about a gas connection provided with a building. Similarly, details of water and electric connections can be located within a specific building, which is made possible by functionality available in GIS. The linking of GIS features to SAP business objects is achieved through foreign-key mapping, which can attach the unique ID for each SAP business object with a corresponding GIS feature.

SAP REFX and GIS are integrated and used in some of the airports where the entire land and real estate space is mapped in GIS to create a visual interface and be integrated with real estate objects. This helps to keep close control over property and also to ensure effective utilization of the property.

Port trust authorities are also using these interfaces to control port trust land, which is large in size and scattered; ensuring a close watch on such land is a challenge. These interfaces are further integrated with DMS, where all the land records, drawings, designs, and agreements are stored along with RE objects, and one can quickly get complete information about it.

Summary

SAP Flexible Real Estate Management provides seamless integration capabilities to connect with other SAP modules—and non-SAP systems also—giving customers the best use of its functionality. SAP REFX combined with GIS/CAD is big value add for many organizations with large real estate assets. They are able to control assets effectively and ensure complete control of them.

CHAPTER 6

Service Charge Settlements

In this chapter we will explain the service charge settlement process and factors influencing it, as well as describe the posting procedures. In this chapter, we will discuss the following:

- Infrastructure of service charge settlements

- Pre-requisites to configuring a service charge settlement

- Configurations for service charge settlements in REFX

- Define RE-specific account properties

Let us understand this using a business scenario.

Let us take an example of a mall where shops are let out on a rental basis to various units, like a fast food restaurant, fashion stores, other retail shops, bank ATMS, offices, and so on, and common facilities are provided and paid for by the lessor. Costs incurred for the maintenance of such facilities are paid by the landlord for the mall as a whole and need to be recovered from all tenants based on usage. This requires a system that will allocate costs among various tenants every month based on agreed upon parameters and debit them for settlement. SAP Flexible Real Estate Management provides fully automated, accurate, and transparent processes to ensure efficient service charge settlement processing. SAP REFX can help manage services, maintenance, and repairs for a particular organization's properties and also for the organization's customers' properties. In SAP all the service charges are generally settled through settlement units, which have to be defined for each service charge that needs to be settled. A new settlement unit has to be created for each type of service charge that is defined in the service charge key and that participates in the settlement.

Another example is an airport where retail space has been let out to various units like duty-free shops, bank ATMs, restaurants, and spas, and where space is also used for the internal operations of airport, like offices, cargo handling unit's break rooms, and so forth. The airport makes a total water and electricity bill payment for the complete property, and that needs to be recovered from each occupant based on usage. Water and electricity meters will provide usage details, and a service charge will be allocated among the tenants and internal units based on usage. The amount needs to be debited to the tenant and to the respective cost center of the internal unit. Apportionment of service charges needs to be clearly defined, as all costs are not apportionable in simple ways, such as we do for water or power where you have meters to capture consumption. Certain costs are not apportionable and need to have a logical, transparent basis for allocation. Elevator charges paid by the airport authority may not be possible to apportion between tenants who are using it—what is the basis for charging for it?

Service charge keys are created for the types of expenses that occur in real estate properties. Some of them are apportionable and some are not. For example, property taxes and water supply costs are allocated to tenants based on actual meters, but how do we allocate costs for the maintenance of elevators? We cannot keep track of the usage of each tenant. We need to use some rational basis for allocation. The next step will be to apportion the service charges among tenants who are liable to pay for the usage of such services. In REFX, you apportion service charges based on the measurements defined in the rental objects. It can be done in a few ways.

© Jayant Daithankar 2016
J. Daithankar, *SAP Flexible Real Estate Management*, DOI 10.1007/978-1-4842-1482-4_6

Various parameters based on which apportionment expenses can be made are:

- Apportionment according to fixed values where a fixed amount that will be charged to each tenant is agreed upon by the parties

- Apportionment according to consumption values wherein you capture the number of units consumed by each tenant for electricity usage and charge based on the total units for which the landlord made a bill payment

- Apportionment according to condition types

- Apportionment according to percentage shares where you agree to share a specific percentage of costs between various units

- Equal apportionment where an equal amount is allocated to each tenant

- Apportionment for vacant rental objects where a rental object—say, a shop—is vacant but you need to pay basis electricity charges and other charges and you need to allocate it to a respective unit/cost center

Once costs are apportioned, a service charge settlement is carried out through contracts and invoices. The tenants and service providers are entered into the system as business partners. The contracts are raised with the business partners and are managed by the contract management system in REFX; the invoices are raised and posted, as REFX is integrated with SAP Finance and Controlling (FICO).

Infrastructure of Service Charge Settlements

We need to create the following master data in order to carry out a service charge settlement.

Participation Group

Transaction Code

RESCPG

The participation group (Figure 6-1) is made up of tenants who are required to share common expenses incurred for all. Rental objects are part of this group that participates in the settlement of one or more cost elements. Example: water charges paid by the mall owner need to be recovered from all the shops that are leased out for rent. We have to define the participation group containing these shops, which are created as rental objects in the system. Business entities, buildings, land, and rental objects can be part of a participation group. If a business entity containing rental objects is assigned, rental objects assigned to it are also automatically assigned to the participation group. The participation group indicates whether the rental object participates in the settlement. All rental objects assigned to a participation group participate in the apportionment of costs, provided that this participation group is assigned to a settlement unit. For example, if a building is assigned to the participation group, all of the rental objects belonging to that building are automatically assigned. We can exclude individual rental objects from a participation group, and also assign individual pooled spaces without including corresponding rental spaces. The apportionment of expenses between the rental objects of a participation group may be done for a defined period. Hence, while creating a participation group, we need to mention its validity period (Figure 6-2). Any expense beyond the validity period will not be allocated to the rental objects within the participation group.

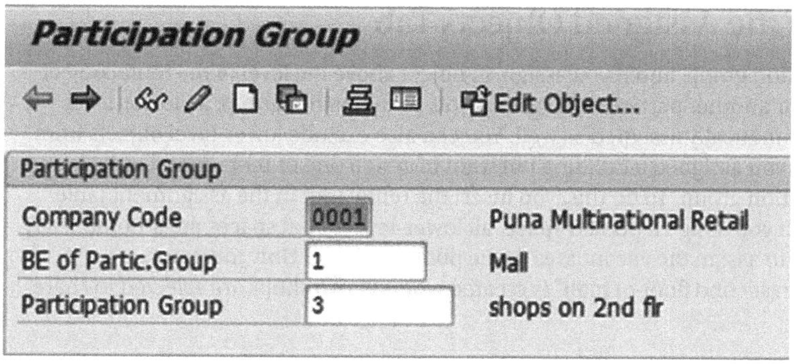

Participation Group

⬅ ➡ | 🔍 ✏ ▯ ▣ | 🖥 ▤ | 🗗 Edit Object...

Participation Group

Company Code	0001	Puna Multinational Retail
BE of Partic.Group	1	Mall
Participation Group	3	shops on 2nd flr

Figure 6-1. *Participation Group screen*

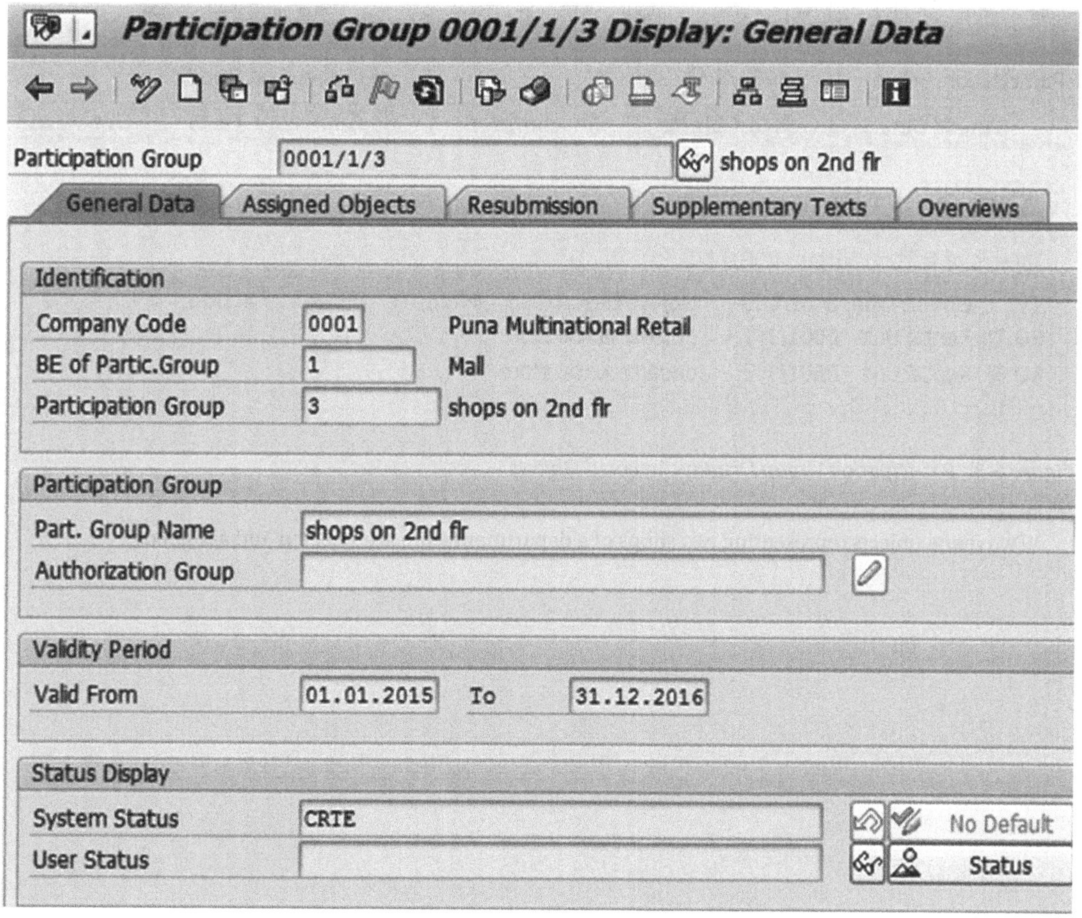

Participation Group 0001/1/3 Display: General Data

⬅ ➡ | ✂ ▯ ▣ ▤ | 🔳 ▱ 🔲 | 🗗 ✒ | 🔩 ▱ ◁ | 🖧 🖥 ▤ | ℹ

Participation Group | 0001/1/3 | 🔍 shops on 2nd flr

| General Data | Assigned Objects | Resubmission | Supplementary Texts | Overviews |

Identification

Company Code	0001	Puna Multinational Retail
BE of Partic.Group	1	Mall
Participation Group	3	shops on 2nd flr

Participation Group

Part. Group Name	shops on 2nd flr
Authorization Group		✏

Validity Period

Valid From	01.01.2015	To	31.12.2016

Status Display

System Status	CRTE		No Default
User Status			Status

Figure 6-2. *Participation Group Display: General Data*

Assign the Objects on the Assigned Objects Tab

Objects form a part of a participation group, and if you assign an object above the level of the rental object (such as building, pooled space, or another participation group) to a participation group, all lower-level objects within that object are automatically assigned as well. You can also exclude lower-level objects from the assignment. For example, say you assigned a building but want to assign one or more rental units from that building to another participation group. To do this, you insert the rental unit in the assignment table and select the Exclude indicator. If you assign a pooled space, all lower-level rental spaces are automatically assigned as well. If you only want to assign the vacant area of the pool, set the PS Only indicator.

Participation group "shops on second floor of mall" is created wherein two shops are selected to share service charge costs (Figure 6-3).

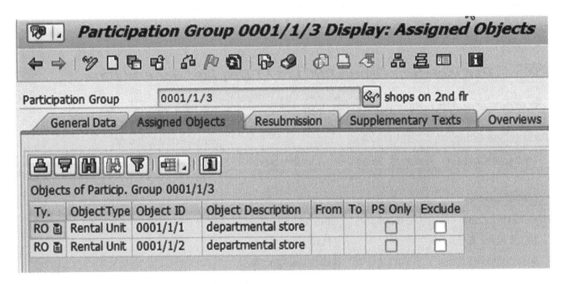

Figure 6-3. *Participation Group Display: Assigned Objects*

Two rental objects representing two shops of a department store are selected and assigned.

Settlement Unit

Transaction Code

RESCSU

We have to create a settlement unit (SU) before we settle service charges. The settlement unit defines the following:

- The settlement period during which settlement is possible, defined in settlement variants found in Customizing

- The type of service charges, such as water or electricity, by means of service charge keys

- Nature and purpose of the service charge apportionment, such as landlord/tenant apportionment or apportionment to tenants with any remainder assigned to landlord

- The measurement, such as electricity consumption in units or water consumption in cubic feet, using units of measurement defined in Customizing

- Rental objects like business entities, buildings, properties, and rental objects that are part of participation groups

We have to create a new settlement unit (Figure 6-4) for each type of service charge mentioned in the service charge key participating in the settlement. Cost collectors are defined for each settlement period to enable costs to be posted to a settlement unit. The costs of a settlement unit are collected on a cost collector for settlement for each settlement period. When we post to a settlement unit, the system determines the cost collector based on the specified settlement reference date (Figure 6-5).

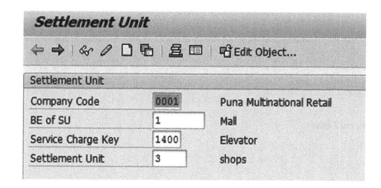

Figure 6-4. *Settlement Unit screen*

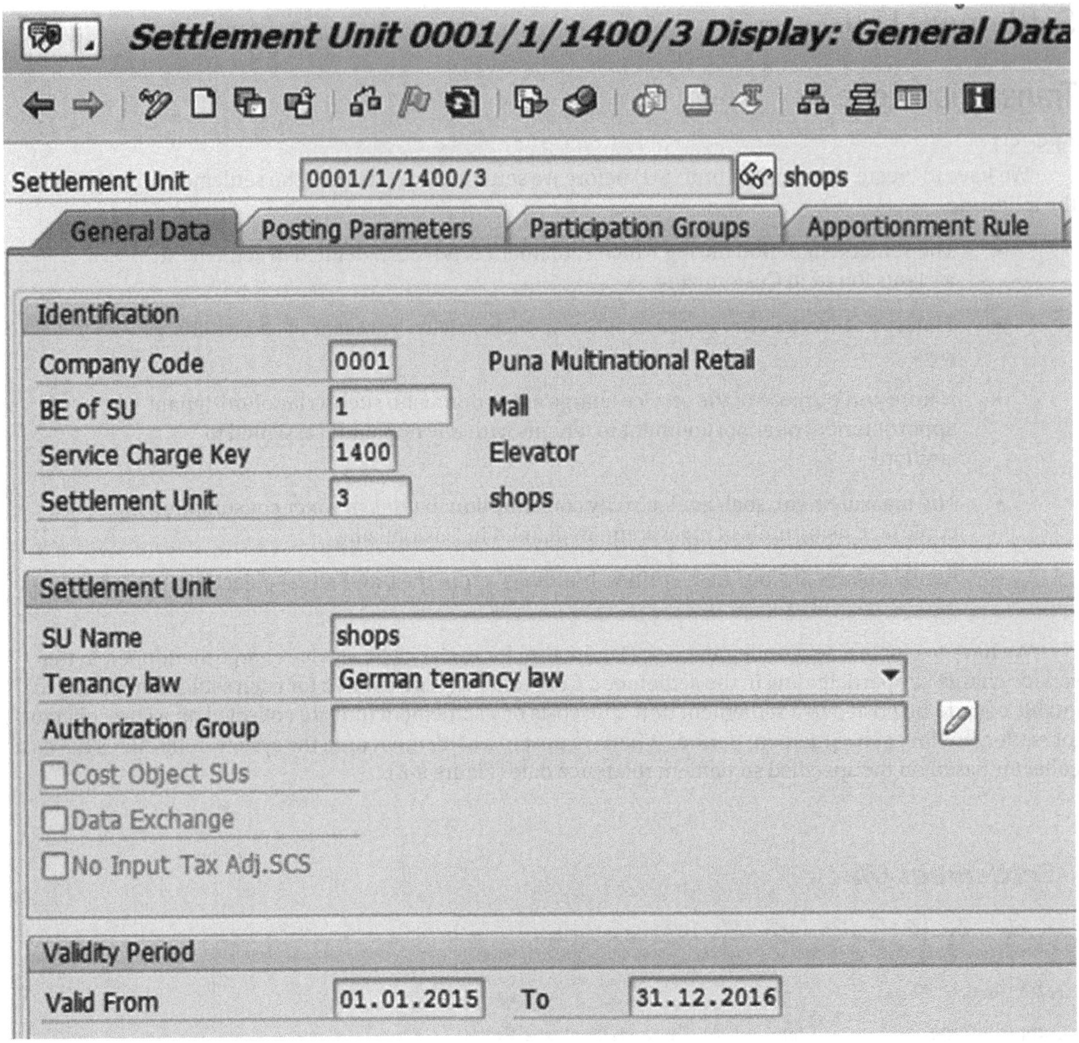

Figure 6-5. *Settlement Unit Display: General Data*

Click on the Participation Groups tab to assign a participation group (Figure 6-6).

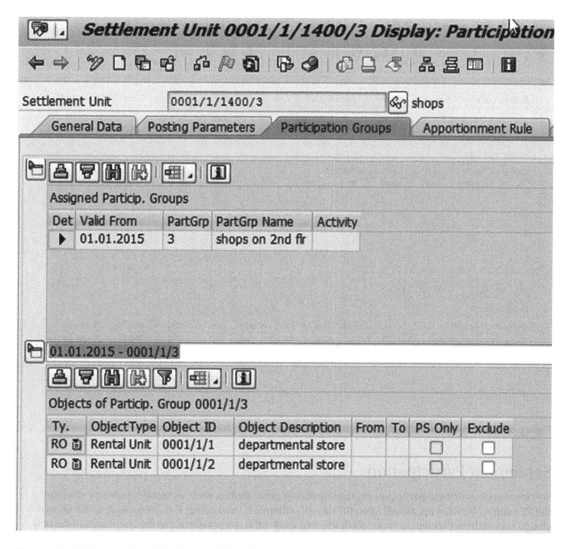

Figure 6-6. Settlement Unit Display: Participation Groups

Click on the Apportionment Rule tab to assign a settlement variant (Figure 6-7).

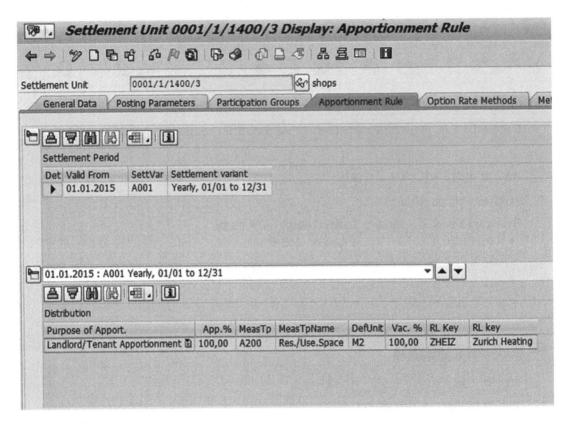

Figure 6-7. *Settlement Unit Display: Apportionment Rule*

Settlement Participation

Service charge settlement participation is automatically generated for each real estate contract each time the RE contract is called up, as well as on the date of settlement. In so doing, the system assigns the service charge keys of the settlement units to which the rental object(s) is/are assigned to the conditions of the real estate contract. In the Contract Processing screen, choose the Settlement Participation tab. The rental objects that are assigned to the contract are listed in the Selectable Objects table. When you have assigned the rental objects to a settlement unit, the settlement participation appears in the Settlement Participation tab for each selected rental object with the status 🔵 Generated. You can change the participation type and the validity period of the generated settlement participation of the rental object (Figure 6-8).

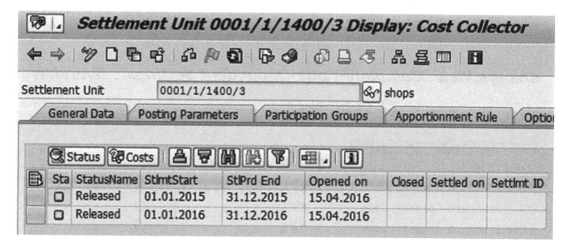

Figure 6-8. *Settlement Unit Display: Cost Collector*

Pre-requisites to Configuring Service Charge Settlement

To enable the use of REFX, we need to define a company code and controlling area at the enterprise level and activate the Financial Extension (Application Indicator EA-FIN) within the SAP R/3 Enterprise extension set. Also, activation of the BTE application (RE) is required to ensure business transactions events (BTE) related to other modules. After this, the real estate extension needs to be activated (Figure 6-9).

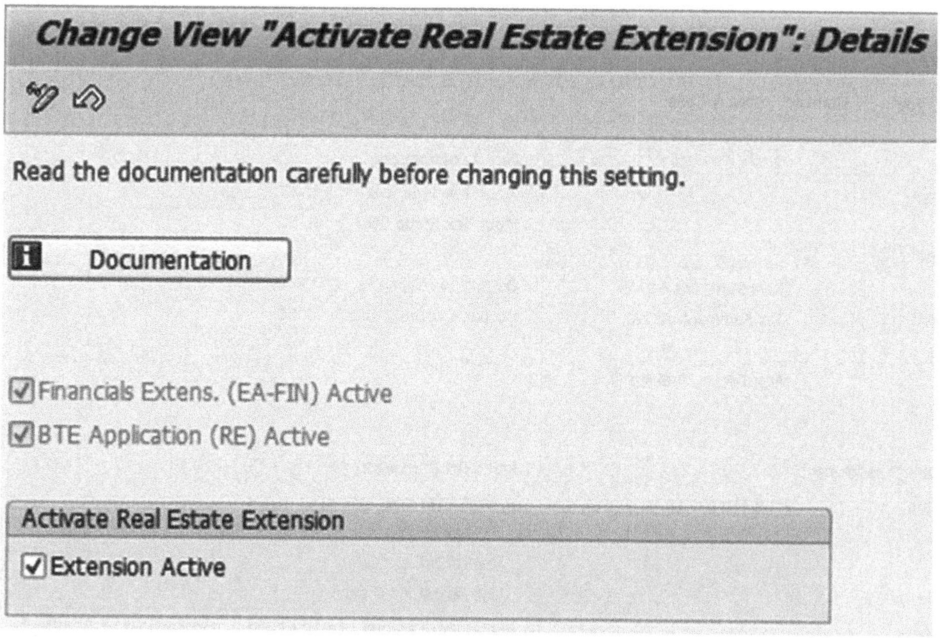

Figure 6-9. *Activate real estate extension*

To enable the use of REFX, the following configuration is required to be set at the company-code level (Figure 6-10):

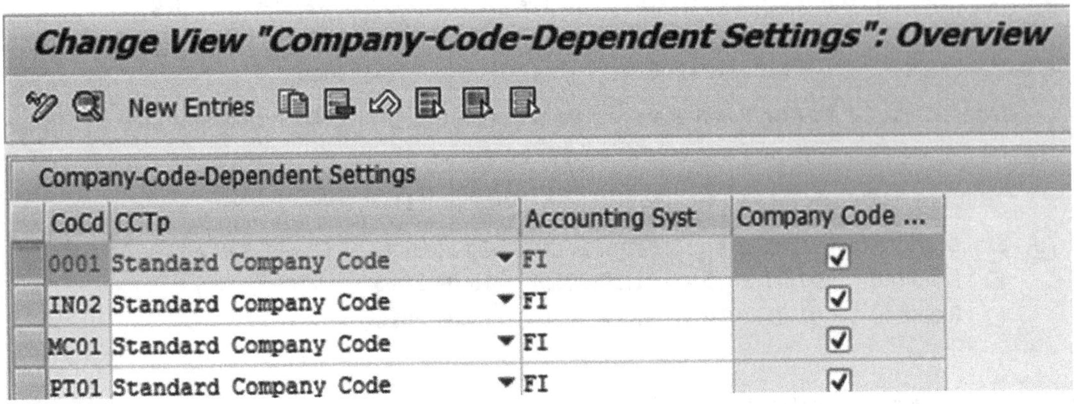

Figure 6-10. *Company-code-dependent settings*

Various company codes can be created. An example is given in Figure 6-11 and Figure 6-12.

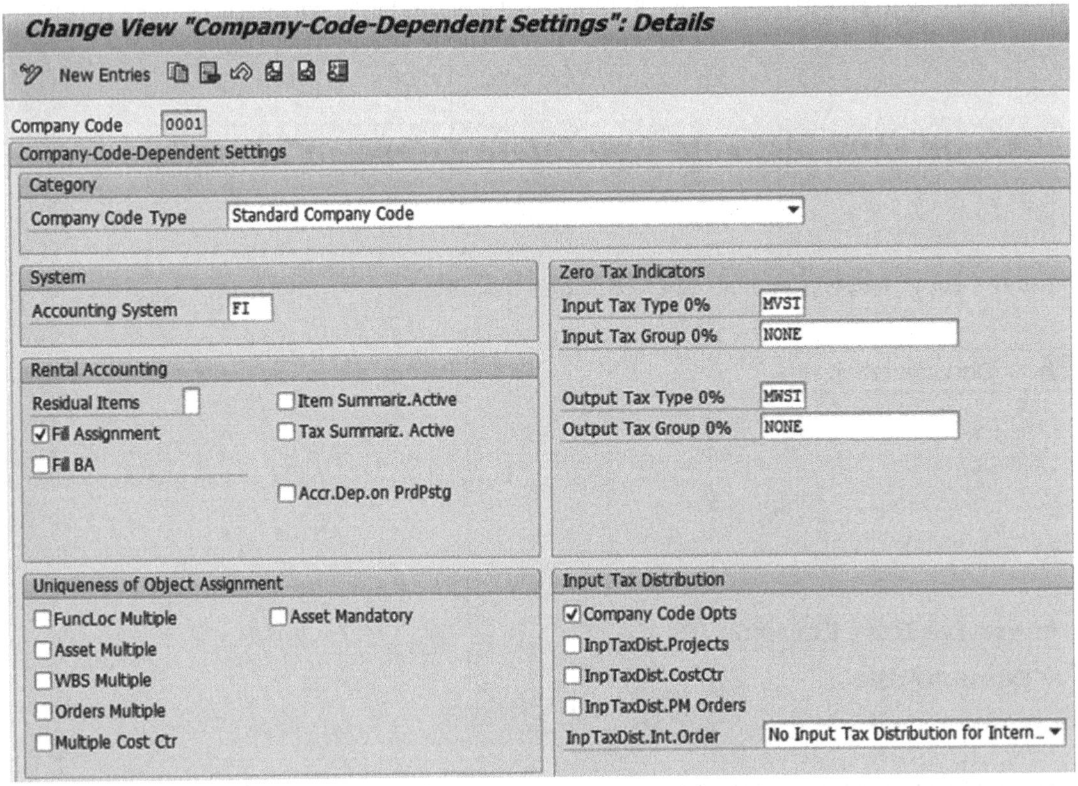

Figure 6-11. *Company-Code-Dependent Settings: Details*

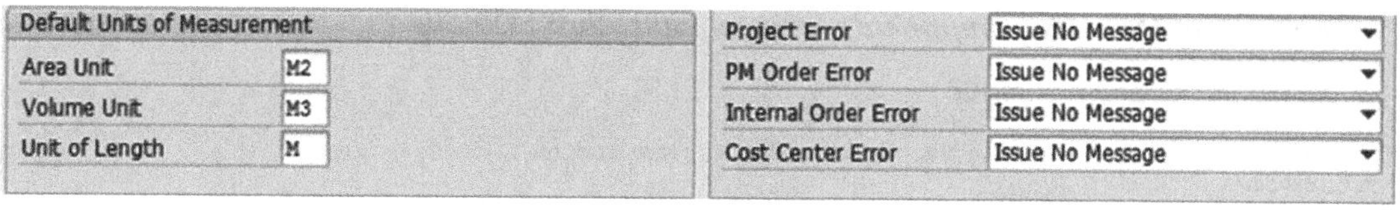

Default Units of Measurement			Project Error	Issue No Message ▾
Area Unit	M2		PM Order Error	Issue No Message ▾
Volume Unit	M3		Internal Order Error	Issue No Message ▾
Unit of Length	M		Cost Center Error	Issue No Message ▾

Figure 6-12. *Company-Code-Dependent Settings: Details (continued)*

- R3-FI has been activated as the Financial Accounting System.

- Input Tax Distribution

  Company Code Opts – If this indicator is set, it means that option rates are to be determined.

- Rental Accounting

  What if indicators are set against each item below?

  - Residual Item – Uncleared balance amount becomes a residual item that is treated as a new open item.

  - Fill Assignment – Document line-item assignment is automatically filled.

  - Item Summarization – Items will be summarized

  - Tax Line Item Summarization – Tax items are summarized based on specified criteria

- Uniqueness of Object Assignment

  It states whether the uniqueness of an object is to be maintained or not. Select checkboxes for Functional Location, Asset Assignment, WBS Multiple, Order Multiple, or Multiple Cost Center, which means you can have multiple real estate objects set in the same time in the same period for the order. No checkmark here means you can assign only one real estate object in the period. Selecting Asset Mandatory means it is mandatory to assign the fixed asset to the real estate object.

- Default Units of Measurement

  Area Unit, Volume Unit, Unit of Length options specify the units of measurement for the area, volume, and length per the company code as a default value for the business entity.

In order to ensure the account's assignment to a real estate object we need to activate real estate management in the Controlling Area screen (Figure 6-13).

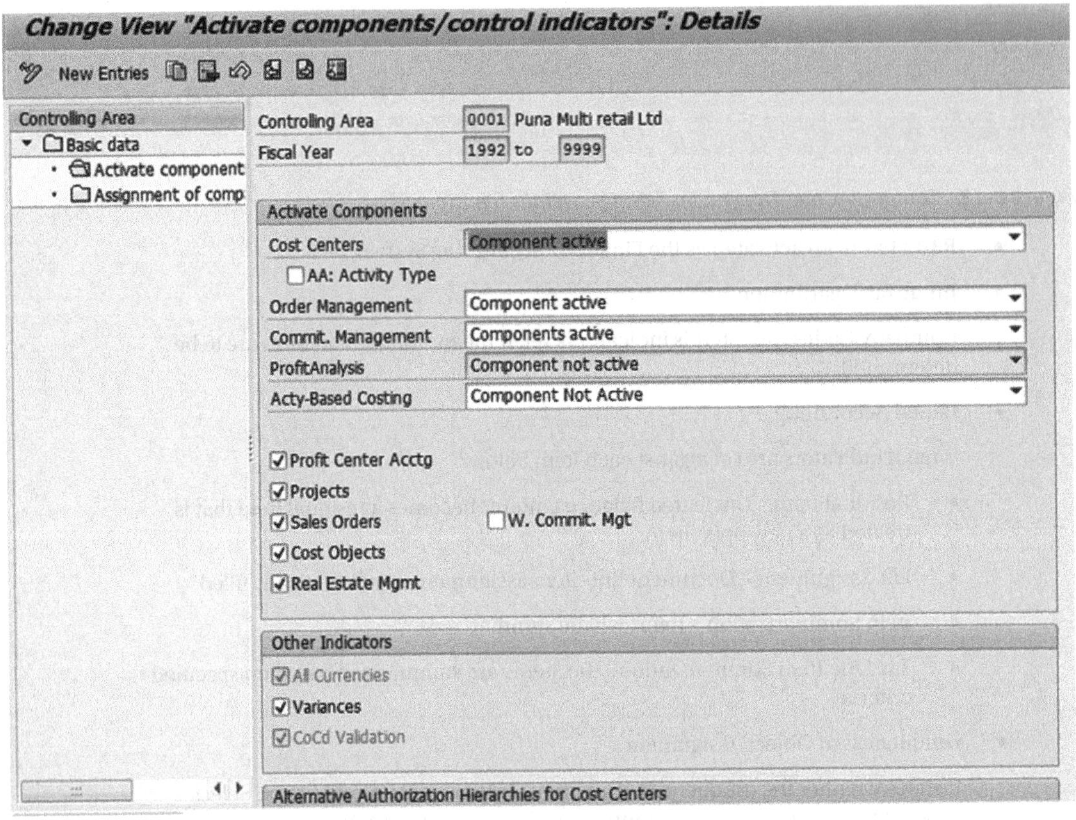

Figure 6-13. *"Activate components/control indicators": Details*

Configurations for Service Charge Settlements in REFX

The Flexible Real Estate module comes under the accounting part of SAP and can be accessed in SPRO as shown in Figure 6-14. SAP service charge settlements are a part of the SAP Flexible Real Estate management module, which enables service charge settlement of all types to be incurred in SAP REFX.

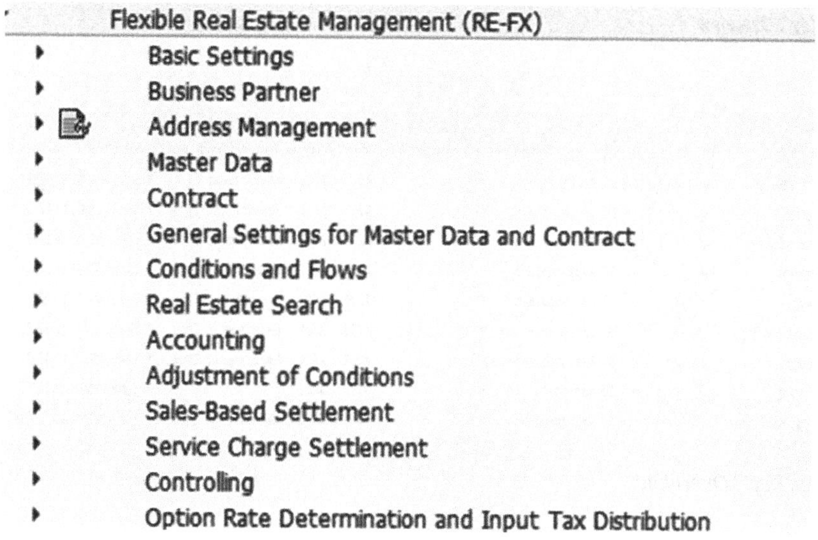

Flexible Real Estate Management (RE-FX)
- ▸   Basic Settings
- ▸   Business Partner
- ▸ 📄 Address Management
- ▸   Master Data
- ▸   Contract
- ▸   General Settings for Master Data and Contract
- ▸   Conditions and Flows
- ▸   Real Estate Search
- ▸   Accounting
- ▸   Adjustment of Conditions
- ▸   Sales-Based Settlement
- ▸   Service Charge Settlement
- ▸   Controlling
- ▸   Option Rate Determination and Input Tax Distribution

Figure 6-14. Service Charge Settlement node is found under Flexible Real Estate Management (REFX) in SPRO

Service Charge Settlement configurations are available in SPRO under:

Menu Path

IMG ➤ Flexible Real Estate Management ➤ Service Charge Settlement

Set Service Charge Keys

The service charge keys determine the type of expenses, and the settlement units determine the various service charges that need to be settled.

Menu Path

IMG ➤ RE-FX ➤ Service Charge Settlement ➤ Master Data of Settlement Unit ➤ Service Charge Keys

Service charge keys are used for the settlement of expenses under different heads. Standard service charge keys are available considering various heads of expenses required to be incurred. However, any new expense head can be added based upon the requirements. Default values can be set for service charge keys (Figure 6-15). The next step would be to enter the measurement details and check the heating value day's indicator.

Change View "Service Charge Key": Overview

New Entries

Service Charge Key

SCK	Description	Short Text	OC	A...	C...	H...	Direct Cost Posting	AcctSymb.CostAc	MeasTp	SettVar	MasterSU DistribType	SettVariant
1000	Property Tax	Property Tax	☑	☑	☐	☐	SU Assignable to ..		A200	A001	Measurement Type	Yearly, 01/01 to 12/31
1100	Property + Liability Insurance	Insurance	☑	☑	☐	☐	SU Assignable to ..		A200	A001	Measurement Type	Yearly, 01/01 to 12/31
1200	Water Supply	Water Supply	☑	☑	☐	☐	SU Assignable to ..		A200	A001	Measurement Type	Yearly, 01/01 to 12/31
1300	Drainage	Drainage	☑	☑	☐	☐	SU Assignable to ..		A200	A001	Measurement Type	Yearly, 01/01 to 12/31
1400	Elevator	Elevator	☑	☑	☐	☐	SU Assignable to ..		A200	A001	Measurement Type	Yearly, 01/01 to 12/31
1500	Street Cleaning	Street Cleaning	☑	☑	☐	☐	SU Assignable to ..		A200	A001	Measurement Type	Yearly, 01/01 to 12/31
1600	Garbage Removal/Disposal	Disposal	☑	☑	☐	☐	SU Assignable to ..		M001	A001	Measurement Type	Yearly, 01/01 to 12/31
1700	Lighting	Lighting	☑	☑	☐	☐	SU Assignable to ..		A200	A001		Yearly, 01/01 to 12/31
1800	Broad Band Cable Network	Broad Band Cab.	☑	☑	☐	☐	SU Assignable to ..		A200	A001	Measurement Type	Yearly, 01/01 to 12/31

Figure 6-15. *"Service Charge Key": Overview*

A service charge key denotes the type of costs that a real estate object incurs. Not all costs incurred are apportionable, and we need to distinguish between costs chargeable to tenants and costs that cannot be charged to them (Figure 6-16).

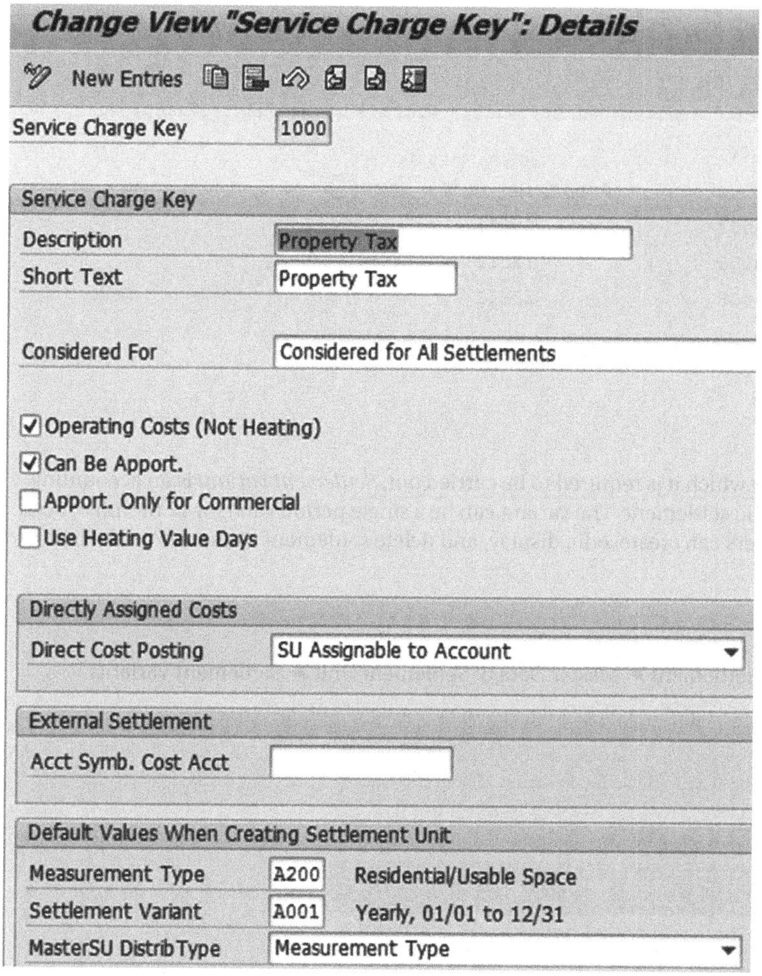

Figure 6-16. *"Service Charge Key": Details*

Default Values for Distribution Rule of Settlement Unit

When a settlement unit is created, the system first checks if an entry was created for the given service charge key. If there is no entry, then the system defaults to the measurement type that was entered in the characteristics of the service charge key. Though default values can be mentioned in the Service Charge Keys link, for some service charge keys that is not enough, since they need to settle, for instance, 60% by usable space and 40% by consumption. In this step you can specify these more complex rules as defaults (Figure 6-17).

Menu Path

IMG ➤ RE-FX ➤ Service Charge Settlement ➤ Master Data of Settlement Unit ➤ Default Values for Distribution Rule of Settlement Unit

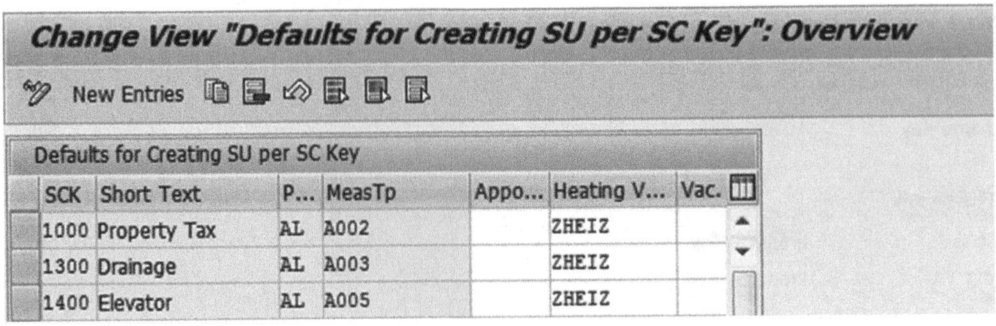

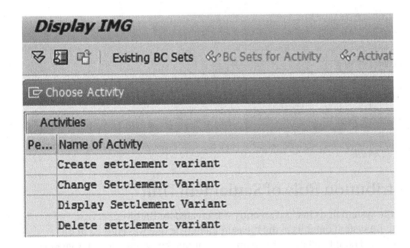

Figure 6-17. *"Defaults for Creating SU per SC Key": Overview*

Settlement Variants

Any settlement needs a period for which it is required to be carried out. *Settlement variant* is an accounting variant created for the period of the settlement. The variant can be a single period valid for 12 months or can be various settlement periods. Users can create, edit, display, and delete settlement variants from the link (Figure 6-18).

Menu Path

IMG ➤ RE-FX ➤ Service Charge Settlement ➤ Master Data of Settlement Unit ➤ Settlement Variants

Figure 6-18. *Settlement variants (create, edit, display, and delete)*

The following is an example of one settlement variant, A005 (Figure 6-19). UM corresponds to the month, UD to the day, and AD to the annual displacement, which is used to determine the settlement year depending on the value date of a document for the service charge settlement.

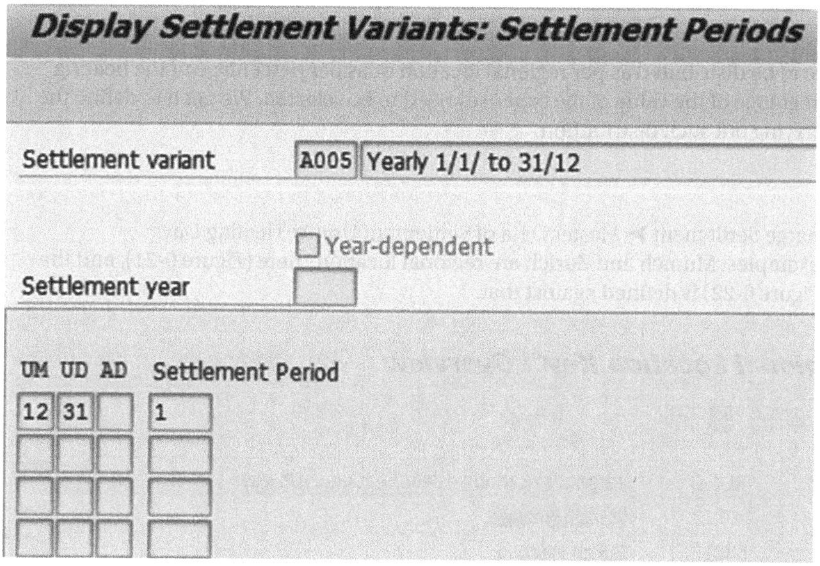

Figure 6-19. *Display Settlement Variants: Settlement Periods*

Tenancy Laws

The tenancy laws of some countries provide rules for the distribution of heating expenses as per the specific location (Figure 6-20). This determines if part of the heating cost will be passed to tenants or whether there is a system to distribute it, as per the regional locations' tenancy laws.

Menu Path

IMG ➤ RE-FX ➤ Service Charge Settlement ➤ Master Data of Settlement Unit ➤ Settings Dependent on Tenancy Law: Apportion Vacancy and Reg. Location Key

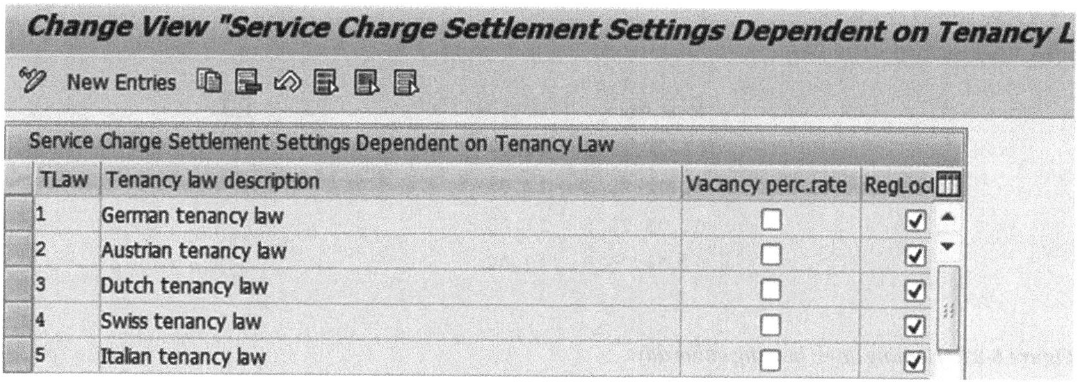

Figure 6-20. *Settings dependent on tenancy law*

Heating Days

In case heating expenses are to be distributed as per regional location or as per percentage of the heating area, the period and the percentage of the value of the expenses need to be selected. We need to define the regional locations before carrying out such distribution.

Menu Path

IMG ➤ RE-FX ➤ Service Charge Settlement ➤ Master Data of Settlement Unit ➤ Heating Days

Refer to the following examples. Munich and Zurich are regional locations here (Figure 6-21), and the heating value percentage (Figure 6-22) is defined against that.

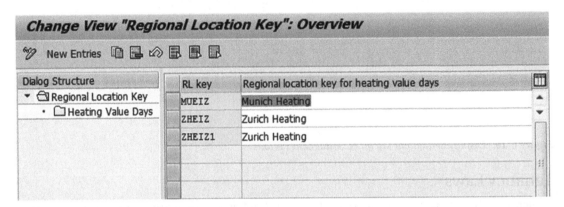

Figure 6-21. *Heating days: regional location key*

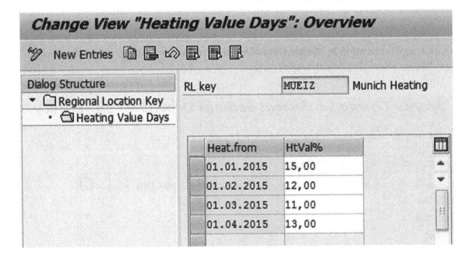

Figure 6-22. *Heating days: heating value days*

Define Default Values for Current Occupancy Principle

We may define for each service charge key which default settings are valid for new settlement units based on the current occupancy principle (Figure 6-23). The Current Occupancy Principle indicator can only be set for rental units and rental spaces, not for pooled spaces.

Menu Path

IMG ➤ RE-FX ➤ Service Charge Settlement ➤ Master Data of Settlement Unit ➤ Define Default Values for Current Occupancy Principle

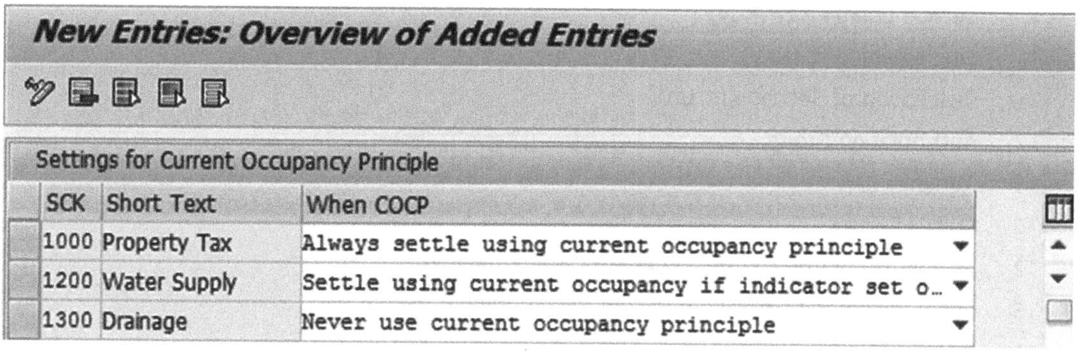

	SCK	Short Text	When COCP	
	1000	Property Tax	Always settle using current occupancy principle ▼	
	1200	Water Supply	Settle using current occupancy if indicator set o… ▼	
	1300	Drainage	Never use current occupancy principle ▼	

Figure 6-23. Settings for current occupancy principle

In certain countries, the current occupancy principle is common for buildings that were constructed prior to certain date, and some specific costs may not be chargeable based on the current occupancy principle. Here you may have to select "Never settle according to current occupancy principle" for the relevant service charge key, as seen for service charge key 1300 in the previous figure.

Dialogs and BAdI

To define the field status, screen sequences, and field status groups, the Dialog link is used. To define any substitutions or validations that would be required in the master data for participation groups, the BAdI link is used.

Menu Path

IMG ➤ RE-FX ➤ Service Charge Settlement ➤ Master Data of Settlement Unit ➤ Dialog ➤ Screen Layout

Field Groups

Field groups specify how the fields are grouped for the Business Data Toolset. Standard settings are available, and you need not make changes unless you want to add some new fields to the master data dialog.

Menu Path

IMG ➤ RE-FX ➤ Service Charge Settlement ➤ Master Data of Settlement Unit ➤ Dialog ➤ Screen Layout ➤ Field Groups ➤ Field Groups

The following (Figure 6-24 and Figure 6-25) are screenshots of some of the configurations.

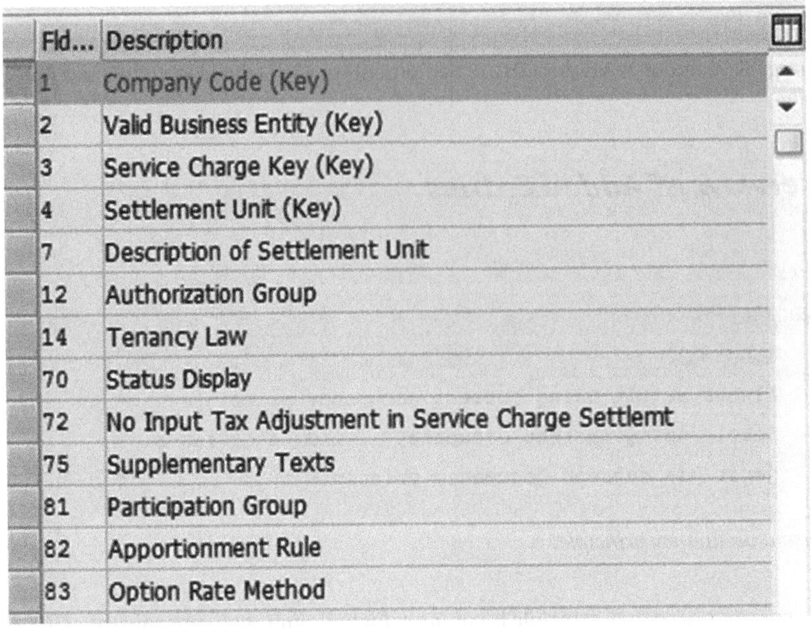
Fld...
Description
1
Company Code (Key)
2
Valid Business Entity (Key)
3
Service Charge Key (Key)
4
Settlement Unit (Key)
7
Description of Settlement Unit
12
Authorization Group
14
Tenancy Law
70
Status Display
72
No Input Tax Adjustment in Service Charge Settlemt
75
Supplementary Texts
81
Participation Group
82
Apportionment Rule
83
Option Rate Method

Figure 6-24. *Configurations*

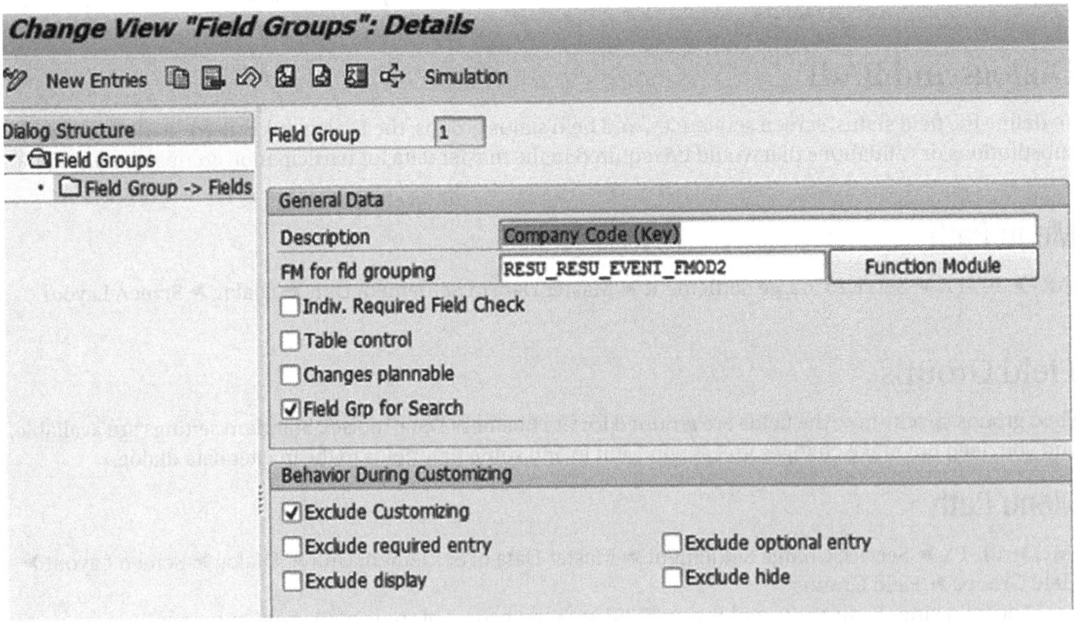
Change View "Field Groups": Details
New Entries
Simulation
Dialog Structure
Field Groups
Field Group -> Fields
Field Group
1
General Data
Description
Company Code (Key)
FM for fld grouping
RESU_RESU_EVENT_FMOD2
Function Module
Indiv. Required Field Check
Table control
Changes plannable
Field Grp for Search
Behavior During Customizing
Exclude Customizing
Exclude required entry
Exclude optional entry
Exclude display
Exclude hide

Figure 6-25. *Field groups*

Field Status

Field statuses are the details that group individual fields into field groups.

Menu Path

IMG ➤ RE-FX ➤ Service Charge Settlement ➤ Master Data of Settlement Unit ➤ Dialog ➤ Screen Layout ➤ Field Groups ➤ Field Status

Figure 6-26. *Field grouping activity*

We can customize the fields that are displayed (Figure 6-26).

Views

We need to specify which field groups are grouped together into a view. We need to group together the field groups that necessarily belong together during a check (Figure 6-27 and Figure 6-28).

Menu Path

IMG ➤ RE-FX ➤ Service Charge Settlement ➤ Master Data of Settlement Unit ➤ Dialog ➤ Screen Layout ➤ Views

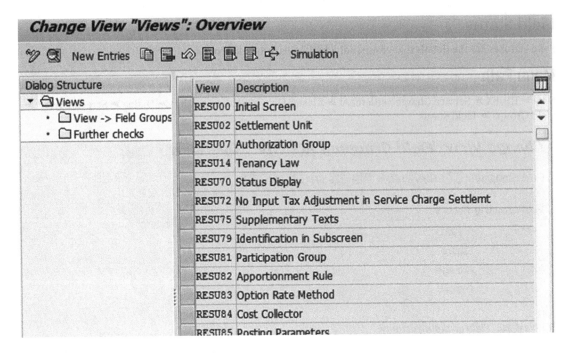

Figure 6-27. *Views*

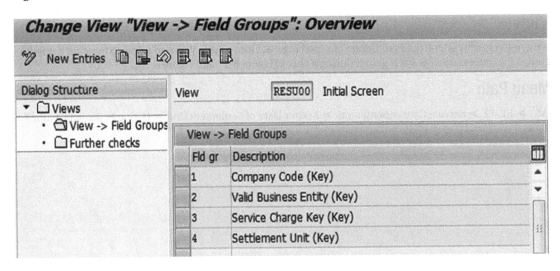

Figure 6-28. *View field groups*

Screens

You can define screens and the sections that go in them. You can create custom tab pages, specifying where the tab pages should appear in the dialog and the sections that make up these tab pages (Figure 6-29).

Menu Path

IMG ➤ RE-FX ➤ Service Charge Settlement ➤ Master Data of Settlement Unit ➤ Dialog ➤ Screen Layout ➤ Screens

Change View "Screens": Overview

🏷️ 🔍 New Entries 📋 🖫 🖉 🖺 🖺 🖺 ⇨ Simulation

Dialog Structure	Screen	Description	Screen title
▼ 📁 Screens	RESU00	Initial Screen	Initial Screen
• 📁 Screen -> Sections	RESU02	General Data	General Data
	RESU03	Assigned Participation Groups	Participation Groups
	RESU04	Apportionment Rule	Apportionment Rule
	RESU06	Settlement Company	Settlement Company
	RESU08	Cost Object	Cost Object
	RESU09	Option Rate Methods	Option Rate Methods
	RESU10	Cost Collector	Cost Collector
	RESU11	Posting Parameters	Posting Parameters
	RESU13	Meter	Meter
	RESU75	Supplementary Texts	Supplementary Texts
	RESU86	Resubmission	Resubmission
	RESU9V	Overviews (Lists)	Overviews
	SUCH42	Settlement Company (CH)	Settlement Company (
	SUFC40	Fuel Level (CH)	Fuel Level (CH)

Figure 6-29. *Screens*

Screen Sequences

A screen sequence consists of different screens. We need to define the screen sequence, including the screens that are part of it (Figure 6-30 and Figure 6-31) and the assignment of a screen sequence category. It provides details of the tab pages that will be used as well as their order.

Menu Path

IMG ➤ RE-FX ➤ Service Charge Settlement ➤ Master Data of Settlement Unit ➤ Dialog ➤ Screen Layout ➤ Screen Sequences

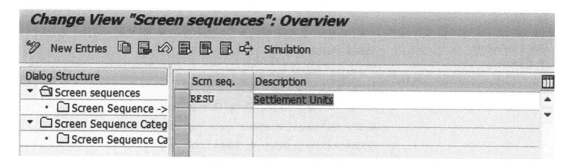

Figure 6-30. *Screen sequences*

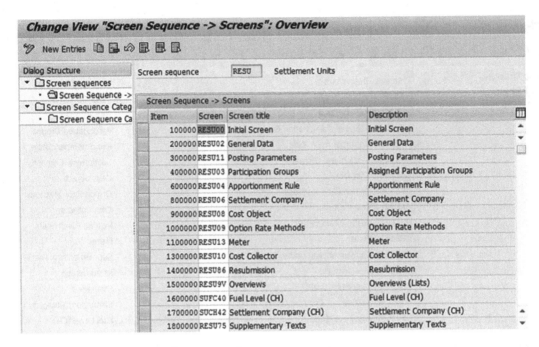

Figure 6-31. *Screen Sequence: Screens overview*

Events

Standard dialogs are provided and should not be changed unless some complex modification is required (Figure 6-32).

Menu Path

IMG ➤ RE-FX ➤ Service Charge Settlement ➤ Master Data of Settlement Unit ➤ Dialog ➤ Screen Layout ➤ Events

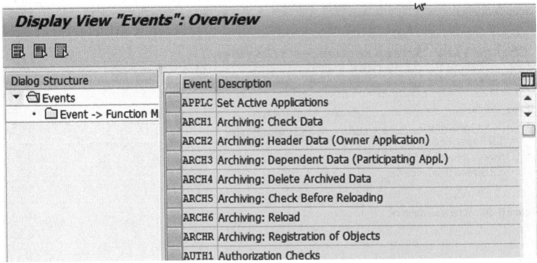

Figure 6-32. *Events*

Tables

Tables may be modified in case of a complex requirement, but it is recommended to not make any changes to the standard settings (Figure 6-33)

Menu Path

IMG ➤ RE-FX ➤ Service Charge Settlement ➤ Master Data of Settlement Unit ➤ Dialog ➤ Screen Layout ➤ Tables

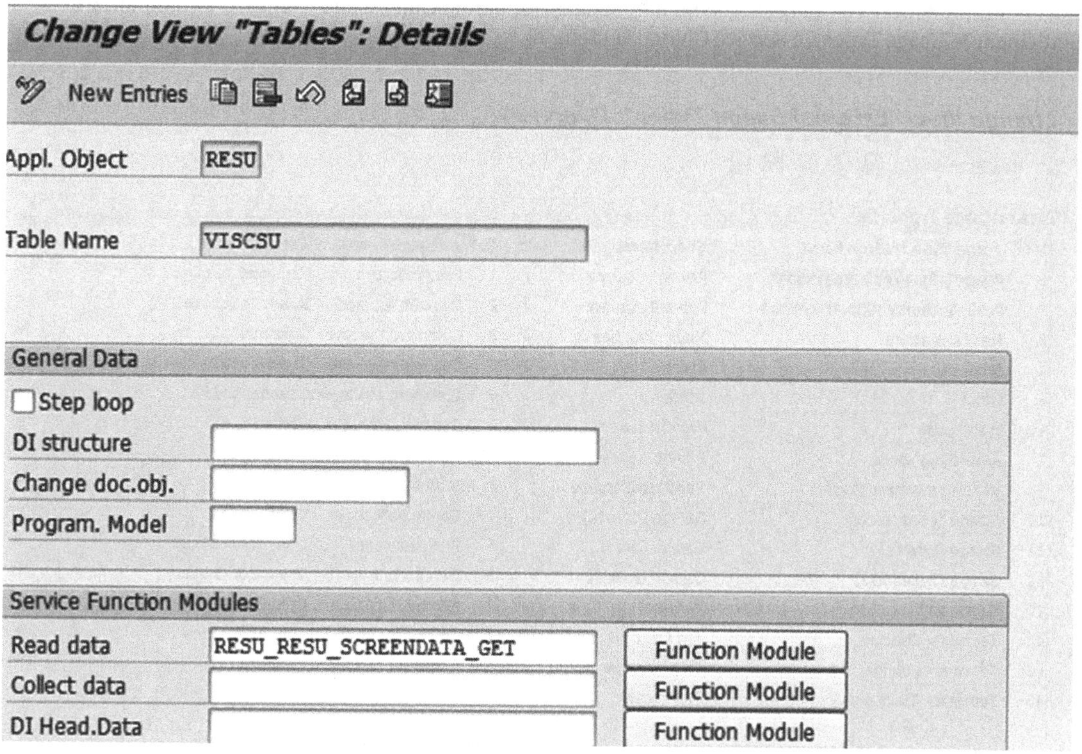

Figure 6-33. Tables

Implement Enhancements (BAdI)

The Business Add-In helps in enhancing the standard functions of real estate contracts without touching codes. We can create a BAdI and implement it for our particular enhancement.

Menu Path

IMG ➤ RE-FX ➤ Service Charge Settlement ➤ Master Data of Settlement Unit ➤ Implement Enhancements (BAdI) ➤ Number Assignment, Validation, Substitution

Usage Types for Service Charge Settlements

We must define all rental objects for which the service charge settlement is to be performed. The user needs to define all usage types that would need a service charge settlement to be performed on them. A usage type against which we set an indicator can participate in the service charge settlement, and those for which you do not set an indicator cannot participate (Figure 6-34). Rental objects are in turn assigned to usage types through participation groups.

Menu Path

IMG ➤ RE-FX ➤ Service Charge Settlement ➤ Settings for Rental Objects and Contracts Participating in Settlement ➤ Usage Types for Service Charge Settlement

Change View "External Usage Types": Overview

♦ New Entries 🗋 🖫 🕼 🖪 🖪 🖪

External Usage Types

UT	Usage Type Medium Name	Short Name	Sett.	IUT	IntUsageTypeNa...	Cat
1	Privately-financed accommodat.	Priv.fin.accomm	☑	1	Priv.fin.accomm	Non-commercial
2	Public-authority supp.accommod	Pub-aut.sup.acc	☑	2	Pub-aut.sup.acc	Non-commercial
3	Medical practice	Medic. practice	☑	3	Commerc.ten.law	Commercial
4	Store	Store	☑	3	Commerc.ten.law	Commercial
5	Office	Office	☑	3	Commerc.ten.law	Commercial
6	Warehouse	Warehouse	☑	3	Commerc.ten.law	Commercial
7	Advertising space	Advert. space	☐	7	Advert. space	Commercial
8	Vending machine space	Vend.mach.space	☐	8	Stand area	Commercial
10	Garage (commercial)	Garage (comm.)	☐	4	Comm.park.space	Commercial
11	Garage (private)	Garage (priv.)	☐	5	Priv.park.space	Non-commercial
12	Garage (mixed use)	Garage (mixed)	☐	9	Gen.parking spc	Used for both
40	Terminal	Terminal	☑	3	Commerc.ten.law	Commercial
41	Terminal - Check-in	Tml Check-in	☑	3	Commerc.ten.law	Commercial
42	Terminal - Lounge	Tml - Lounge	☑	3	Commerc.ten.law	Commercial
43	Terminal - Trading stall	Tml - Stall	☑	3	Commerc.ten.law	Commercial

Figure 6-34. *External usage types*

Define Measurement Types

Measurements are used to record the measurable part of objects. The measurement type indicates the type of trait that is being measured. The measurements of a rental object are used in service charge settlement for determining apportionment. In the case of real estate objects, we can have total area, office area, parking area, and so on, which are occupying a specific area of total available space and are created as measurement types (Figure 6-35 and Figure 6-36).

Menu Path

IMG ➤ RE-FX ➤ Service Charge Settlement ➤ Settings for Rental Objects and Contracts Participating in Settlement ➤ Define Measurement Types

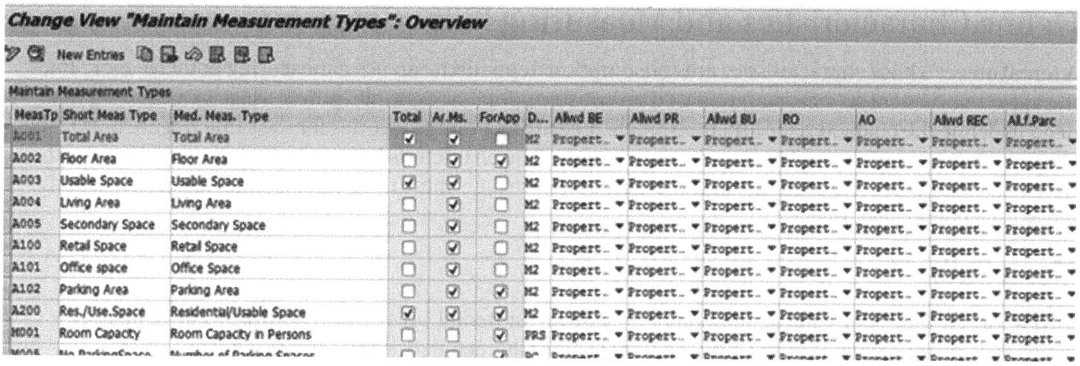

Change View "Maintain Measurement Types": Overview

⍋ ☶ New Entries 🗈 🖩 ⟳ 🖩 🖩 🖩

Maintain Measurement Types

MeasTp	Short Meas Type	Med. Meas. Type	Total	Ar.Ms.	ForApp	D...	Allwd BE	Allwd PR	Allwd BU	RO	AO	Allwd REC	ALf.Parc
A001	Total Area	Total Area	☑	☑	☐	M2	Propert.. ▾	Propert.. ▾	Propert.. ▾	Propert.. ▾	Propert.. ▾	Propert.. ▾	Propert.. ▾
A002	Floor Area	Floor Area	☐	☑	☑	M2	Propert.. ▾	Propert.. ▾	Propert.. ▾	Propert.. ▾	Propert.. ▾	Propert.. ▾	Propert.. ▾
A003	Usable Space	Usable Space	☑	☑	☐	M2	Propert.. ▾	Propert.. ▾	Propert.. ▾	Propert.. ▾	Propert.. ▾	Propert.. ▾	Propert.. ▾
A004	Living Area	Living Area	☐	☑	☐	M2	Propert.. ▾	Propert.. ▾	Propert.. ▾	Propert.. ▾	Propert.. ▾	Propert.. ▾	Propert.. ▾
A005	Secondary Space	Secondary Space	☐	☑	☐	M2	Propert.. ▾	Propert.. ▾	Propert.. ▾	Propert.. ▾	Propert.. ▾	Propert.. ▾	Propert.. ▾
A100	Retail Space	Retail Space	☐	☑	☐	M2	Propert.. ▾	Propert.. ▾	Propert.. ▾	Propert.. ▾	Propert.. ▾	Propert.. ▾	Propert.. ▾
A101	Office space	Office Space	☐	☑	☐	M2	Propert.. ▾	Propert.. ▾	Propert.. ▾	Propert.. ▾	Propert.. ▾	Propert.. ▾	Propert.. ▾
A102	Parking Area	Parking Area	☐	☑	☑	M2	Propert.. ▾	Propert.. ▾	Propert.. ▾	Propert.. ▾	Propert.. ▾	Propert.. ▾	Propert.. ▾
A200	Res./Use.Space	Residential/Usable Space	☑	☑	☑	M2	Propert.. ▾	Propert.. ▾	Propert.. ▾	Propert.. ▾	Propert.. ▾	Propert.. ▾	Propert.. ▾
M001	Room Capacty	Room Capacty in Persons	☐	☐	☑	PRS	Propert.. ▾	Propert.. ▾	Propert.. ▾	Propert.. ▾	Propert.. ▾	Propert.. ▾	Propert.. ▾
M005	No. ParkingSpace	Number of Parking Spaces	☐	☐	☑	PC	Propert.. ▾	Propert.. ▾	Propert.. ▾	Propert.. ▾	Propert.. ▾	Propert.. ▾	Propert.. ▾

Figure 6-35. *Maintain measurement types*

Change View "Maintain Measurement Types": Details

⍋ New Entries 🗈 🖩 ⟳ 🖩 🖩 🖩

easurement Type   A001

Maintain Measurement Types

Name

Med. Meas. Type   Total Area
Short Meas Type   Total Area

Default Unit   M2
☑ Total Measurement
☑ Area Measurement

Restrictions

Allowed for AO	Property Is Allowed for Object	▾	☐ No Exception
Allowed for RO	Property Is Allowed for Object	▾	☐ No Exception
Allowed for BE	Property Is Allowed for Object	▾	
Allowed for PR	Property Is Allowed for Object	▾	
Allowed for BU	Property Is Allowed for Object	▾	
Allowed for Contract	Property Is Allowed for Object	▾	☐ No Exception
Object Reference	Object Reference Allowed	▾	
Allowed for Parcel	Property Is Not Allowed for Object	▾	

Service Charge Settlement Properties

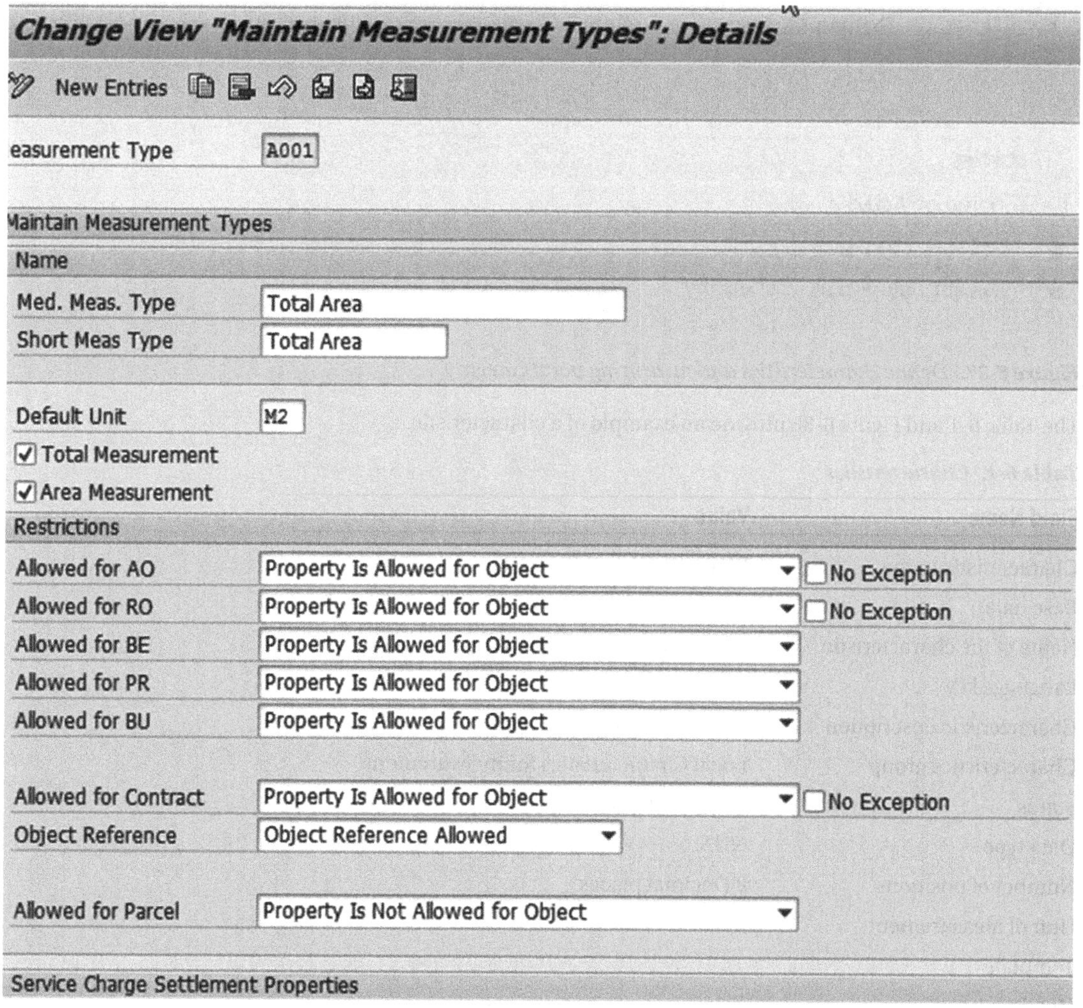

Figure 6-36. *"Maintain Measurement Types": Details screen*

Define Characteristics and Measuring Point Category

A rental object whose characteristics are consumption dependent can use a measuring point category for the apportionment of service charges based on consumption; for example, power usage in a building. We need to define the characteristic and then create measuring point categories for the same (Figure 6-37). The characteristics can be created in characteristic classes. The characteristics cannot be transported, but rather have to be manually created in the target system. Here, we determine the characteristics for meters and the measuring point categories.

Menu Path

IMG ➤ RE-FX ➤ Service Charge Settlement ➤ Settings for Rental Objects and Contracts Participating in Settlement ➤ Apportionment by Consumption: Define Characteristics and Measuring Point

Figure 6-37. Define characteristics and measuring point category

The Table 6-1 and Figure 6-38 provide an example of a characteristic.

Table 6-1. Characteristics

Field Name	Value
Characteristic name	POWERCONSUMPTION
Base data:	
Name of the characteristic	POWERCONSUMPTION
Language key	E
Characteristic description	Power consumption
Characteristics group	Local Characteristics for measurement
Status	1 released
Data type	NUM
Number of positions	8 Decimal places
Unit of measurement	m3
Template	__.__.__.__
Heading 1	Power
Heading 2	Consumption

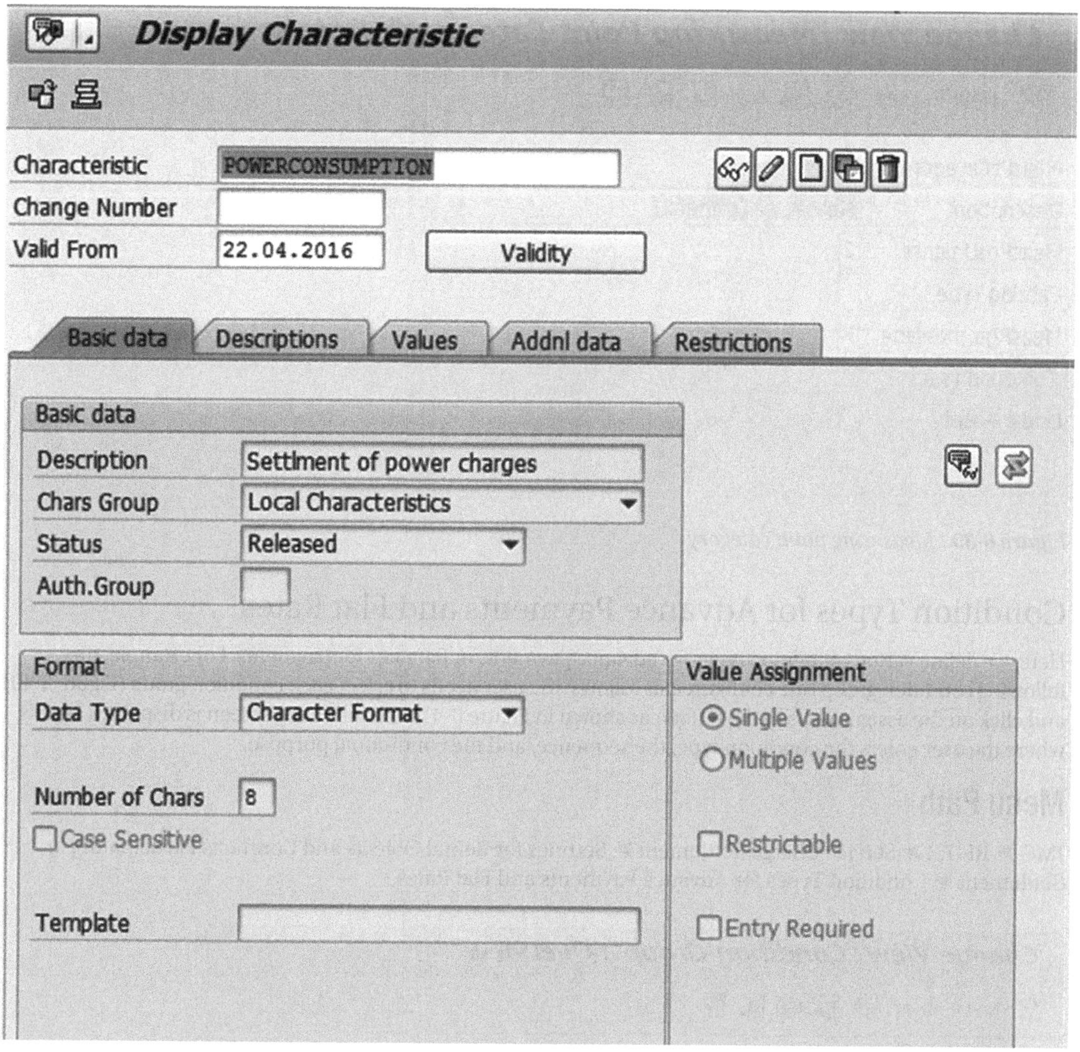

Figure 6-38. *Characteristic data*

Figure 6-39 provides an example of a measuring point category.

Change View "Measuring Point Category": Details

New Entries 📋 📑 🔗 📇 📄 📊

MeasPtCategory	M
Description	MeasPoint (general)
MeasPosUniqnss	2
Catalog type	
MeasRge message	W
TolPeriod (sec)	
Linear Asset	☐

Figure 6-39. *Measuring point category*

Condition Types for Advance Payments and Flat Rates

Here, we define various condition types for advance payments or flat rates for payments. For example, the following condition groups are configured as follows: the user needs to select each condition group (Figure 6-40) and click on the assignments in the left tab as shown in Figure 6-41. The following screen is displayed, and is where the user enters the condition type, the sequence, and the conditional purpose.

Menu Path

IMG ➤ RE-FX ➤ Service Charge Settlement ➤ Settings for Rental Objects and Contracts Participating in Settlement ➤ Condition Types for Advance Payments and Flat Rates

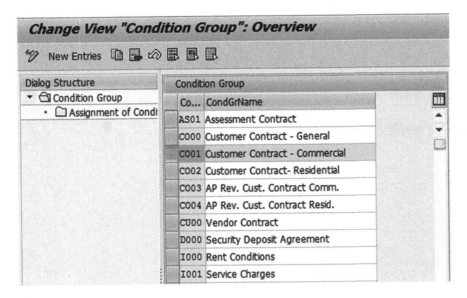

Figure 6-40. *Condition group*

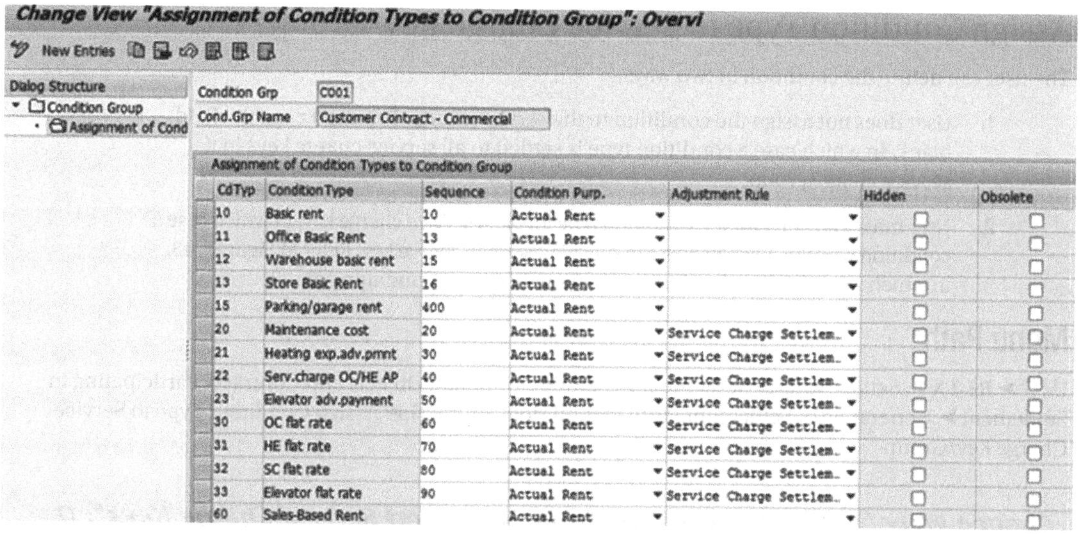
Change View "Assignment of Condition Types to Condition Group": Overvi

New Entries

Dialog Structure
- Condition Group
  - Assignment of Cond

Condition Grp: C001
Cond.Grp Name: Customer Contract - Commercial

Assignment of Condition Types to Condition Group

CdTyp	ConditionType	Sequence	Condition Purp.	Adjustment Rule	Hidden	Obsolete
10	Basic rent	10	Actual Rent		☐	☐
11	Office Basic Rent	13	Actual Rent		☐	☐
12	Warehouse basic rent	15	Actual Rent		☐	☐
13	Store Basic Rent	16	Actual Rent		☐	☐
15	Parking/garage rent	400	Actual Rent		☐	☐
20	Maintenance cost	20	Actual Rent	Service Charge Settlem..	☐	☐
21	Heating exp.adv.pmnt	30	Actual Rent	Service Charge Settlem..	☐	☐
22	Serv.charge OC/HE AP	40	Actual Rent	Service Charge Settlem..	☐	☐
23	Elevator adv.payment	50	Actual Rent	Service Charge Settlem..	☐	☐
30	OC flat rate	60	Actual Rent	Service Charge Settlem..	☐	☐
31	HE flat rate	70	Actual Rent	Service Charge Settlem..	☐	☐
32	SC flat rate	80	Actual Rent	Service Charge Settlem..	☐	☐
33	Elevator flat rate	90	Actual Rent	Service Charge Settlem..	☐	☐
60	Sales-Based Rent		Actual Rent		☐	☐

Figure 6-41. *Assignement of condition types to condition group*

Assign Default Condition Type to Service Charge Key

The assignment of a condition type to a service charge key enables the determination of flow type, which in turn helps in account determination (Figure 6-42).

Menu Path

IMG ➤ RE-FX ➤ Service Charge Settlement ➤ Settings for Rental Objects and Contracts Participating in Settlement ➤ Assign Default Condition Type to Service Charge Key

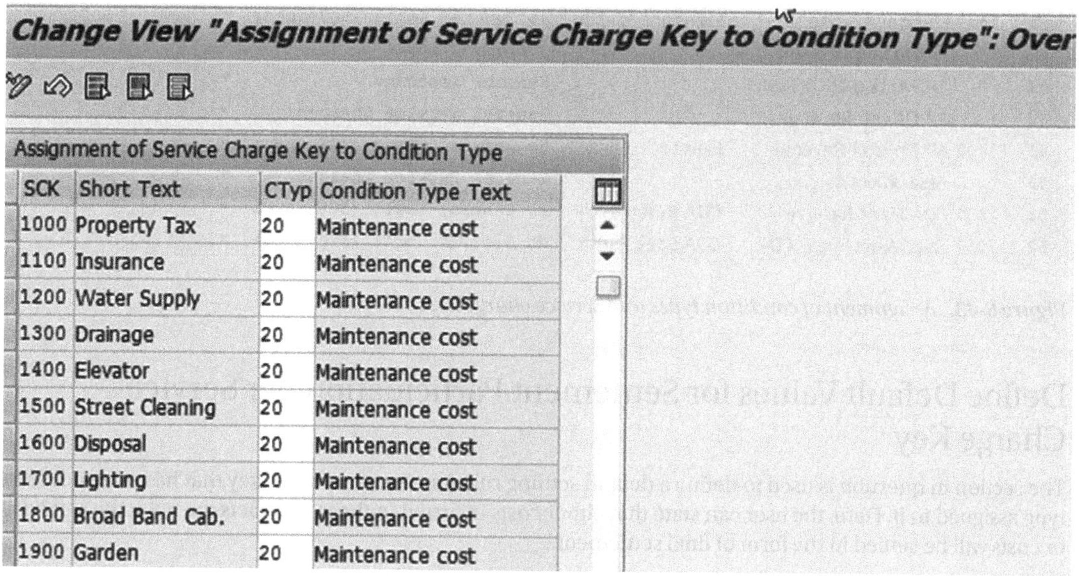
Change View "Assignment of Service Charge Key to Condition Type": Over

Assignment of Service Charge Key to Condition Type

SCK	Short Text	CTyp	Condition Type Text
1000	Property Tax	20	Maintenance cost
1100	Insurance	20	Maintenance cost
1200	Water Supply	20	Maintenance cost
1300	Drainage	20	Maintenance cost
1400	Elevator	20	Maintenance cost
1500	Street Cleaning	20	Maintenance cost
1600	Disposal	20	Maintenance cost
1700	Lighting	20	Maintenance cost
1800	Broad Band Cab.	20	Maintenance cost
1900	Garden	20	Maintenance cost

Figure 6-42. *Assignement of service charge key to condition type*

Assign Condition Type to Service Charge Key/Group

The user can define the condition in two ways:

1. User does not assign the condition to the service charge key and keeps the field blank, in which case a condition type is settled to all service charge keys in a service charge group.

2. User makes an entry for the condition type for each service charge key, in which case a condition type is settled against the specified service charge key. Refer to Figure 6-43, in which service charge key 1400 is mentioned against Condition type 23

Menu Path

IMG ➤ RE-FX ➤ Service Charge Settlement ➤ Settings for Rental Objects and Contracts Participating in Settlement ➤ Generating of Settlement Participation (for Contract) ➤ Assign Condition Type to Service Charge Key/Group

Change View "Assignment of Condition Types and Service Charge Keys": 0

New Entries

Assignment of Condition Types and Service Charge Keys

CTyp	SCK	Condition Type Text	Short Text	Service Charge Cat.	OC	Apb	Co...	H...
20		Maintenance cost		Operating Costs ▼	☐	☐	☐	☐
21		Heating exp.adv.pmnt		Heating Expenses ▼	☐	☐	☐	☐
22		Serv.charge OC/HE AP		General Service Charges ▼	☐	☐	☐	☐
23	1400	Elevator adv.payment	Elevator	No General Costs (SCS-Speci... ▼	☑	☑	☐	☐
30		OC flat rate		Operating Costs ▼	☐	☐	☐	☐
31		HE flat rate		Heating Expenses ▼	☐	☐	☐	☐
32		SC flat rate		General Service Charges ▼	☐	☐	☐	☐
33	1400	Elevator flat rate	Elevator	No General Costs (SCS-Speci... ▼	☑	☑	☐	☐
40		AP Op.Costs Revenue		Operating Costs ▼	☐	☐	☐	☐
41		AP Heating Costs Rev		Heating Expenses ▼	☐	☐	☐	☐
42		AP OC+HC Revenue		General Service Charges ▼	☐	☐	☐	☐
43	1400	AP Elevator Revenue	Elevator	No General Costs (SCS-Speci... ▼	☑	☑	☐	☐
50		Assessment		General Service Charges ▼	☐	☐	☐	☐
51	7400	COA Maint.Reserve	COA Reserves	No General Costs (SCS-Speci... ▼	☑	☐	☐	☐
52	7910	Spec.Assessment COA	COA Spec.Assmt	No General Costs (SCS-Speci... ▼	☑	☐	☐	☐

Figure 6-43. *Assignment of condition types and service charge keys*

Define Default Values for Settlement Participation per Service Charge Key

The section in question is used to define a default settling rule for a service charge key that has no condition type assigned to it. Here, the user can state that either costs incurred in those contracts are not to be settled or costs will be settled in the form of final settlement.

Menu Path

IMG ➤ RE-FX ➤ Service Charge Settlement ➤ Settings for Rental Objects and Contracts Participating in Settlement ➤ Generating of Settlement Participation (for Contract) ➤ Define Default Values for Settlement Participation per Service Charge Key

Define Settlement Parameters

Defining the parameters for a settlement (Figure 6-44 and Figure 6-45) can be done by selecting the following checkboxes. This helps users, as they need not define parameters on their own.

- Active: The parameters can be used for selection only if the Active checkbox is checked.

- Standard: You can set a parameter as the default for settlement when Standard checkbox is selected.

- Open AP: Open AP checkbox determines how advance payments that were agreed upon but not paid will be settled.

- Country-Specifics: Settlement for each country may vary depending on legal requirements of each country; hence, it is better that individual settlement parameters for each country are created by respective users.

- Post Balance: If the requirement is to offset the down payments received with receivables, then this checkbox needs to be selected.

- Tenant Service Charge Settlement: If we have to settle rental agreements and rental units with the current occupancy principle indicator in the service charge, this checkbox needs to be checked.

- Leave Unpaid Advance Payments Open (Planned Principle): Unpaid advance payments in settlements will not be cleared if checkbox is selected.

- Print Separate: This will check whether correspondence is to be printed manually or automatically.

Menu Path

IMG ➤ RE-FX ➤ Service Charge Settlement ➤ Settlement Process ➤ Define Settlement Parameters

Change View "Settlement Parameters": Overview

%⁄ 🔍 New Entries 📋 🖫 🔊 🖺 🖺 🖺

Settlement Parameters

Stt. Schema	Key Name
AT	Austria, Current Occupancy Principle
ATHK	Austria, w/o Current Occupancy Principle (Heating Expense)
CH	Switzerland
DE	Actual Down Payments
DE2	Target Down Payments
DESS	Balance + Debited Advance Payments (Standard)
DEWG	Germany COA: Balance, Debited Advance Payments, COCP

Figure 6-44. Settlement parameters

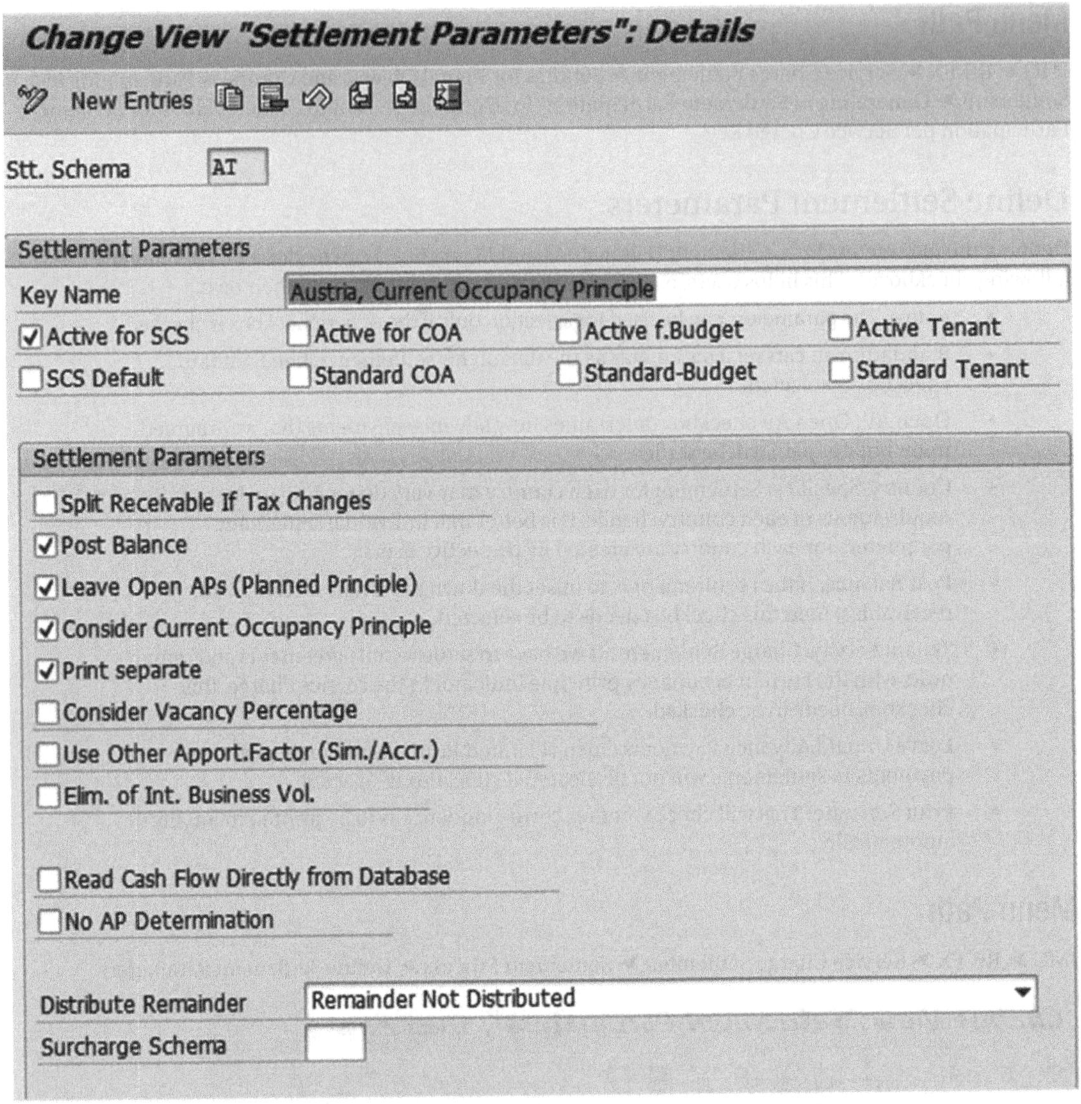

Figure 6-45. *"Settlement Parameters": Details screen*

Define RE-Specific Account Properties

Accounts assignment is dependent on account groups, but here we define the accounts that can be used for real estate objects (Figure 6-46). Accounts can be used for all real estate objects except those for which no further settings are made. However, you cannot directly post service charge settlements in such accounts.

The following settings are needed:

- Account properties: Key in identifying the properties of an account

- Name of account property

- Indicator for "Applicable for Business Entity"

- Indicator for "Applicable for Property"

- Indicator for "Applicable for Building"

- Indicator for "Rental Object"

- Indicator for "Contract"

- Indicator for "Settlement Unit"

- Service charge key

- Service charge key name

- Direct cost postings

Menu Path

IMG ➤ RE-FX ➤ Service Charge Settlement ➤ Settlement Process ➤ Accounting: Account Determination and Accounts for Apportionable Costs ➤ Define RE-Specific Account Properties

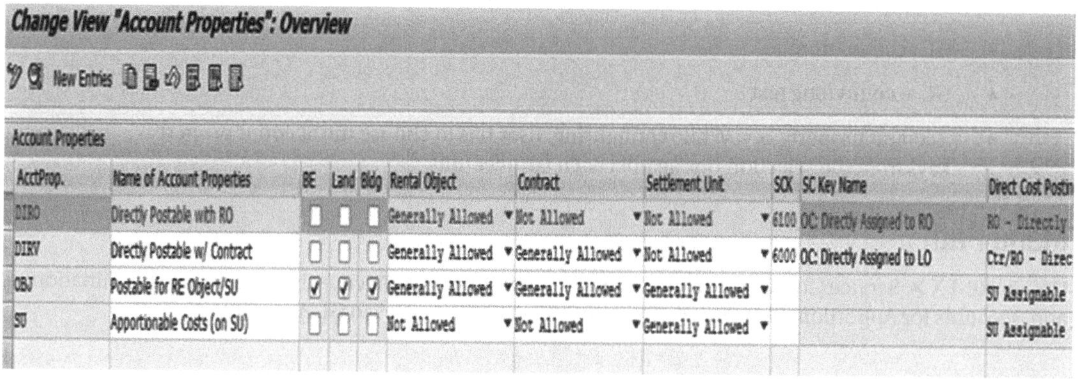

Figure 6-46. *Account properties*

Define Accounts Allowed for Individual Service Charge Keys

We can define certain accounts for settlement units with specific service charge keys (Figure 6-47). The following settings are needed:

- Account properties: Key in identifying the properties of an account

- Name of account property

- Service charge key

- Short text

Here, one has to specify all service charge keys for which a posting has to be done; in particular, account properties.

Menu Path

IMG ➤ RE-FX ➤ Service Charge Settlement ➤ Settlement Process ➤ Accounting: Account Determination and Accounts for Apportionable Costs ➤ Define Accounts Allowed for Individual Service Charge Keys

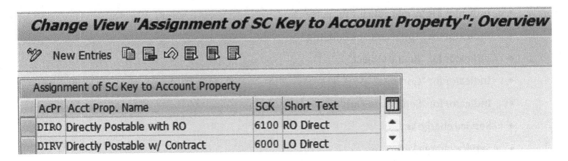

Figure 6-47. Assignment of SC key to account property

Assign RE-Specific Properties to GL Account

We have seen how account properties are defined, and here we assign the particular accounts that can be used for real estate (Figure 6-48). The following settings are needed:

- Chart of accounts

- GL account number

- GL account long text

- Account property key: While configuring, user has to choose the account property keys from the selection box against each GL account

Menu Path

IMG ➤ RE-FX ➤ Service Charge Settlement ➤ Settlement Process ➤ Accounting: Account Determination and Accounts for Apportionable Costs ➤ Assign RE-Specific Properties to GL Accounts

Change View "Account Properties": Overview

New Entries

	ChAc	Cost Element	Description	AcPr	Acct Prop. Nam
	INT	470000	Occupancy costs	OBJ	Postable for RE
	INT	470400	RE Apportionable operating costs	SU	Apportionable C
	INT	470410	RE Apport. Oper. Costs Assignable to RO	DIRO	Directly Postable
	INT	470420	RE App. Op. Costs Assignable to Contract	DIRV	Directly Postable
	WEG	470000	Office/Facility Expense	OBJ	Postable for RE
	WEG	470400	RE Apportionable Costs COA	SU	Apportionable C

Figure 6-48. Account properties

Assign Clearing Accounts to Cost Account

Here, we define clearing accounts to be used for the cost accounts. These accounts need to be created as cost elements. The following configurations, as given in Figure 6-49 and Figure 6-50, are required for a new entry to the preceding table

Menu Path

IMG ➤ RE-FX ➤ Service Charge Settlement ➤ Settlement Process ➤ Accounting: Account Determination and Accounts for Apportionable Costs ➤ Assign Clearing Accounts to Cost Account

Change View "Allocation of clearing accts to cost acct": Overview

New Entries

Allocation of clearing accts to cost acct

Ch...	Cost Acct	Description
CABE	619400	RE Apportionable operating costs
CANA	630400	IS-RE Assessment-related costs
GKR	470400	RE Apportionable operating costs
IKR	670400	RE Apportionable operating costs

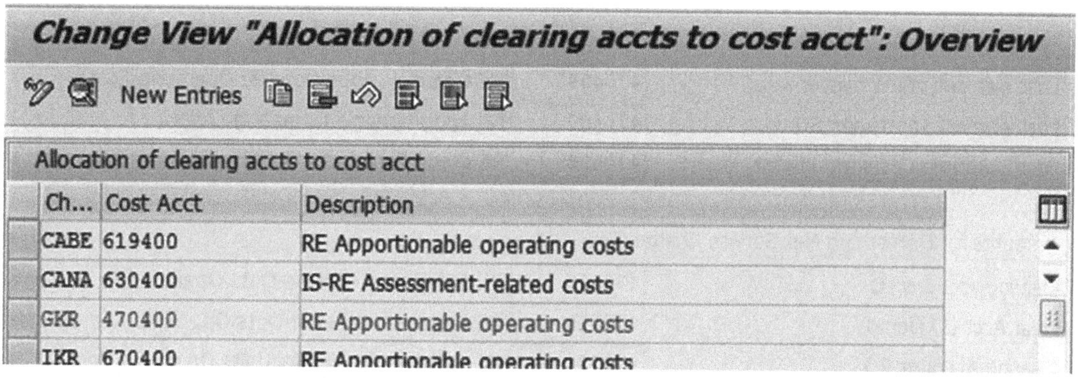

Figure 6-49. *Allocation of clearing accounts to cost account*

Change View "Allocation of clearing accts to cost acct": Details

🖉 New Entries 🗋 🗒 🖎 🗐 🗐 🗐

| Cost Acct | 470400 | Chart of Accts | GKR |
| | RE Apportionable operating costs | | |

Crediting of Settlement Units

| SU credit account | 470499 | RE Clearing - Apportionable Operating Costs |

Accounts for Breakdown Postings for Master Settlement Units

Cost element credit master SU	470499	RE Clearing - Apportionable Operating Costs
Cost element for master SU recip.	470400	RE Apportionable Operating Costs
Cost El.Remain.Costs frm Predist.	470498	RE Credit Remainder Op. Costs Master Sett. Unit

Accounts for Distributing Net Service Charges

Clearing account LO	470500	RE Settlement - Lease-Outs Operating C
Clear.Acct LO Nonall	470510	RE Settlement- Lease-Outs Op. Costs w/o Clg
Clearing Account RO	470520	RE Settlement - Rental Units Operating Costs

Input Tax

Clear.acct.non-deduc	470950	RE Settlement Non-Deduct. Input Tax OC SU
Clearing Acct Non-Ded.InpTax Ctr		
Clearing Acct Non-Ded.InpTx RO		
Credit acct non-ded.	470999	RE Adj. Non-Deductible Input Tax Op.Costs SU

Figure 6-50. *"Allocation of Clearing Accounts to Cost Account": Details screen*

Assign Default Condition Type to Service Charge Key

We need to assign a condition type to a service charge key. This type is used to set the flow type in case either explicit settlement participation for a contract has not been defined or there is no condition defined for settlement units in a contract. If a settlement unit contains more than one object, this setting is used.

Menu Path

IMG ➤ RE-FX ➤ Service Charge Settlement ➤ Settlement Process ➤ Accounting: Account Determination and Accounts for Apportionable Costs ➤ Assign Default Condition Type to Service Charge Key

The configuration seen in Figure 6-51 is required.

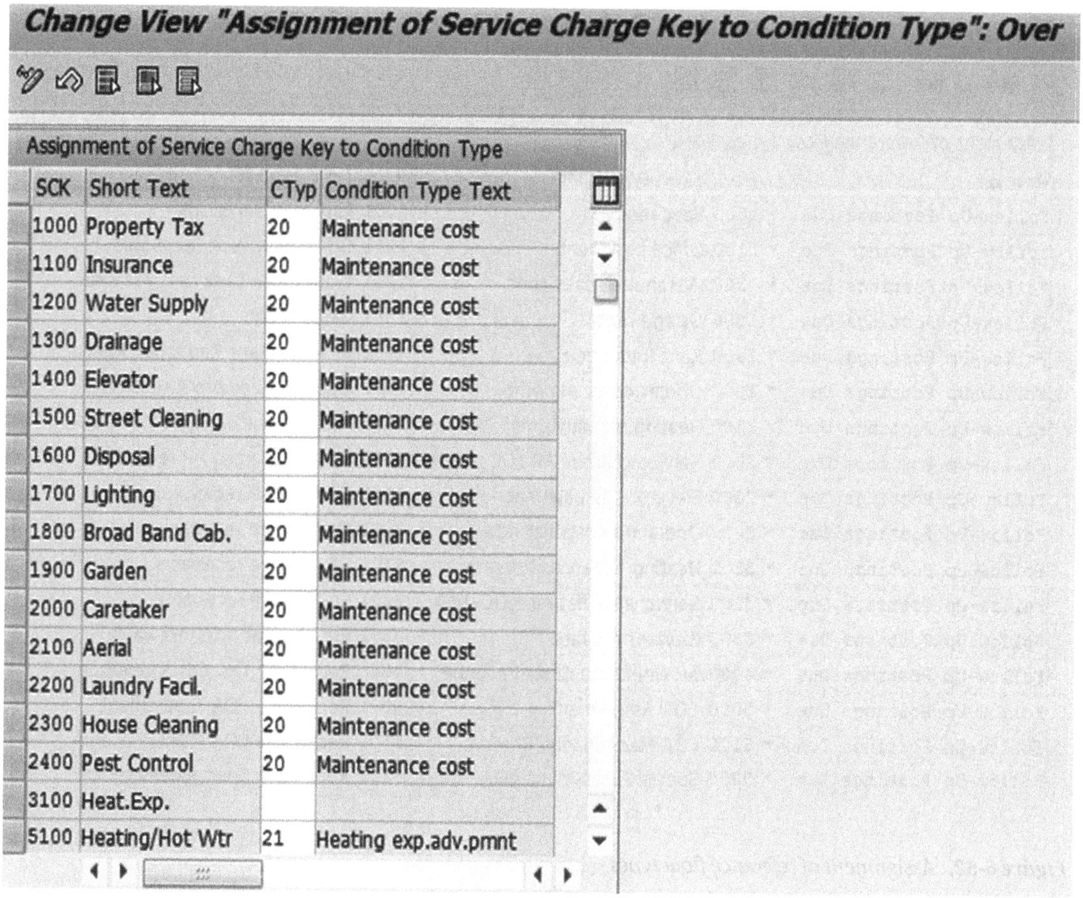

SCK	Short Text	CTyp	Condition Type Text
1000	Property Tax	20	Maintenance cost
1100	Insurance	20	Maintenance cost
1200	Water Supply	20	Maintenance cost
1300	Drainage	20	Maintenance cost
1400	Elevator	20	Maintenance cost
1500	Street Cleaning	20	Maintenance cost
1600	Disposal	20	Maintenance cost
1700	Lighting	20	Maintenance cost
1800	Broad Band Cab.	20	Maintenance cost
1900	Garden	20	Maintenance cost
2000	Caretaker	20	Maintenance cost
2100	Aerial	20	Maintenance cost
2200	Laundry Facil.	20	Maintenance cost
2300	House Cleaning	20	Maintenance cost
2400	Pest Control	20	Maintenance cost
3100	Heat.Exp.		
5100	Heating/Hot Wtr	21	Heating exp.adv.pmnt

Figure 6-51. *Assignment of service charge key to condition type*

Assign Reference Flow Types for Receivables/Credit from SCS

This setting is required so as to assign a reference flow type to the flow type for service charge settlements (Figure 6-52). The relationship between the flow type and the reference flow type needs to be selected from the drop-down box. The user can specify the reference flow type in this field, which will allow the system to refer to this flow type and follow the process as mentioned in this flow type.

Menu Path

IMG ➤ RE-FX ➤ Service Charge Settlement ➤ Settlement Process ➤ Accounting: Account Determination and Accounts for Apportionable Costs ➤ Assign Reference Flow Types for Receivables/Credit from SCS

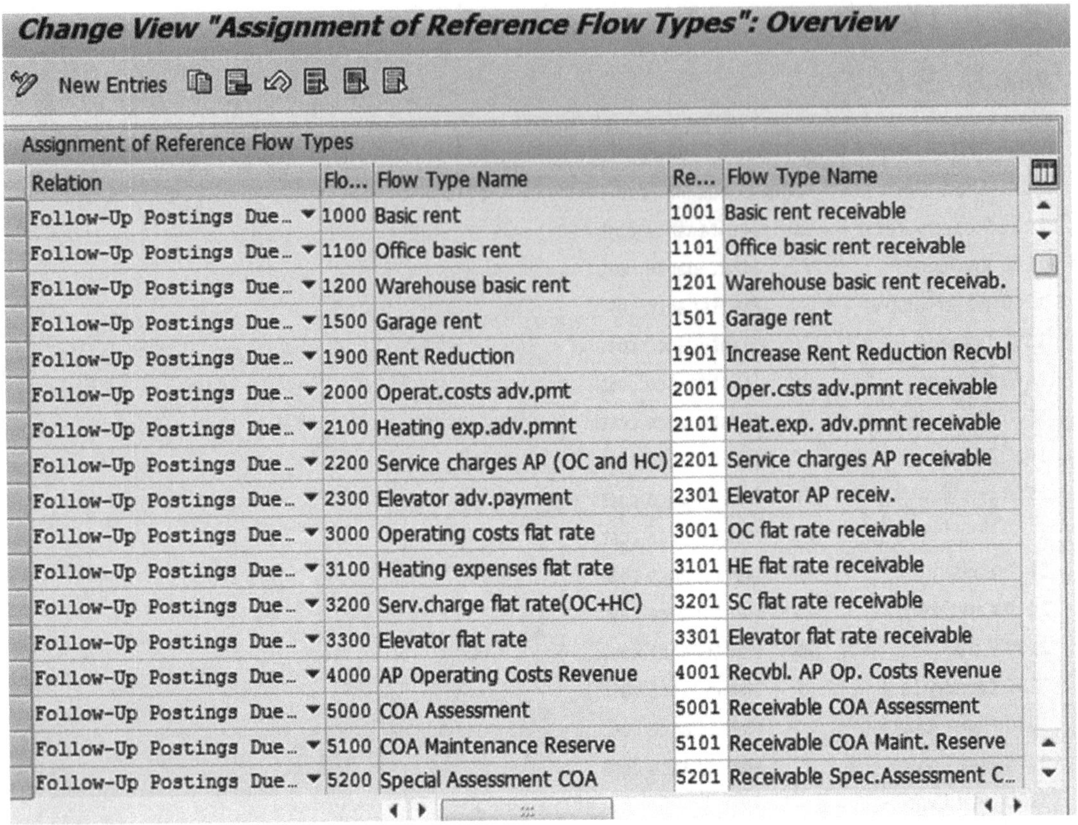

Change View "Assignment of Reference Flow Types": Overview

New Entries

Assignment of Reference Flow Types

Relation	Flo...	Flow Type Name	Re...	Flow Type Name
Follow-Up Postings Due...	1000	Basic rent	1001	Basic rent receivable
Follow-Up Postings Due...	1100	Office basic rent	1101	Office basic rent receivable
Follow-Up Postings Due...	1200	Warehouse basic rent	1201	Warehouse basic rent receivab.
Follow-Up Postings Due...	1500	Garage rent	1501	Garage rent
Follow-Up Postings Due...	1900	Rent Reduction	1901	Increase Rent Reduction Recvbl
Follow-Up Postings Due...	2000	Operat.costs adv.pmt	2001	Oper.csts adv.pmnt receivable
Follow-Up Postings Due...	2100	Heating exp.adv.pmnt	2101	Heat.exp. adv.pmnt receivable
Follow-Up Postings Due...	2200	Service charges AP (OC and HC)	2201	Service charges AP receivable
Follow-Up Postings Due...	2300	Elevator adv.payment	2301	Elevator AP receiv.
Follow-Up Postings Due...	3000	Operating costs flat rate	3001	OC flat rate receivable
Follow-Up Postings Due...	3100	Heating expenses flat rate	3101	HE flat rate receivable
Follow-Up Postings Due...	3200	Serv.charge flat rate(OC+HC)	3201	SC flat rate receivable
Follow-Up Postings Due...	3300	Elevator flat rate	3301	Elevator flat rate receivable
Follow-Up Postings Due...	4000	AP Operating Costs Revenue	4001	Recvbl. AP Op. Costs Revenue
Follow-Up Postings Due...	5000	COA Assessment	5001	Receivable COA Assessment
Follow-Up Postings Due...	5100	COA Maintenance Reserve	5101	Receivable COA Maint. Reserve
Follow-Up Postings Due...	5200	Special Assessment COA	5201	Receivable Spec.Assessment C...

Figure 6-52. *Assignment of reference flow types*

Summary

We have seen how the service charge settlement functionality provided by SAP REFX caters to business requirements, as well as how it is configured in the system. We also learned how the infrastructure of service charge settlements is created; this infrastructure enables the settlement process.

CHAPTER 7

Sales-Based Contracts

In this chapter, we will explain the options available for sales-based contracts, the steps required to carry out sales-based settlements, and the different options available for those settlements. In this chapter, we will discuss the following:

- Sales rule and reporting rule

- Sales-based contract

- Sales-based rent settlement

Let us understand this using a business scenario.

Take a fast food restaurant that is let out by the company Purna Multinational Retail Limited to Samurai Fireworks Limited for monthly rent. It can be either fixed monthly rent or variable rent, which is based on the sales effected at the restaurant and varies from month to month. There is a minimum rent clause dictating that the tenant has to pay even if no sales take place. Also, the receivable varies based on the sales slab, and a percentage can be defined for different slabs. The functionality is also useful in places like airports, where rent is charged based on sales in duty-free shops. We need to calculate rent based on sales figures for a particular period.

Sales Rule and Reporting Rule

The sales-based rent condition is used to specify which objects of the sales-based rent agreement form the basis for sales-based rent. A sales rule defines the selection of parameters for carrying out a sales-based settlement. For example, in order to settle all sales promotion expenses, a sales rule needs to be created. We must specify sales rules for sales-based rent conditions, otherwise settlement is not possible. A contract can have more than one sales rule, but each rule needs to be assigned to sales-based rent conditions. We can assign a sales rule from zero to any number of minimum sales-based rent conditions.

The reporting rule is used to determine which sales types are considered for calculating the sales-based rent. We may have different sales types, like food sales, beer sales, clothing, and so on, that have to be defined in the reporting rule to enable the calculation of rent against those sales.

We can also enter the following:

- Gross/net sales numbers in field for net or gross sales reported

- The minimum and maximum sales amount based on which rent is calculated can be defined in the contract as a simple amount or as per a grading method in which we define for what sales slab what percentage of rent is charged. If the sales-based rent is to be calculated using a linear (not x-graded) calculation on the basis of sales, then the % rate (percentage rate) needs to be defined. With graded sales-based rent, sales limits are required to be entered; i.e., from maybe 1,000 to 5,000, 5,000 to 10,000, and so on.

- Minimum/maximum quantitative sales in units or measures can be entered, and system calculates rent based on units or measures

Sales-based rent contract creation and settlement steps are shown in detail next.

Sales-Based Agreement

In order to post receivables to the customer account in case any space has been leased out to alliance partners based on a sales-based agreement, a contract needs to be created in SAP. In such cases, it will be a lease-out contract.

Trigger

The creation of contract in SAP should only be done after the agreement has been signed between business partners and all necessary approvals have been obtained by the respective role holders.

Prerequisites

Before the contract can be created, necessary master data objects should have been created in the system, like the business entity, pooled space, and rental space. A business partner role also needs to be created for the customer with whom the alliance has been made.

Menu Path

SAP Easy Access Menu ➤ Accounting Flexible real estate management ➤ Accounting ➤ Flexible Real Estate Management ➤ Contract ➤ Process Contract

Transaction Code

RECN

Helpful Hints

The contract type to be used for creating contracts shall be as follows:

- CO01 – Commercial lease-out contract

For a sales-based contract, on the General Data tab page of the contract, activate the checkbox by ticking the "Relevant to Sales" button. An additional tab for Sales-Based Agreement gets activated, and the sales-based agreement values can be captured there.

In case of retail contracts where more than one object will be assigned to the contract, we can create an object group in the object assignment and add the rental objects to this object group.

Procedure

Follow these steps to create a sales-based agreement:

1. Start the transaction using either the menu path or the transaction code.

   Double-click ⬡ **RECN - Process Contract** as shown in Figure 7-1.

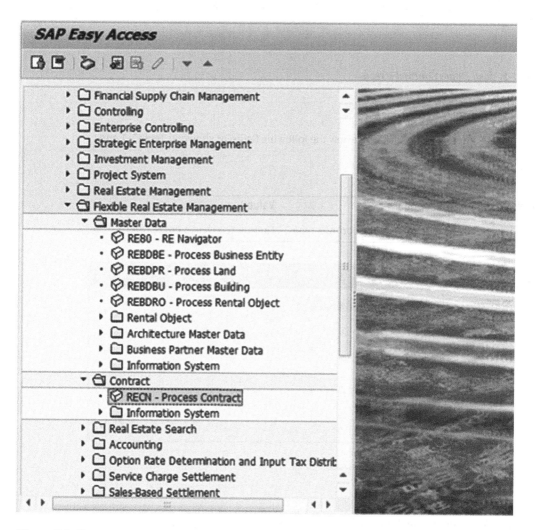

Figure 7-1. *Process contract*

2. Enter the company code (Figure 7-2).

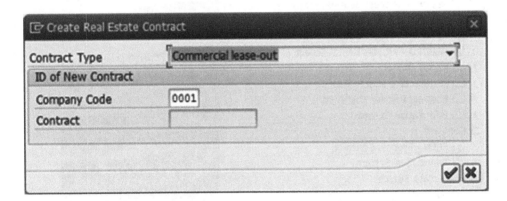

Figure 7-2. *Real Estate Contract screen*

3. Click ⬚.

As required, complete and review the following fields, as shown in Table 7-1 and Figure 7-3.

Table 7-1. *Create Real Estate Contract*

Field Name	Description	Value
Contract Type	Description of the contract type	Commercial lease-out (CO01)

Figure 7-3. *Create Real Estate Contract screen*

4. Click ✓.

5. As required, complete and review the following fields, as shown in Table 7-2 and Figure 7-4.

Table 7-2. *Create: General Data with Fast Entry*

Field Name	Description	Value
Contract name	Description of the contract name	Fast food restaurant at mall
Relevant to Sales	Description of relevant to sales	Select
Not Applicable	-	Select

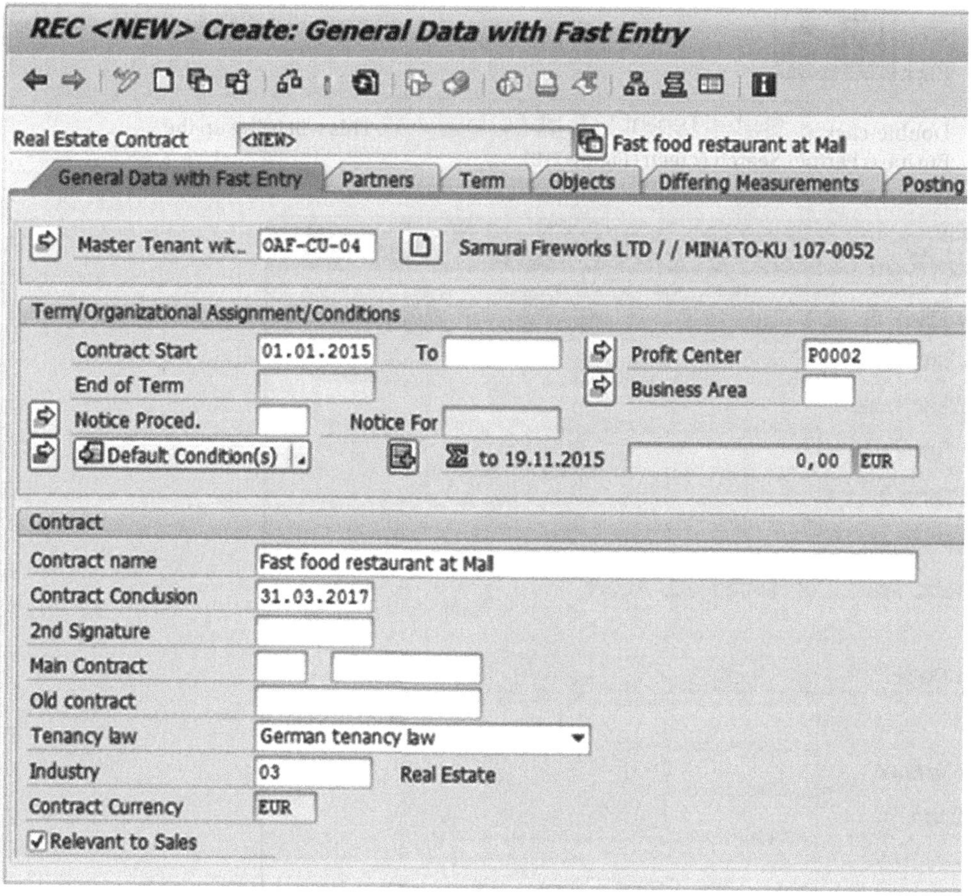

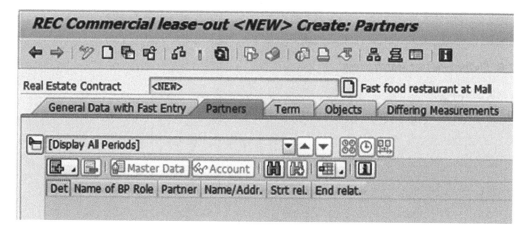

Figure 7-4. *Commercial lease out: General Data with Fast Entry tab*

6. Click Partners (Figure 7-5).

Figure 7-5. *Commercial lease out: Partners tab*

7.   Click .

8.   Double-click ☐ **Master Tenant w.Cust.Acct** . This will bring up the Business Partner Search screen (Figure 7-6).

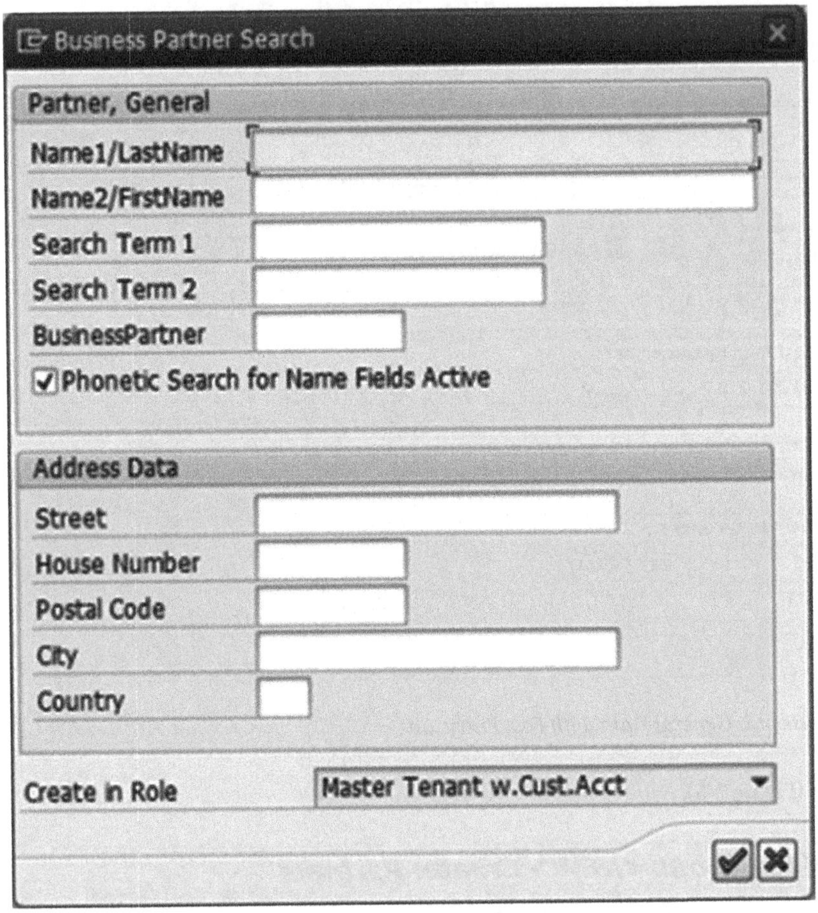

🖻 Business Partner Search   ✕

Partner, General

Name1/LastName	
Name2/FirstName	
Search Term 1	
Search Term 2	
BusinessPartner	

☑ Phonetic Search for Name Fields Active

Address Data

Street	
House Number	
Postal Code	
City	
Country	

Create in Role   Master Tenant w.Cust.Acct   ▼

                                              ✅ ❎

Figure 7-6. *Business Partner Search screen*

9.   Click ✅. It will provide list of all partners (Figure 7-7).

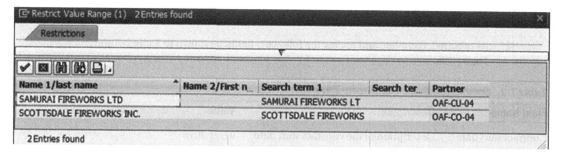

Figure 7-7. Business partner search result

10. Double-clicking

| SAMURAI FIREWORKS LTD | SAMURAI FIREWORKS LT | OAF-CU-04 |

will add the partner (Figure 7-8).

REC Commercial lease-out <NEW> Create: Partners

| Real Estate Contract | <NEW> | | Fast food restaurant at Mall |

General Data with Fast Entry / Partners \ Term \ Objects \ Differing Measurements \ Posting Parameters

[Unlimited]

Det	Name of BP Role	Partner	Name/address	Strt rel.	End relat.
▶	Master Tenant w.Cust.Acct	OAF-CU-04	Samurai Fireworks LTD / / MINATO-KU 107-0052		

BP Role	TR0600	Master Tenant w.Cust.A...
BusinessPartner	OAF-CU-04	Samurai Fireworks LTD / / MINATO-KU 107-0052
Start reltnship		End of relat.	
Address Type		
Customer	34	Samurai Fireworks LTD / / MINATO-KU 107-0052

Figure 7-8. Commercial Lease-Out Create: Partners screen

11. Click Term .

12. As required, complete and review the following fields, as shown in Table 7-3 and Figure 7-9.

Table 7-3. *Commercial Lease-Out: Create Term*

Field Name	Description	Value
Contract start date	Description of the contract start date	01.01.2015
1st Contract End	Description of the first contract end	31.03.2017

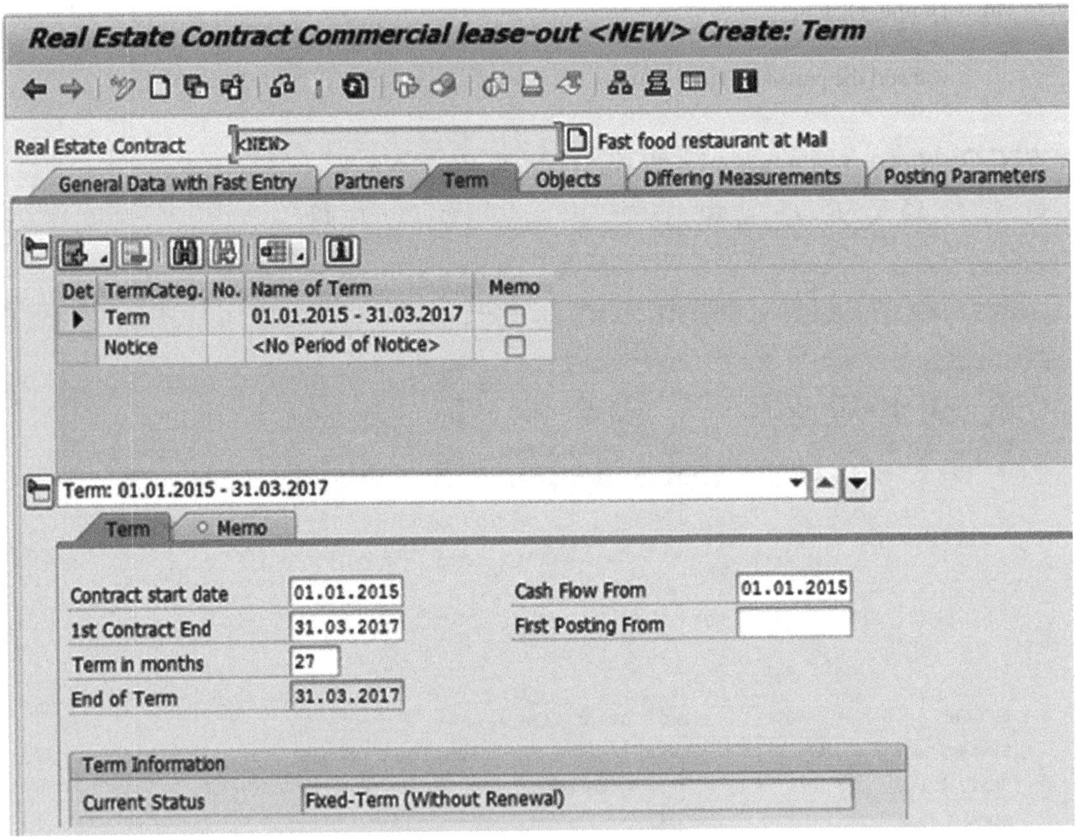

Figure 7-9. *Commercial Lease-Out Create: Term screen*

13. Click Objects (Figure 7-10).

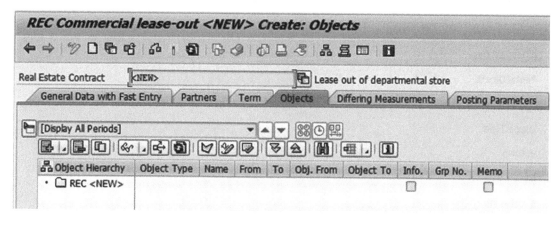

Figure 7-10. *Commercial Lease-Out Create: Objects screen*

14. Click ⏹. This will show a list of object types (Figure 7-11).

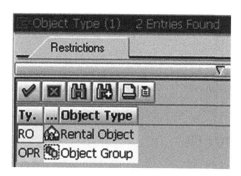

Figure 7-11. *Commercial Lease-Out Create: Objects—search object type*

15. Double-clicking 🏠Rental Object will bring up the rental object search screen (Figure 7-12).

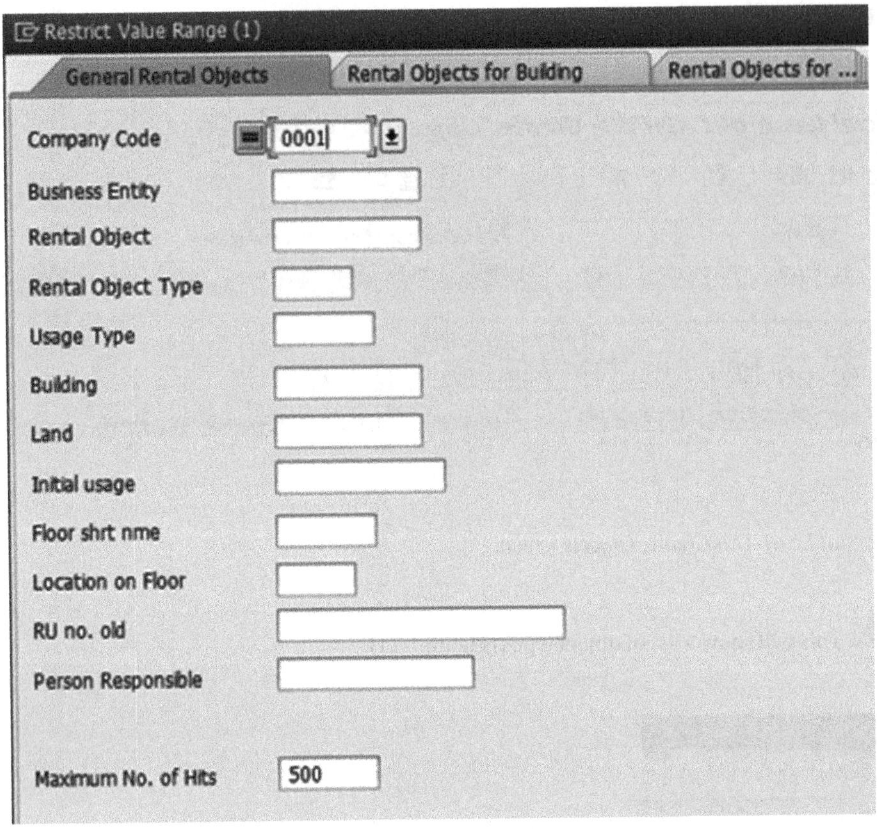

Figure 7-12. *Commercial Lease-Out Create: Objects—search rental objects*

16. Click ![checkmark]. This will show a list of rental objects (Figure 7-13).

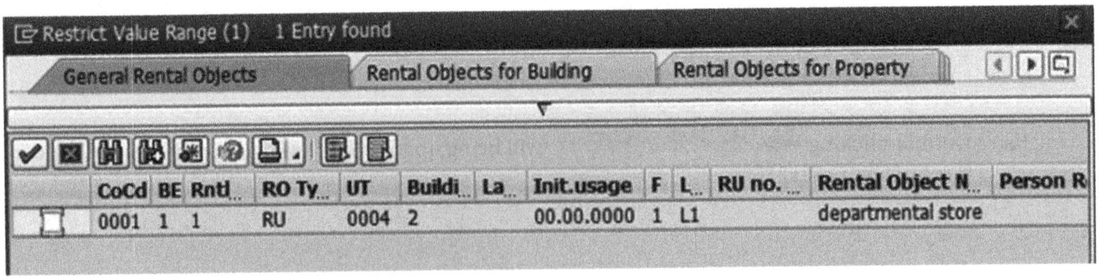

Figure 7-13. *Commercial Lease-Out Create: Objects—search result*

For a retail business, in the object assignment we can create an object group first and then add the rental objects and assign them to this object group. Only rental objects belonging to the same territory can be assigned to an object group, and only to one object group per contract. For example, Fast Food mall has counters in many regions In this case, contracts will have to be created, one per region, with all the rental objects assigned to one object group in the contract.

17. Select 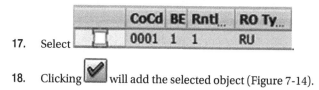.

18. Clicking ✅ will add the selected object (Figure 7-14).

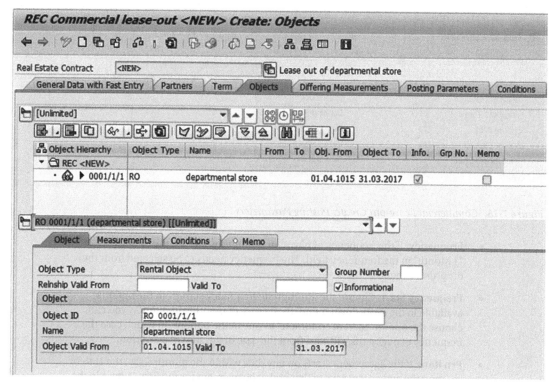

Figure 7-14. *Commercial Lease-out Create: Objects, after adding the rental objects*

19. Click **Posting Parameters** (Figure 7-15).

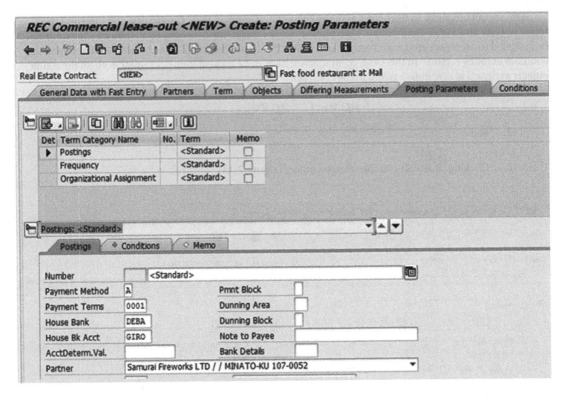

Figure 7-15. *Commercial Lease-out Create: Posting Parameters*

- **Frequency**: If the frequency of payment is monthly, choose the option "1 Month" in the frequency field. The frequency needs to be selected from the drop-down menu.

- **Frequency Start**: Choose the appropriate frequency start from the options available in the drop-down menu. In the case of monthly frequency, you can choose the option "Start of condition" as one of the options, in which case the frequency of payments will start from the date of the start of condition.

- **Pro Rata**: If the agreement starts on any date within the month—say, the 16th or so—and the agreement says to first make the payment for the first 14 days in the current month and then pay on a monthly basis, the pro rata option "contract or rental object start of end date" needs to be chosen.

- **Amount Reference**: Choose the option from the drop-down entries for monthly, yearly, or cyclical amounts, as the case may be.

- **Calc. Method**: Whether the calculation of the amount is based on an exact number of days in a month or a fixed 30 days in a month. Choose the appropriate option as the case may be.

- **Payment Form**: Whether the payment is received at the beginning of the month for the month or at the end of the month. Choose the option "In Advance" or "In Arrears," respectively, as the case may be.

20.   Click **Conditions** (Figure 7-16).

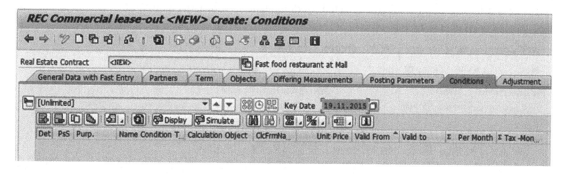

Figure 7-16. Commercial Lease-out Create: Conditions screen

21.   Click 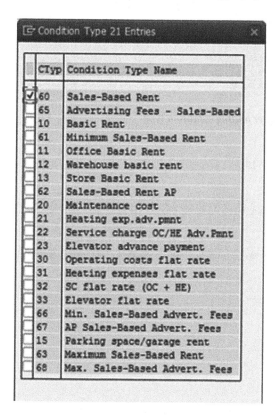 to add condition type (Figure 7-17).

CTyp	Condition Type Name
60	Sales-Based Rent
65	Advertising Fees - Sales-Based
10	Basic Rent
61	Minimum Sales-Based Rent
11	Office Basic Rent
12	Warehouse basic rent
13	Store Basic Rent
62	Sales-Based Rent AP
20	Maintenance cost
21	Heating exp.adv.pmnt
22	Service charge OC/HE Adv.Pmnt
23	Elevator advance payment
30	Operating costs flat rate
31	Heating expenses flat rate
32	SC flat rate (OC + HE)
33	Elevator flat rate
66	Min. Sales-Based Advert. Fees
67	AP Sales-Based Advert. Fees
15	Parking space/garage rent
63	Maximum Sales-Based Rent
68	Max. Sales-Based Advert. Fees

Figure 7-17. Commercial Lease-out Create: Conditions—condition type search

22. Select ☑ 60 | Sales-Based Rent .

23. Clicking will add the selected condition type, as shown in Figure 7-18.

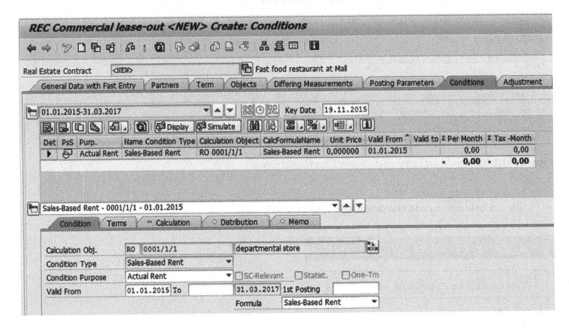

Figure 7-18. *Commercial Lease-out Create: Conditions, after adding condition type*

24. Click **Sales-Based Rent Agreement** (Figure 7-19).

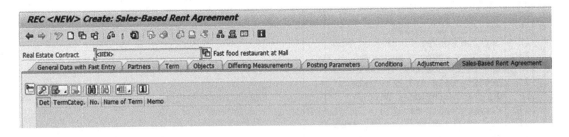

Figure 7-19. *Create: Sales-Based Rent Agreement screen*

25. Click (Figure 7-20).

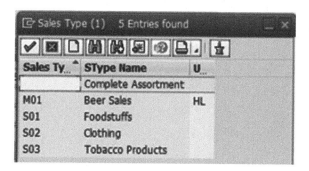

Figure 7-20. *Fast Entry for New Sales Rule screen*

26. As required, complete and review the following fields, as shown in Table 7-4.

Table 7-4. *Create: Sales-Based Rent Agreement, Fast Entry for New Sales Rule*

Field Name	Description	Value
Valid From	Description of valid from date	01.01.2015

27. Click 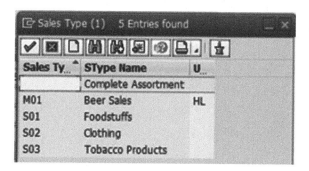 next to Sales Type (Figure 7-21).

Figure 7-21. *Fast Entry for New Sales Rule, sales type search*

28. Double-click `M01      Beer Sales                    HL` .

29. As required, complete and review the following fields, as shown in Table 7-5 and Figure 7-22.

Table 7-5. *Create: Sales-Based Rent Agreement, Fast Entry for New Sales Rule, Reporting Frequency Section*

Field Name	Description	Value
Frequency	Description of frequency	3

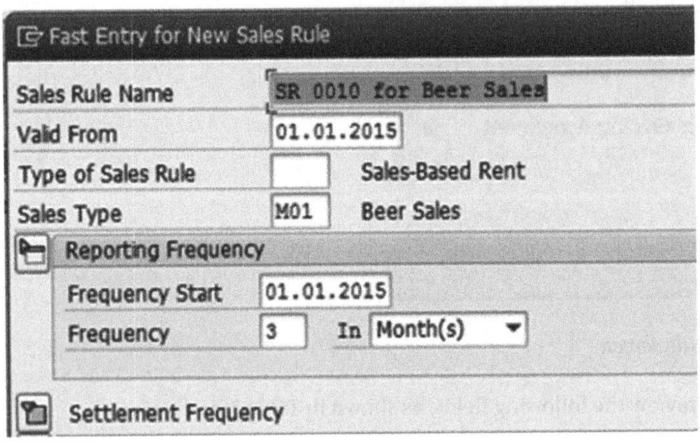

Figure 7-22. *Fast Entry for New Sales Rule, Reporting Frequency section*

30. Click  (Figure 7-23).

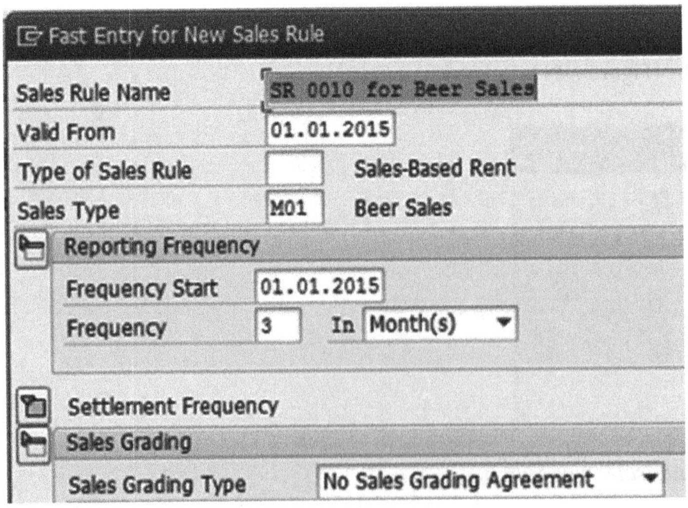

Figure 7-23. *Fast Entry for New Sales Rule, Sales Grading section*

31. As required, complete and review the following fields, as shown in Table 7-6.

Table 7-6. *Create: Sales-Based Rent Agreement, Fast Entry for New Sales Rule, Sales Grading Section*

Field Name	Description	Value
Sales Grading Type	Description of sales grading type	Sales Grading Agreement (01)

32. As required, complete and review the following fields, as shown in Table 7-7 and Figure 7-24.

Table 7-7. *Create: Sales-Based Rent Agreement, Fast Entry for New Sales Rule, Sales Grading Section, First Combination*

Field Name	Description	Value
Min. Rent	Description of minimum rent	10000
Sales From	Description of sales from	100000

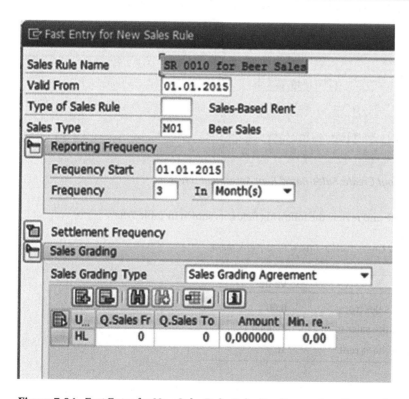

Figure 7-24. *Fast Entry for New Sales Rule, Sales Grading section, first combination*

33.   Click ⊞ as required, and complete and review the following fields, as shown in Table 7-8 and Figure 7-25.

Table 7-8. *Create: Sales-Based Rent Agreement, Fast Entry for New Sales Rule, Sales Grading Section, Second Combination*

Field Name	Description	Value
Sales To	Description of sales to	200000

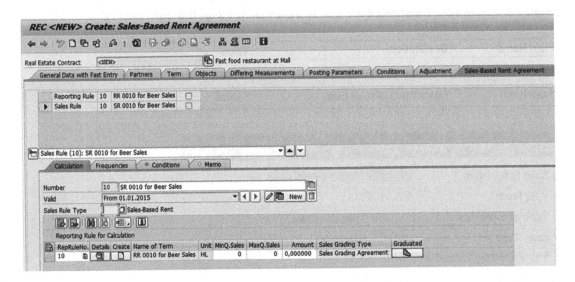

Figure 7-25. *Commercial Lease-out Create: Sales-Based Rent Agreement screen*

34.   As required, complete and review the following fields, as shown in Table 7-9.

Table 7-9. *Commercial Lease-out Create: Sales-Based Rent Agreement, Reporting Rule for Calculation*

Field Name	Description	Value
Sales From	Description of sales from	0.00
Sales To	Description of the sales to	200000
% Rent	Description of the % rent	10

35. Click on "Graduated" and click 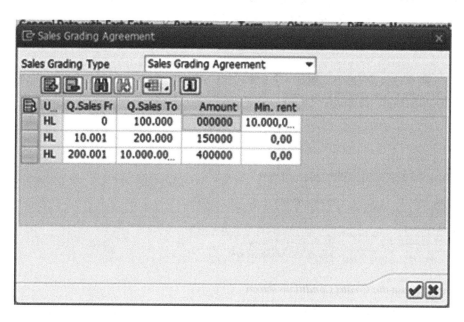 (Figure 7-26).

Figure 7-26. *Commercial Lease-out Create: Sales-Based Rent Agreement, Sales Grading Agreement screen*

36. Click [✓].

37. Click [Conditions].

38. Click [Terms].

39. As required, complete and review the following fields, as shown in Table 7-10 and Figure 7-27.

Table 7-10. *Commercial Lease-out Create: Conditions, Terms*

Field Name	Description	Value
Sales Rule	Description of sales rule	10

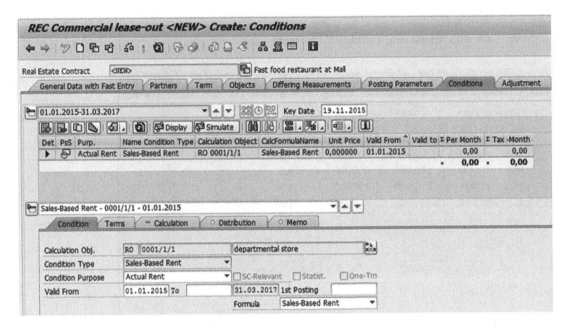

Figure 7-27. Commercial Lease-out Create: Conditions screen

40.   Click **Sales-Based Rent Agreement** (Figure 7-28 and Figure 7-29).

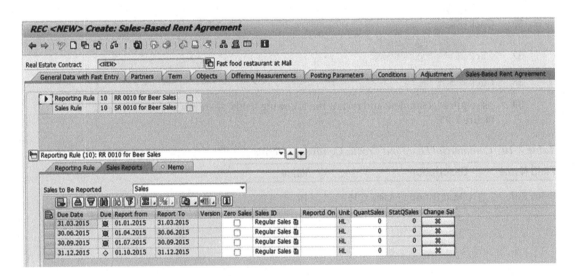

Figure 7-28. Commercial Lease-out Create: Sales-Based Rent Agreement, Sales Reports tab

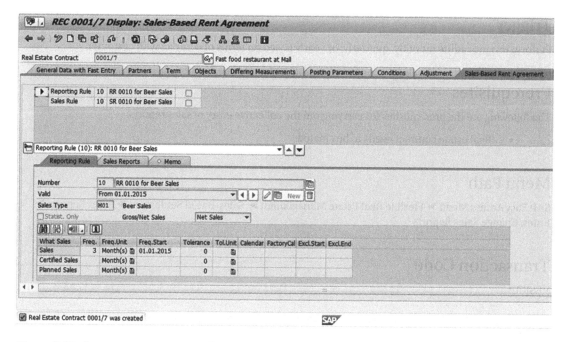

Figure 7-29. *Lease-out contract created*

41. Click 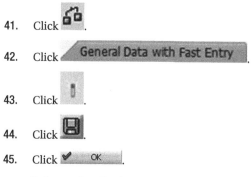.

42. Click ![General Data with Fast Entry].

43. Click ![icon].

44. Click ![save icon].

45. Click ![OK].

   Information: Real estate contract 0001/7 was created and activated.

46. You have completed this transaction.

Result

Real estate contract created successfully.

Collective Entry of Sales Reports

Use this procedure to enter sales figures into the contract so that a sales-based settlement can be run.

Trigger

Perform this procedure monthly, quarterly, or yearly based on terms of contract with customer.

Prerequisites

The following are the prerequisites for carrying out the collective entry of sales reports:

- Real estate contract needs to be created

Menu Path

SAP Easy Access Menu ➤ Flexible Real Estate Management ➤ Sales-Based Settlement ➤ Sales Reports ➤ Enter/Change Sales Reports

Transaction Code

RESRRP

Procedure

Follow these steps to carry out of the collective entry of sales reports:

1. Start the transaction using either the menu path or the transaction code (Figure 7-30).

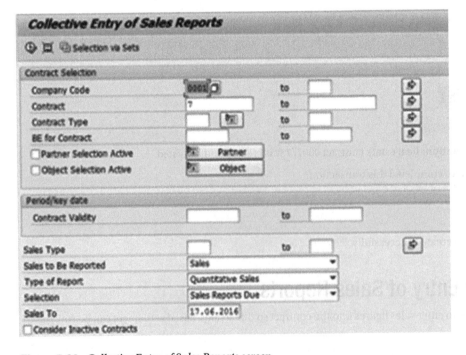

Figure 7-30. *Collective Entry of Sales Reports screen*

2. Clicking  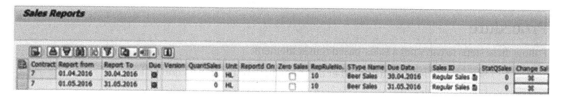 will display the sales reports due wherein sales figures need to be entered (Figure 7-31).

Sales Reports

Contract	Report from	Report To	Due	Version	QuantSales	Unit	Reportd On	Zero Sales	RepRuleNo.	SType Name	Due Date	Sales ID	StatQSales	Change Sal
7	01.04.2016	30.04.2016	⊠		0	HL		☐	10	Beer Sales	30.04.2016	Regular Sales ▣	0	✖
7	01.05.2016	31.05.2016	⊠		0	HL		☐	10	Beer Sales	31.05.2016	Regular Sales ▣	0	✖

Figure 7-31. *Sales reports due*

3. Enter the sales figures (Figure 7-32).

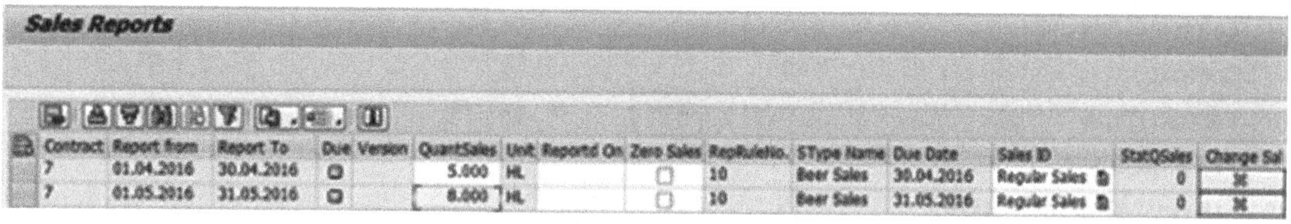

Sales Reports

Contract	Report from	Report To	Due	Version	QuantSales	Unit	Reportd On	Zero Sales	RepRuleNo.	SType Name	Due Date	Sales ID	StatQSales	Change Sal
7	01.04.2016	30.04.2016	❑		5.000	HL		☐	10	Beer Sales	30.04.2016	Regular Sales ▣	0	✖
7	01.05.2016	31.05.2016	❑		8.000	HL		☐	10	Beer Sales	31.05.2016	Regular Sales ▣	0	✖

Figure 7-32. *Sales Reports screen after entering the sales figures*

Result

We have entered the sales figures and are ready to run the sales-based rent settlement.

Sales-Based Rent Settlements

Use this procedure to post rent receivables dependent on sales. The settlement process will calculate rent receivables due from the customer and post a financial document debiting customer and crediting the income account.

Trigger

Perform this procedure monthly, quarterly, or yearly based on terms of contract with customer.

Prerequisites

The following are the prerequisites for carrying out s sales-based rent settlement:

- Real estate contract needs to be created
- Sales figures need to be reported

Menu Path

SAP Easy Access Menu ➤ Flexible Real Estate Management ➤ Sales-Based Settlement ➤ Settlement

Transaction Code

RESRSE

Procedure

Follow these steps to carry out a sales-based rent settlement:

1. Start the transaction using either the menu path or the transaction code (Figure 7-33).

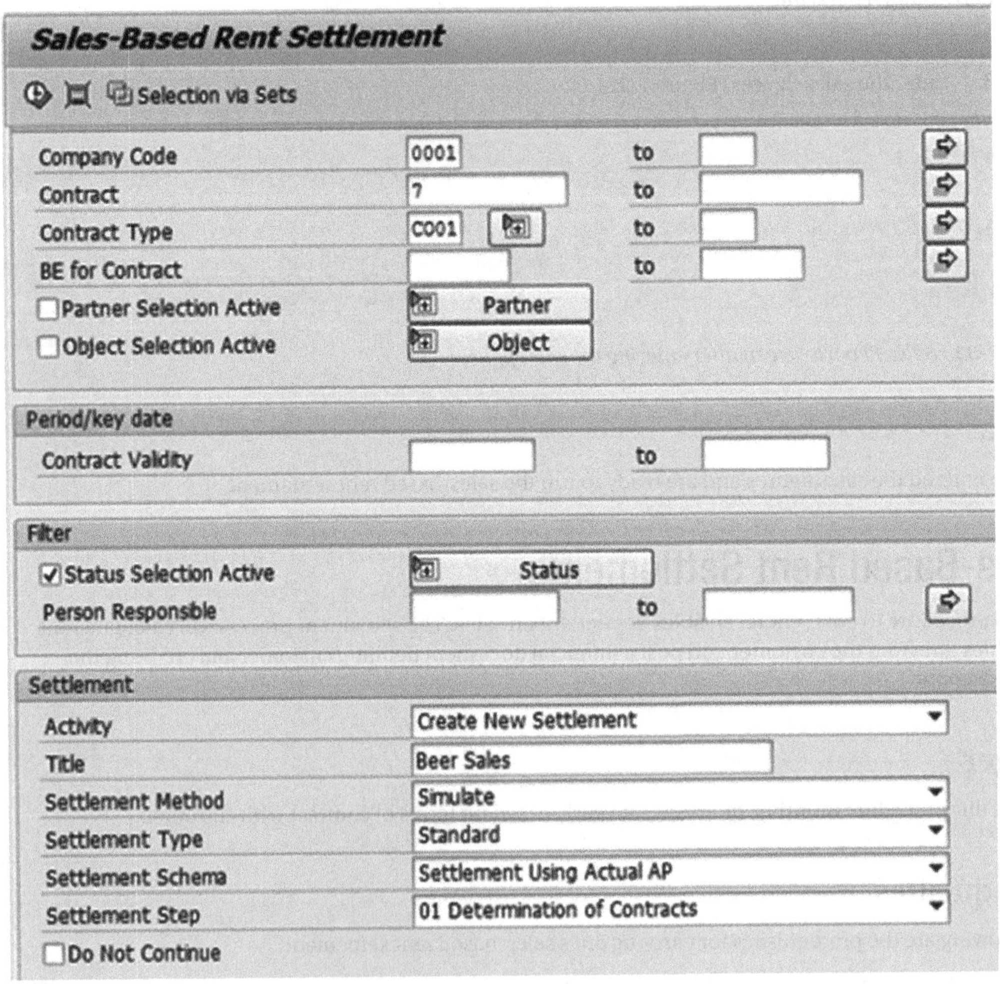

Figure 7-33. *Sales-Based Rent Settlement screen*

2. As required, complete and review the following fields, as shown in Table 7-11 and Figure 7-34.

Table 7-11. Sales-Based Rent Settlement, Settlement Section

Field Name	Description	Value
Contract Number	Description of the contract number	0001/7
Title	Description of the title	Beer sales
Settlement Method	Description of settlement method	Execute (EX)
Settlement Step	Description of settlement step	Determination of Contracts (01)

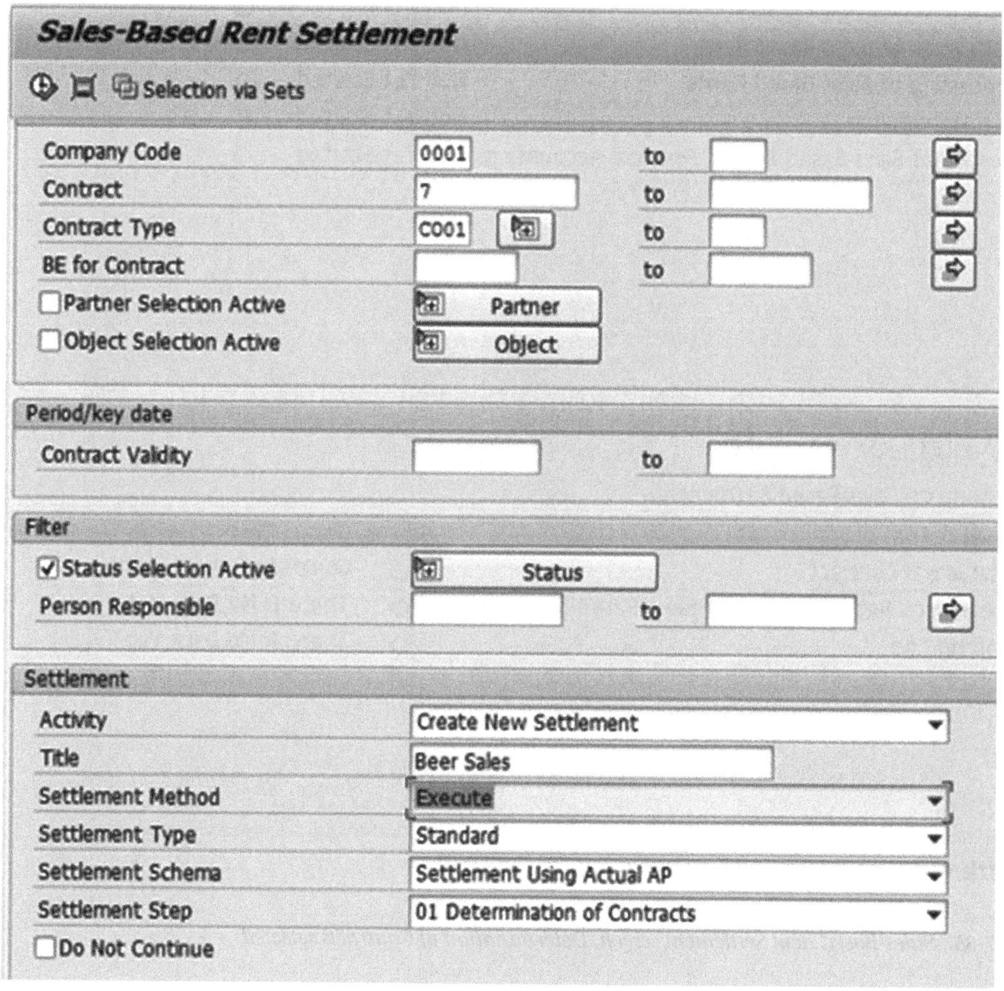

Figure 7-34. Sales-Based Rent Settlement screen, Settlement section

3. Clicking 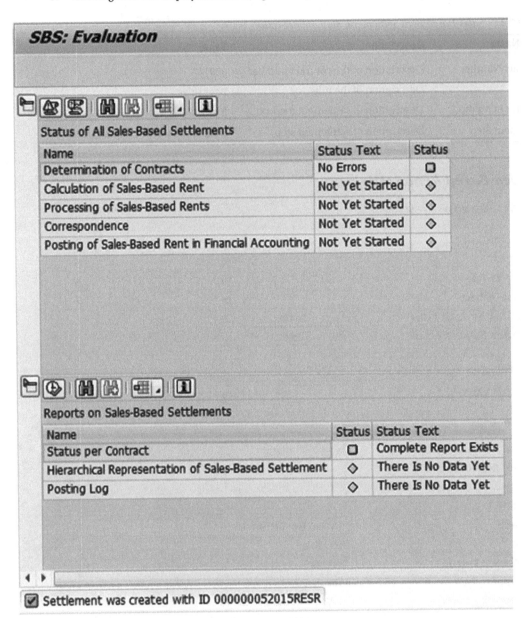 will display the result (Figure 7-35).

Figure 7-35. Sales-Based Rent Settlement screen, Determination of Contracts selected

4. As required, complete and review the following fields, as shown in Table 7-12 and Figure 7-36.

Table 7-12. *Sales-Based Rent Settlement, Settlement Section (Settlement Step: Calculation of Sales-Based Rent)*

Field Name	Description	Value
Settlement Step	Description of settlement step	Calculation of Sales-Based Rent (02)

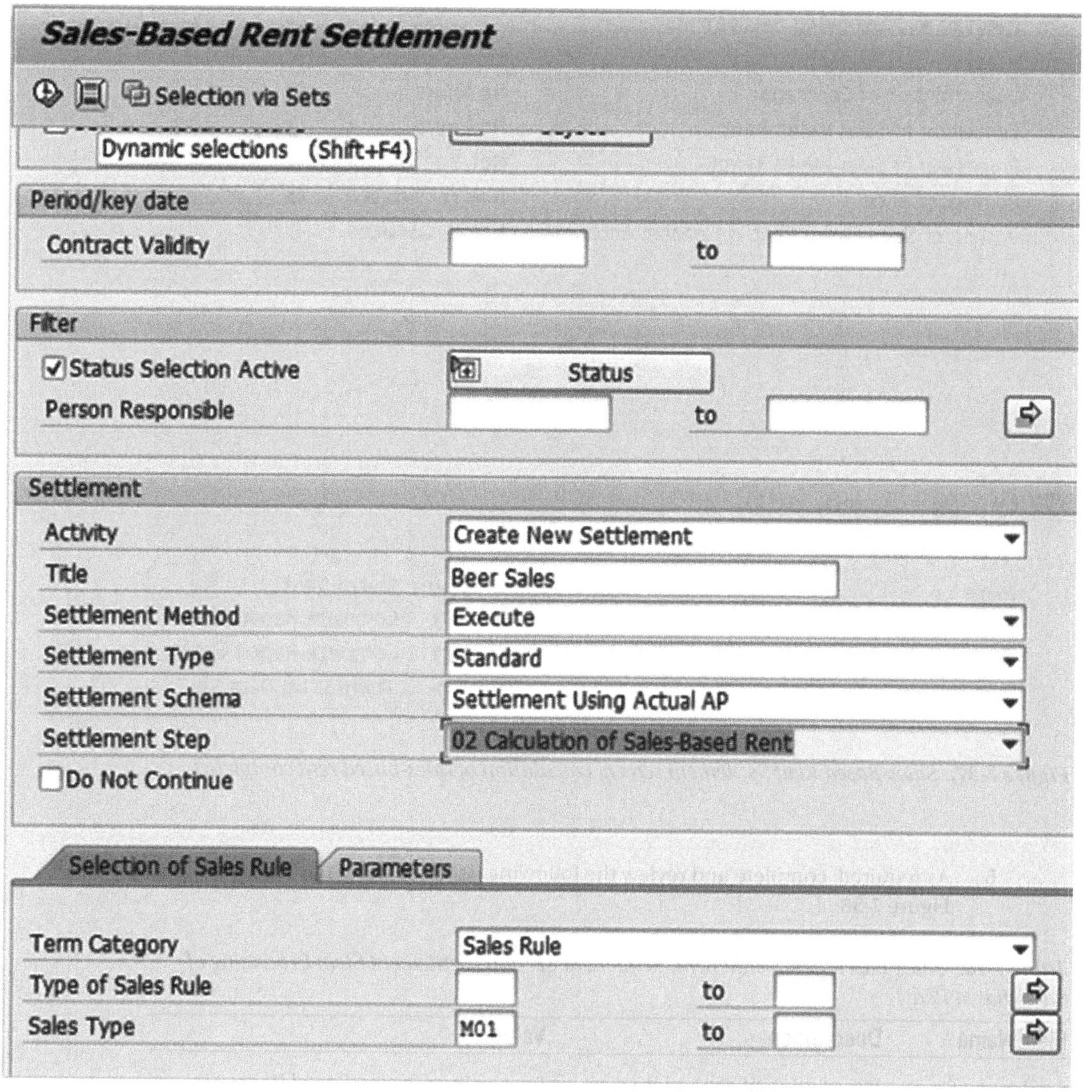

Figure 7-36. *Sales-Based Rent Settlement screen, Settlement Step: Calculation of Sales-Based Rent completed*

5.　Clicking 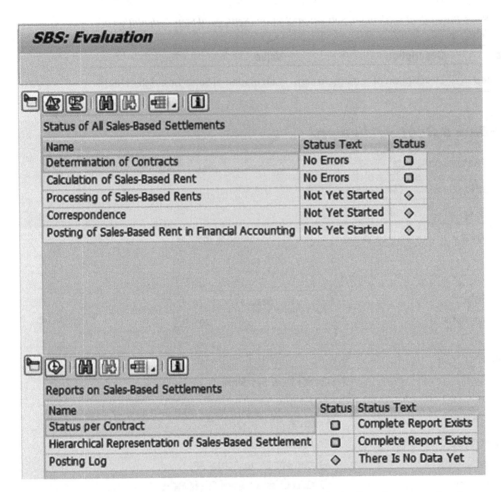 will display the result (Figure 7-37).

Figure 7-37. Sales-Based Rent Settlement screen, calculation of sales-based rent completed

6.　As required, complete and review the following fields, as shown in Table 7-13 and Figure 7-38.

Table 7-13. Sales-Based Rent Settlement, Settlement Section (Settlement Step: Processing of Sales-Based Rent)

Field Name	Description	Value
Settlement Step	Description of settlement step	Processing of Sales-Based Rent (03)

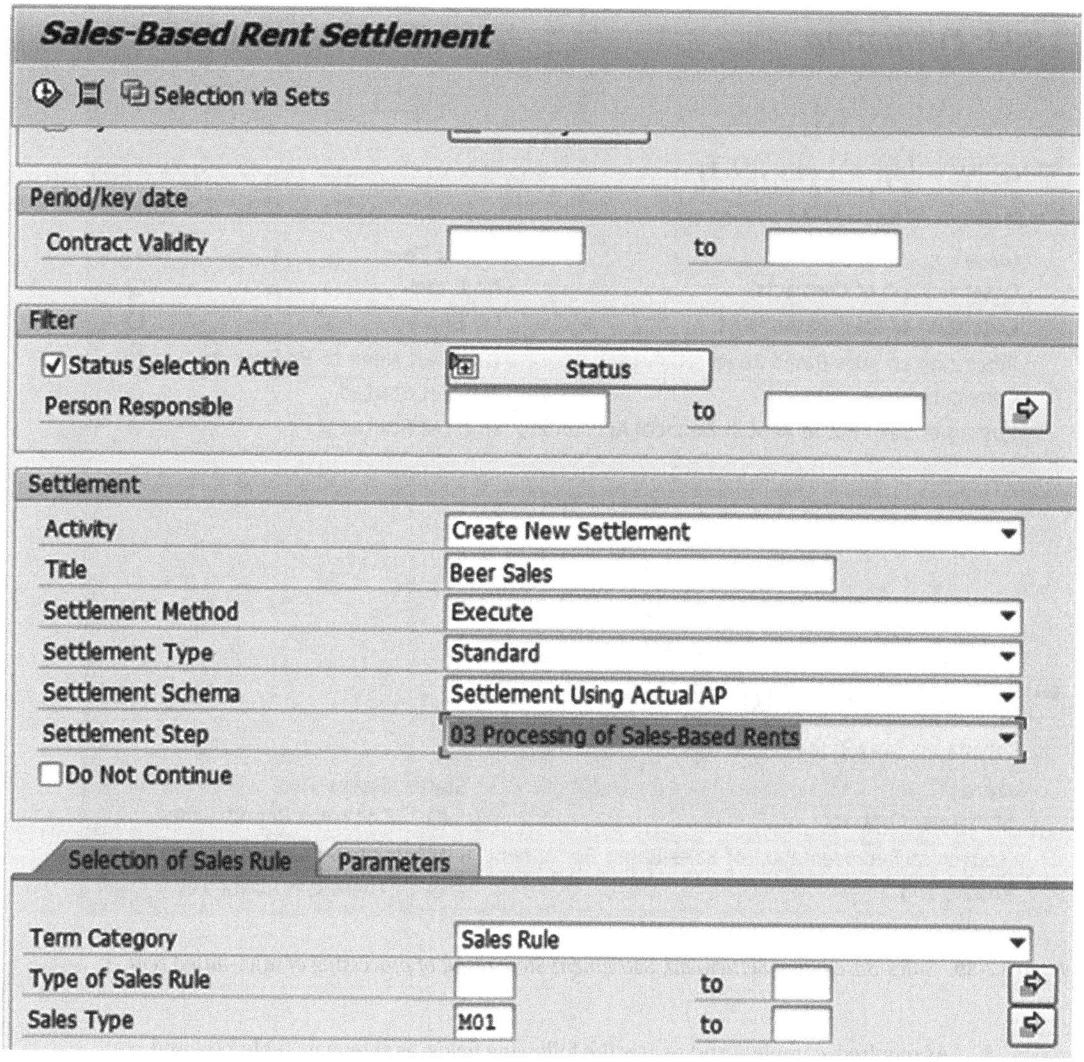

Sales-Based Rent Settlement

⊕ 冝 ⊕ Selection via Sets

Period/key date

Contract Validity   [　　　　]   to   [　　　　]

Filter

☑ Status Selection Active   [⊞]   Status

Person Responsible   [　　　　]   to   [　　　　]   ⇨

Settlement

Activity	Create New Settlement ▼
Title	Beer Sales
Settlement Method	Execute ▼
Settlement Type	Standard ▼
Settlement Schema	Settlement Using Actual AP ▼
Settlement Step	03 Processing of Sales-Based Rents ▼
☐ Do Not Continue	

| Selection of Sales Rule | Parameters |

Term Category	Sales Rule	▼
Type of Sales Rule	[　] to [　]	⇨
Sales Type	M01 to [　]	⇨

Figure 7-38. *Sales-Based Rent Settlement screen, Settlement Step: Processing of Sales-Based Rent*

7.   Clicking ⊕ will display the result (Figure 7-39).

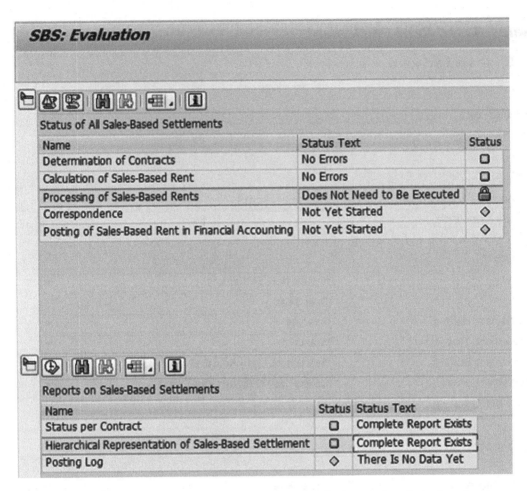

Figure 7-39. *Sales-Based Rent Settlement, Settlement Step: result of processing of sales-based rent*

8. As required, complete and review the following fields, as shown in Table 7-14 and Figure 7-40.

Table 7-14. *Sales-Based Rent Settlement, Settlement Section (Posting of Sales-Based Rent in Financial Accounting)*

Field Name	Description	Value
Settlement Step	Description of settlement step	Posting of Sales-Based Rent in Financial Accounting (BC06)

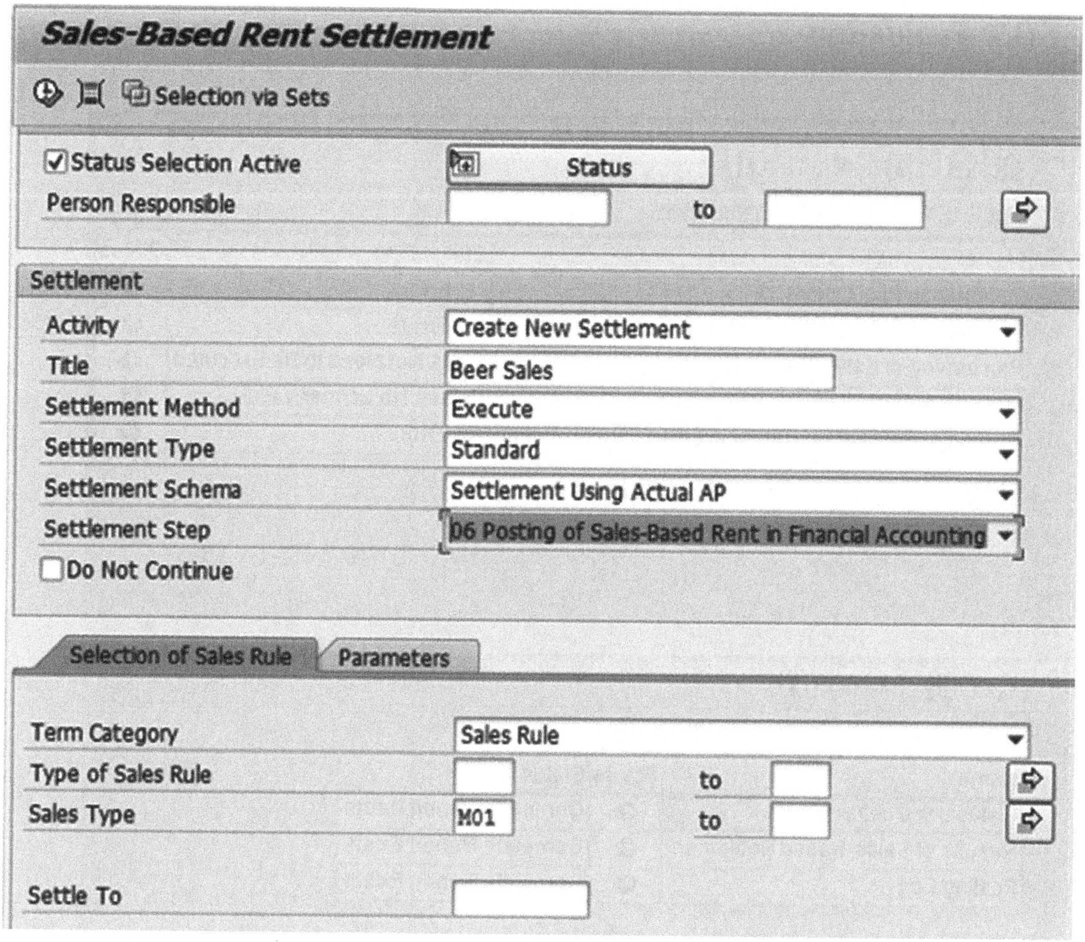

Figure 7-40. *Sales-Based Rent Settlement, Settlement Step: Posting of Sales-Based Rent in Financial Accounting*

9. Click `Parameters`. As required, complete and review the following fields, as shown in Table 7-15.

Table 7-15. *Sales-Based Rent Settlement, Parameters Tab*

Field Name	Description	Value
Posting Date	Description of posting date	19.11.2015
Document Date	Description of document date	19.11.2015

10. Clicking ⊕ will display the result (Figure 7-41).

Settlement ID generated 000000052015RESR

SBS: Evaluation

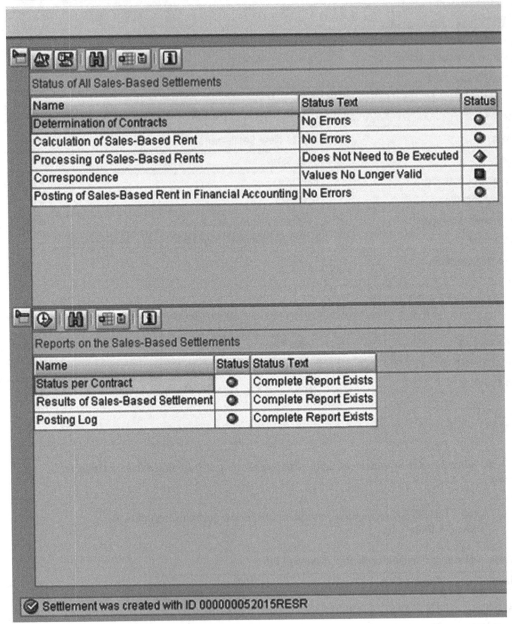

Figure 7-41. Sales-Based Rent Settlement, SBS: Evaluation screen

11. Click ✔ OK .

12. Double-clicking Complete Report Exists will display the posting log (Figure 7-42).

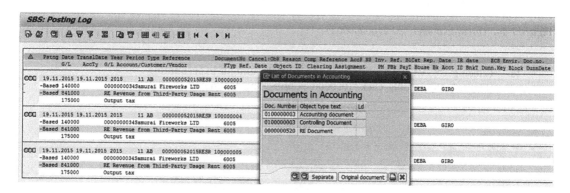

Figure 7-42. *Sales-Based Rent Settlement, SBS: Posting Log*

13. Clicking 100000003 will provide a list of documents in accounting (Figure 7-43).

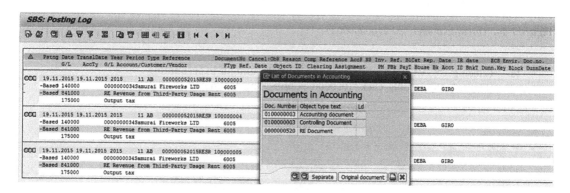

Figure 7-43. *List of Documents in Accounting (100000003)*

14. Double-click "10000003: Accounting document" to get the document overview (Figure 7-44).

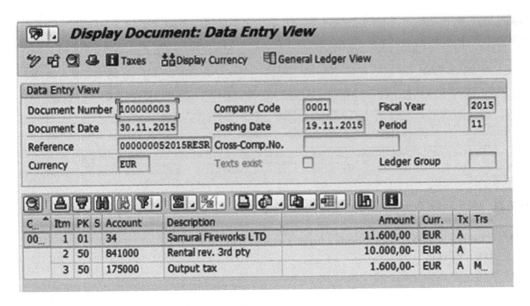

Figure 7-44. *Document overview (100000003)*

15. Clicking ⬅ will take you back to the list of documents in accounting (Figure 7-45). Double-click "10000003: Controlling document" (Figure 7-46).

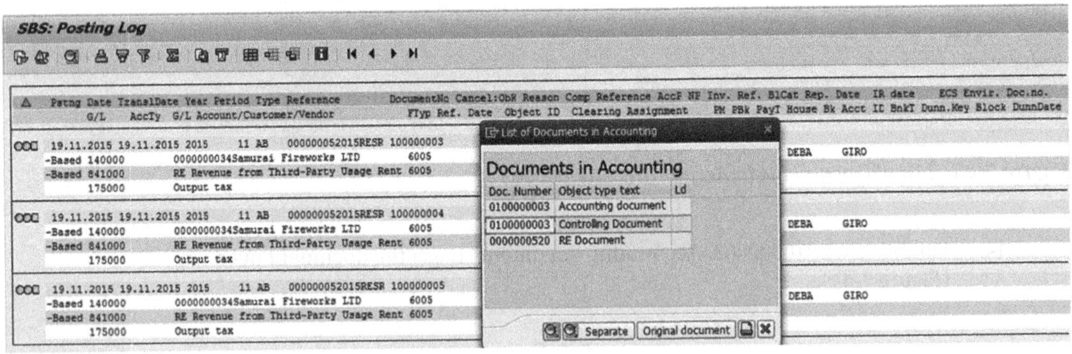

Figure 7-45. *List of Documents in Accounting screen: Controlling Document (100000003)*

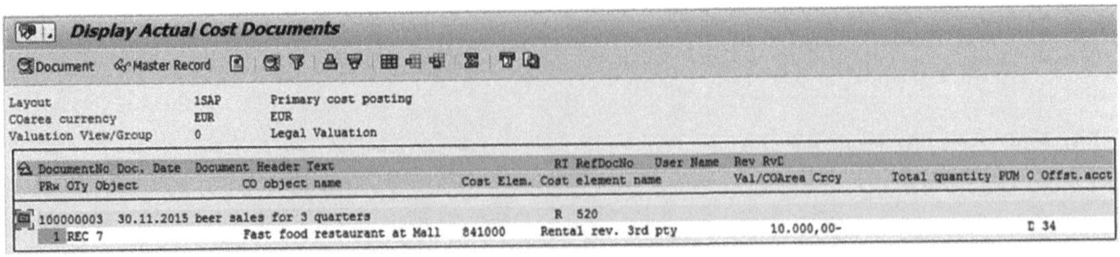

Figure 7-46. *Display Actual Cost Documents screen (100000003)*

16. Clicking 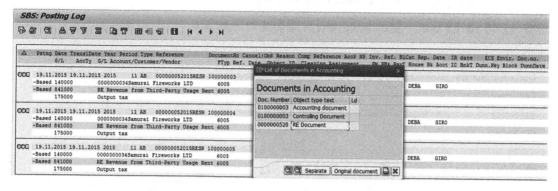 will take you back to the list of documents in accounting (Figure 7-47). Double-click "0000000520: RE document" (Figure 7-48).

Figure 7-47. *List of Documents in Accounting screen: RE Document (0000000520)*

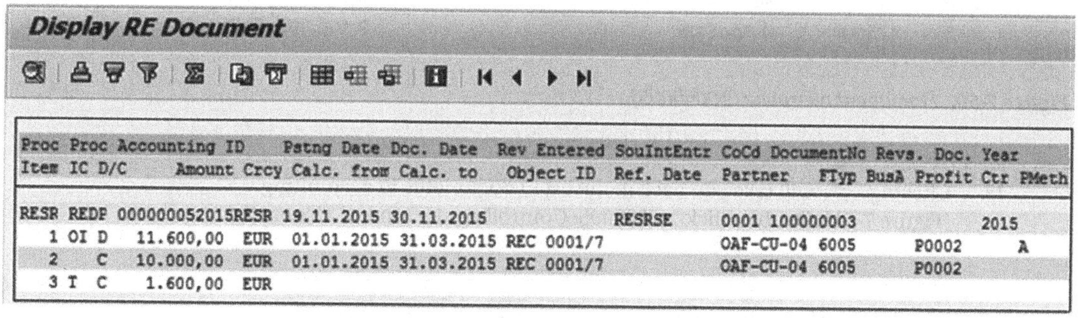

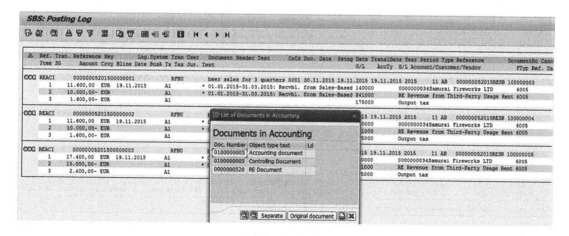

Figure 7-48. *Display RE Document (0000000520)*

17. Clicking on document number 10000005 will provide a list of documents in accounting (Figure 7-49).

Figure 7-49. *List of Documents in Accounting screen (10000005)*

18. Double-click "10000005: Accounting document" (Figure 7-50).

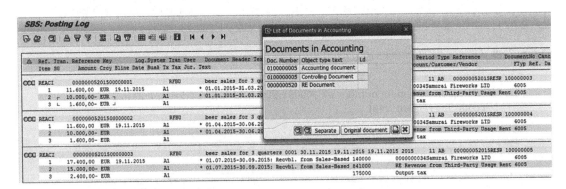

Display Document: Data Entry View

🔍 Taxes 🔁 Display Currency 🔲 General Ledger View

Data Entry View

Document Number	100000005	Company Code	0001	Fiscal Year	2015
Document Date	30.11.2015	Posting Date	19.11.2015	Period	11
Reference	000000052015RESR	Cross-Comp.No.		
Currency	EUR	Texts exist ☐	Ledger Group	

C..	Itm	PK	S	Account	Description	Amount	Curr.	Tx	Trs
00..	1	01		34	Samurai Fireworks LTD	17.400,00	EUR	A	
	2	50		841000	Rental rev. 3rd pty	15.000,00-	EUR	A	
	3	50		175000	Output tax	2.400,00-	EUR	A	M..

Figure 7-50. Document overview (10000005)

19. Clicking ⬅ will take you back to the list of documents in accounting (Figure 7-51). Double-click "10000005: Controlling document" (Figure 7-52).

SBS: Posting Log

Documents in Accounting

Doc. Number	Object type text	Ld
0100000005	Accounting document	
0100000005	Controlling Document	
0000000520	RE Document	

Separate | Original document

Figure 7-51. List of Documents in Accounting screen: Controlling Document (10000005)

Display Actual Cost Documents

Document | Master Record

Layout	1SAP	Primary cost posting
COarea currency	EUR	EUR
Valuation View/Group	0	Legal Valuation

DocumentNo Doc. Date Document Header Text	RI RefDocNo User Name Rev RvE
PRw QTy Object CO object name	Cost Elem. Cost element name Val/COArea Crcy Total quantity PUM C Offst.acct
100000005 30.11.2015 beer sales for 3 quarters	R 520

Figure 7-52. Display Actual Cost Documents screen (10000005)

20. Clicking 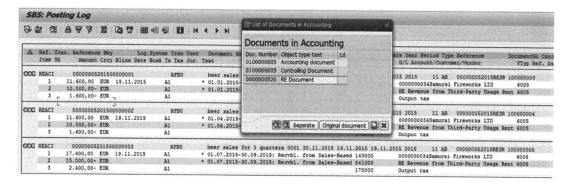 will take you back to the list of documents in accounting (Figure 7-53). Double-click "0000000520: RE document" (Figure 7-54).

Figure 7-53. List of Documents in Accounting screen: RE Document (0000000520)

Figure 7-54. Display RE Document screen (0000000520)

21. Click 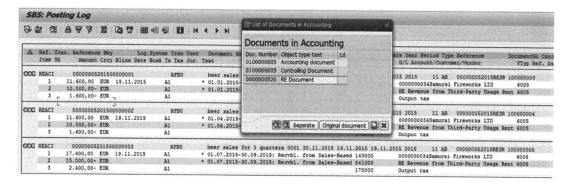 .

22. You have completed this transaction.

Result

You have calculated the amount receivable from the customer based on sales figures and posted it to accounting documents so as to post to the customer account. Also, you have processed one more document, transferring income from the RE contract to the rental object.

Customer Line Item Display

A customer line item display shows the amount that has been posted to the customer account (Figure 7-55).

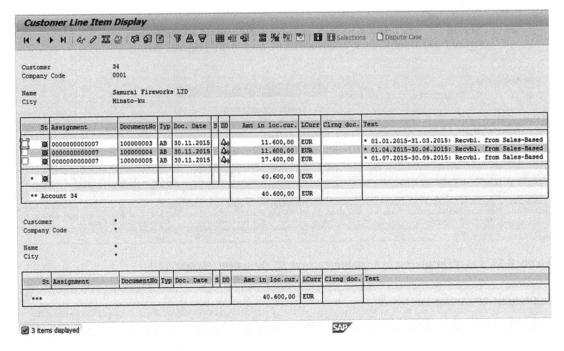

Figure 7-55. Customer line item display

Summary

In this chapter, we studied how sales-based rent contracts are created in the system and how we can use them for business requirements to calculate rent based on different parameters. We also saw how to settle these contracts by using the periodic posting functionality, where rent is calculated based on various criterions.

CHAPTER 8

■ ■ ■

Industry Best Practices

This chapter will explain industry best practices for implementation/rollout and maintenance of SAP REFX, the team composition and skillset required, and competency building. The chapter is divided into the following topics:

- Best practices for implementation/rollout
- Team composition and skill matrix required
- Competency building

Best Practices for Implementation/Rollout

In this chapter, we will discuss the best practices for implementation/rollout of SAP REFX, specifically in the following aspects:

- Approaches for speedy and effective implementation of SAP REFX
- The value of organizational preparedness
- The need for strong executive sponsorship
- The importance of documented processes, business cases, and training
- Key success factors
- Living with SAP REFX

Organizations planning on replacing legacy systems that are unable to keep up with increasing business require a state-of-the-art integrated solution, such as SAP REFX. Organizations are always looking to find answers to a variety of questions relating to the solution, such as its necessity, its functionalities, and, more important, how it can meet the firm's needs. Best practices and effective approaches for speedy and effective implementation are other considerations.

SAP REFX implementation is a key transformation initiative, and successful implementation is the responsibility of all who are part of organization. Companies must ask themselves the following questions:

- What are key success factors for the success of the initiative?
- Do we have strong executive sponsorship, ideally from the business organization, to ensure strong business team support?
- Do we have a sufficient budget sanctioned for such an initiative?

© Jayant Daithankar 2016
J. Daithankar, *SAP Flexible Real Estate Management*, DOI 10.1007/978-1-4842-1482-4_8

- Are all critical business requirements in functional areas met for this implementation?

- Have we identified key resources from business and other functions that will form the core group and ensured their availability for the implementation initiative?

- Are we prepared for managing the training needs of the organization?

Based on responses to the preceding questions, one can judge if more work needs to be done to prepare the organization for change or if it is ready to start the transformation journey. A roadmap of the organization post–REFX implementation needs to be thought out and visualized before the initiation of the preparatory phase. To begin, all persons on the implementation team have to be aware of the broader vision of the organization, its goals, and how the SAP REFX initiative will help in achieving that vision. What are the organization's goals and the vision it carries, and how can the SAP REFX implementation enable it to achieve these goals?

Since you are thinking of replacing the legacy system of your organization, you need an integrated system that will be scalable and functionally rich to support your vision of the organization. A solution should be capable of improving productivity, customer centricity, and the effectiveness of communication within the organization's ecosystem.

When is the right time to start implementation? The answer is certainly not *immediately*, but rather only after considering some key aspects.

Executive Commitment

Executive commitment is crucial to ensuring a successful, on-schedule implementation that is within the sanctioned budget, and hence it is important to know the project sponsor's place in the organization and how much influence he or she has within the organization. Many project sponsors do not focus on the project and are busy in regular business activities, considering implementation as a side activity. However, regular contact with the executive sponsor is a must; the sponsor should be involved from the kickoff to the end. The best project sponsors take a keen interest and spend the requisite time on the project. Obtaining a full commitment from all stakeholders is essential and needs to be ensured before the start of the project. Typically, executives will say that they support such transformation initiatives, but when it comes to releasing funds and key resources for the project, they may not support the project team completely. It is a good practice to conduct review meetings to discuss progress and pending tasks so as to reiterate the commitment made at the start of the project. The project sponsor should begin the kickoff meeting by clearly communicating the vision of the organization and business case for the initiative to make sure everyone is aware of their responsibilities and the deliverables expected from them.

Build a Business Case for Positive Return on Investment

The rationale behind building a business case is to justify the investment requested for the project. Also, it helps in onboarding correctly skilled resources from business functions on a dedicated basis. Business needs may entail achieving cost reduction, greater customer service, improving system performance, or reducing processing time. We have to ensure that we have a sound business case that details the background of the project, benefits envisaged, and how it is going to contribute to the overall vision of the organization. A business case is a presentation of data with views from relevant stakeholders. A new SAP REFX system provides your organization with fresh opportunities to use and refine new business processes, and a business case–building exercise is the first activity in this journey. A business case should talk of business drivers, pain areas, improvement expected by suggested solution, competition, and change-management requirements, if any, due to the impact of new initiatives. The team can help educate the organization's business team on technologies that can help them to achieve business objectives in an easy way. Return on investment needs to be presented, and senior management's concerns need to be addressed. As the owner of the business case and guardian of the investors' interests, the project sponsor must be the one to secure buy-in from every stakeholder.

Build a Case

The project sponsor should share his or her vision and communicate to the larger part of the organization as to what the team is planning to do, how you are going to do this, what help you need, and how it will bring about change for the better. The project sponsor should reach out to the maximum number of people by organizing meetings, conducting workshops where key team members will speak to clarify any doubts, sharing his or her own thoughts about the initiative, and improving overall understanding. This will help to reduce any resistance employees have and address any concerns that might prevent them from participating wholeheartedly.

Core Group Formation

You need to onboard the best talent from various organizational units to create a core group that will be responsible for ensuring successful implementation/rollout. The core group has to drive the transformation initiative by using their experience in the organization; the group has to be formed with the right mix of talent to ensure continued success throughout the journey and thereafter. The core group should consist of the right mix of senior and junior members—senior and experienced individuals who have deep business knowledge and younger people to provide energy and optimism; seniors may offer insights gained from experience. We may create the following four groups in the core team:

- Steering committee (two to three members): To facilitate, monitor, and guide the rest of the teams

- Change control board (three to four members): To review and approve changes to the scope

- Selection committee (four to five members): To select the appropriate solution

- Project teams and leadership: Choose a program manager and project leaders for every project team.

Ensure Resource Commitment

SAP implementation is perceived as a corporate initiative launched from the head office, and employees in the other offices tend to believe that it is the core team's responsibility to implement the change. No initiative will be successful unless end organizations are aligned to initiatives and onboarded correctly. Besides corporate, we need commitment and involvement from branches, factories, and other units, and to get this commitment, we need to conduct regional-level workshops to which we should invite participation from the all locations and support functions.

Manage Change

New initiatives like implementation will bring about a change in the system, processes, or way in which the organization is operating. New business models will require a change in the way business operations are managed. People who are used to a specific way of working may need to understand and adopt new ways aligned to the initiative. This is possible only if it is communicated clearly to employees and all stakeholders who are impacted. We need to make sure that every employee, irrespective of designation, role, location, seniority, and skill set, is made aware of the changes. People must gain an understanding of why the change in strategy or in culture is needed and how it will affect them, covering in particular modifications in their roles, responsibilities, location, and teams. People generally resist change in the beginning. This is when the respective managers must act and connect with them and communicate the benefits of such a change in technology and process, and explain the need for it.

Manage Own Expectations

Business requirements are changing, as are statutory and compliance requirements. You have been making changes to cope with these changes. All this is either captured in one of the systems or is part of the manual work being carried out by your teams. You should not expect everything to undergo change in one attempt, certainly not at the size of transformation we are discussing. There may not be any single solution that meets all business-specific requirements, and customization (major or minor) may be required. You need to set expectations internally as to what the new system can support, what workaround is required, and what process changes may be necessary. Acceptance from users will likely be greater if they are aware of what to expect from the transformation and what not to expect.

Identify Potential Risk

Every project is exposed to risks; you cannot have a project without risk. If we do not mitigate even a small risk, it can become a major hurdle to optimally delivering the project. Therefore, the identification of risk at an early stage is essential. Thorough analysis of risks and initiating appropriate preventive measures is a must to avoid risks. Deviations, short supply, idle time, inadequate communication, lack of preparedness, and overruns are some of the risks you should be able to identify easily.

Have Clear Interface Requirements

Identify every single interface requirement of these processes with respect to give and take of data, frequency, use, size, volume, and current mechanism. This will help you in building a conference room pilot or testing rollouts. Real challenges are mentioned here:

- The system landscape is not the same at every location.
- The processes are different.
- The level of automation is different.
- Regulatory requirements differ from place to place.
- Many processes are not documented, or are incomplete.
- No central team has been appointed to control the version or approve changes.

Use Reports, Key Performance Indicators, and Dashboards

You need to keep an inventory of reports on your organization's processes as well as the distribution list agreed upon. You may need different kinds of reports based on your organization's requirements. You will also want to identify key performance indicators by process, creating a matrix of tasks or activities by role for the dashboard. The REFX system's strong reporting provides most of the reporting needs to fulfill real estate's requirements. Moreover, you may use this opportunity to look into these reports to see if any can be consolidated or eliminated altogether.

Clean the Master Data

Most of the organizations today are struggling to keep track of master data and avoid duplication of it. A lot of investment is made in ensuring master data is correctly maintained so as to get a single version of truth. A disciplined approach is required to ensure the correctness of this data. It is the responsibility of the organization to ensure the quality of master data on land, building, rental objects, and other real estate objects is maintained. A centralized team managing the maintenance and creation of master data is recommended. It should not be left to many agencies to maintain and create master data in order to avoid duplication. It is suggested that you clean master data and synchronize them with the REFX application before we start implementation.

Role-Based Access Control

Granting access to a user for the SAP REFX system will depend on his assigned role and responsibilities. The right to create real estate master data may reside with a central team. Some users may get access to read transactions but not to modify them. It is required to do a complete analysis and create a matrix to identify roles based on the responsibilities of each employee. The segregation of duties needs to be ensured, and you may observe conflicts during the data-collection process. You need to document all such findings and address these conflicts during role creation.

Validate the Solution Against Architecture Guiding Principles

Every organization has certain guiding principles, and any new solution must be reviewed and validated against them. Deviations must be identified and their impact reviewed and agreed on. This needs to be discussed with a solution architect. Bring to his or her notice any deviation and find a workaround before moving forward with the new solution. Every location may have different processes and a different understanding of the solution, but your organization likely needs to work on the following:

- Have a globally standardized process, with localization (permissible only in the case of statutory or compliance requirements) in documented form and controlled at a central location by team

- Ensure updating and modifications to its processes to accommodate what it desires to achieve

- Create an internal knowledge portal where these processes are captured and anybody can refer to them

Team Composition and Skill Matrix Required

Successful project delivery largely depends on having a competent team; getting the right set of experienced people is a major challenge. Project sponsors struggle to get SAP REFX–specific functional and technical consultants to work on the project, but existing and past implementations bring an experienced pool of resources into the market. Ideally, the team should be composed of a reasonable number of domain consultants with a comprehensive knowledge and understanding of real estate processes who are able to validate business requirements and identify deviations from the standard offering of the product. In other words, consultants who are capable of ensuring error-free delivery. Your organization should select the right service providers to ensure experienced resources for the various roles required.

Process harmonization is the first step in getting ready for such a major transformation initiative. Harmonized and standardized processes should also consider local needs in the area of taxation and country/product-specific documentation. This helps in having complete and comprehensive blueprinting for SAP REFX. These documented processes help as a reference guide for every individual in the organization. Based on the preceding factors and the importance of such a program, we recommend the following roles at the corporate and program level.

Steering Committee

The steering committee needs to be formed by the project sponsor once management approves the business case. The steering committee should consist of identified leaders from various departments, such as production, finance, procurement, sales, services, risk and compliance, quality control, business development, planning, and technology. The chief information officer (CIO) generally heads the committee and reports to the project sponsor on a regular basis. The function of the committee is to steer the program, guide the team, resolve conflicts, and decide on critical issues to help with the smooth running of the program. The committee is responsible for vendor selection and contracting with them, and monitoring the progress of the program. The committee is required to evaluate if expenditures are within budget and objectives planned initially are achieved. It is suggested that the committee meets once a month and reviews progress.

Enterprise Architect

An enterprise architect plays an important role in a transformation program like SAP REFX and needs to be supported by functional and technical architects. Business architects will work on changes and impact on business due to the new system, suggest areas of improvement, and ensure harmonization of processes. Technical architects will ensure that design principles are followed and architecture guidelines are adhered to. They understand both the existing technology landscape and the proposed system and vision provided in the business case. Both business and technical architects work under the leadership of the enterprise architect to ensure smooth implementation of the SAP REFX program. It is also advisable that a detailed review of the architecture framework by industry experts be undertaken, as new technology platforms, offerings, and models are evolving rapidly.

Program Manager

The program manager is a single point of contact (SPOC) for the program. He or she is a person who is recommended to have experience in managing large programs, preferably in the area of real estate. Experience in delivering large SAP programs is a plus.

The project sponsor should appoint the program manager at the time when the steering committee is being formed. The program manager creates scope documents for appointing vendors, identifies the risks associated with the program, and provides a mitigation plan. He or she is also involved in creating change-management and critical-resource plans; capturing dependencies; and devising a program organization structure, measurement criteria, an induction plan, and a reporting mechanism.

Whether it be a pilot, a partial implementation, or an organizational-level implementation, these roles are necessary at the corporate level to achieve success with your program.

Domain Consultant (SME)

Domain consultant is a key role for the success of an SAP REFX implementation. A consultant who has worked in a real estate organization can appreciate the challenges and difficulties faced by different roles within a company. He or she is therefore properly equipped to capture requirements correctly and helps in providing the right solution. A domain consultant with experience in implementing SAP REFX is preferable; however, a consultant with experience implementing SAP FICO can also meet project needs with some grooming and training. It is a challenge to get a consultant who has a thorough understanding of both domain and technology; i.e., SAP REFX. Therefore, based on implementation strategy, we need to select domain consultants either by line of business or by business processes. Domain consultants can conduct workshops and will be able to connect with business users easily, as they will talk in the same language as business understands. He or she can capture information like various roles played by consultant, data requirements, pain areas, compliance needs, localization requirements, if any, and volume of transactions.

SAP REFX Functional Consultant

An SAP REFX functional consultant should have good SAP FI knowledge and should be a hands-on person. He or she should know AR, AP, GL, and Asset accounting thoroughly. How vendor and customer accounting is handled, how transactions are posted in FI system, how revenue and cost are recorded, and so on should be clear to him or her. Domain knowledge is also desirable, but at least core SAP FI and basic controlling knowledge is required. The main responsibility of an SAP REFX functional consultant is to work with the domain consultant, map business requirements in SAP REFX, and configure systems that meet business requirements.

SAP REFX Technical Consultant

The SAP REFX technical consultant must have strong knowledge of advanced business application programming (ABAP) and hands-on experience with the SAP REFX ecosystem.

SAP Process Integration (PI) Consultant

An SAP PI has to connect SAP REFX with non-SAP systems, whether ERP or not, and third-party products if used in organization by vendors, customers, and other agencies. The SAP PI consultant builds these interfaces to ensure seamless integration of data flow between both systems. SAP REFX also requires interfacing with GIS, business intelligence (BI), and other systems. A, SAP PI consultant with hands-on experience should be brought on board.

SAP Finance and Controlling (FICO) Consultant

SAP REFX is part of SAP FI, and you may need an SAP FICO consultant to do basic FICO settings. The SAP FICO consultant is needed to configure financial settings in SAP REFX. If SAP FICO is already implemented, you may have the configuration ready in the system. REFX is integrated with Finance and Controlling for managing customer receipts and vendor payments through accounts receivable (AR), accounts payable (AP), general ledger (GL), cost center, and profit center.

Quality Assurance Consultant

The quality assurance consultant is somebody who knows business better than any external agency does. We should onboard the position from internal senior and experienced team members. In case your organization outsources testing activity and appoints an external vendor to run your test factory, he or she should be one experienced with both the testing and the domain. Testing and quality control are important, because REFX interfaces with most of your landscape as well as outside it. Ensure that batch processes are running as expected and all the interfaces, functionalities, and custom-built functionalities are working. It is recommended you collocate your entire program team for better coordination.

Rollout Team

Rollout partners are best enlisted toward the last phase of implementation of the global template. They should shadow the implementation team during the warranty stage at the first site. You need all the skills of the implementation team to carry out the rollouts, but not in the same numbers. We need to choose consultants from the existing team who will continue in rollouts. Retain consultants with multiple skill sets. Also, the competency level required for implementation is higher than that needed for rollout. Rollout consultants should have knowledge of the implementing country or site-specific localization. Different countries have different legal and statutory requirements; these must be addressed while rolling out the standard template. Forms and documents may also be required in the local language(s) and format. The implementation team conducts workshops to share solution details, architecture aspects, environment, configuration, user setup, and documentation with rollout leadership.

The corporate team continues throughout the rollouts. It is good practice to retain a few key resources from the implementation team for the initial rollouts. These resources can act as mentors to the rollout teams. The steering committee appoints one or more rollout partners and release-management partners, depending on the number of sites and time allotted.

SAP REFX Team Ramp-Up and Competency-Building Plan

SAP REFX implementation is a key initiative for organizations and requires a number of experienced and trained SAP REFX resources to manage implementation and multiple rollouts and provide support. We need to build competency by choosing good SAP Finance consultants and training them on the REFX module. This should cover all end-to-end processes that the team may need to configure in sand box and carry all posting, settlement runs, and other routine postings through to REFX.

Summary

We explained best practices for SAP REFX implementation and rollouts, team composition and skill matrix required, and competency building plan.

■ ■ ■

CHAPTER 9

Transformation Impact of SAP REFX Implementation

This chapter will explain transformation impact on a business post–REFX implementation and the impact of new-dimension products like S4 HANA, big data, Mobility, analytics, and social media on SAP REFX. The chapter is divided into the following topics:

- Business transformation

- New-dimension products

- Business case justification for investment

Business Transformation

What is business transformation? It is a major organizational change to plan and aligns the People, Process, and Technology initiatives of a company with its business strategy and vision. It is a strategic and holistic transformation process across the business aiming toward achieving the corporate vision. A key enabler for business transformation is technology. Big data, the Cloud, Internet Of things, social media emergence, and mobility have changed the rules of the game and the competitive scenario by evolving new business models and value chains. The transformation of the IT landscape to make it adaptive to new business models is a key focus going forward. Typical transformation projects include mergers and acquisitions, outsourcing and offshoring, restructuring, value-chain optimization, and information systems redesign. These involve external consulting firms to carry out a major transformation within the organization. IT transformation is no longer a separate initiative, but rather is a major component of any overall business transformation. Innovation is one of the key drivers of transformation. Managing global real estate assets is a challenge due to ever-changing rules and regulations from country to country as well as rising customer expectations, both of which are forcing real estate players to innovate. In the development of trade and commerce, efficient management of real estate assets is essential to staying competitive in the market, and any failure on this point can result in loss. Hence, players managing real estate are under constant pressure to ensure cost-effective operations with reduced complexity. They need to improve efficiency via better forecasting and gaining more insight into market trends.

Generally, real estate players are expected to do the following:

- Enhance usage of the real estate portfolio through efficient space utilization strategies, locating vacant and unutilized space in the portfolio that can be either leased or sold and having an accurate and prompt reporting system that reflects vacant and unoccupied space in order to manage it effectively

- Optimize space utilization of the leased and owned real estate portfolio

© Jayant Daithankar 2016
J. Daithankar, *SAP Flexible Real Estate Management*, DOI 10.1007/978-1-4842-1482-4_9

- Keep close control over lease agreements and expirations, reduce operating costs, have strategies for reducing utility expenses

- Prepare a short-term and a long-term plan for effective management and utilization of real estate and facilities inventory

- Taxes and other statutory payments are accurately worked out for space and amenities owned/occupied and no excess payment is made

- Generate accurate operational reports to help prompt decision making

In order to meet the preceding expectations, real estate players are looking out for integrated solutions that meet organizations' transformational aspirations and investing in software solutions that support standard processes, provide best practices for the industry, and reduce customization so as to deliver maximum return on investment.

We strongly suggest you select a solution and invest in it if it provides the following benefits:

- Real-time availability of data for meaningful analysis and quick corrective action is expected from a new solution. For example, the availability of real-time information of real estate assets like land, building, plant, and other assets will help in ensuring predictive maintenance and replacement readiness.

- The ability to analyze large volumes of data to generate meaningful insights; for instance, real estate master data analytics to determine utilization of assets, vacant objects, lease administration, forecasting of valuations, and minimizing overhead costs.

- Integrated solutions providing a single view of data throughout the organization, ensuring a single source of truth and effective control. Real estate master data like property, building, and rental spaces should be providing the same view to all stakeholders.

- Ability to quickly respond to customers by capturing, interpreting, and analyzing feedback on social media sites.

In nutshell, you need integrated solutions that provide real-time information about the status of assets, enabling analytical support to interpret structured and unstructured data. Hence, we suggest the SAP REFX solution, which is strong enough to address these requirements. We also believe that the implementation of SAP REFX can help you obtain early return on investment.

New-Dimension Products

Let us see in detail the transformation impact of new-dimension products such as big data, HANA, mobility, Cloud, and social media in detail.

Big Data

Big data is a large volume of structured and unstructured data and can be analyzed to improve decision making and strategic business moves. The amount of data that's generated and stored is growing at an alarming pace, but we are able to capture and analyze only a small percentage of data that can help decision making. It is a big challenge for any organization to capture information that flows into it and interpret it to improve efficiency. Customer relationship building is critical to the real estate industry—and that can be achieved by managing big data in an effective manner.

Today's organizations are challenged by increasing costs—construction, infrastructure, and facility overhead are substantial expense categories for many organizations. Real estate players try to reduce the total cost of occupancy through strategies and finding new ways to leverage that information to enhance consumer satisfaction. In-memory databases like SAP HANA allow you to extract an enormous volume of structured and unstructured data from a single place and analyze it in an efficient manner. Advanced analytics enable you to quickly analyze that data to provide better insights and predict future trends. Cloud platforms can make the resulting insights available to the right people at the right time and at an affordable cost. Investments in the retail sector are generally based on the area where the property is situated, but based on behavior trends of actual consumers, you can make smarter decisions about where to acquire or develop a property and start a venture, and if property is owned or leased, what kinds of rents are appropriate, and more. All the new data we are acquiring can help to attract more and more customers in innovative ways. Both the retailer and mall owner will benefit, as retailers will be able to maximize revenues and mall owners will be able to increase rental income and have better retention of tenants.

Organizations with extensive lease portfolios are faced with the huge task of tracking numerous leases with varying expiration dates and different terms of tenancy. The chance for errors is high if we use manual systems to keep track of these requirements. Customer complaints, inaccurate information, missed renewal dates, monetary penalties, and so on are possible in a manual system. Facility management is a major cost factor for businesses since buildings, especially large office blocks, consume enormous amounts of electricity, water, and gas and need regular maintenance. Better insights into the data and the factors influencing a building's performance can help significantly reduce resource consumption and improve environmental performance.

SAP HANA Solutions

SAP HANA is an in-memory platform for processing a large amount of data in real time. It is at the center of SAP's technology strategy, with new innovations like S4 HANA, which is based on the HANA database. SAP HANA enables businesses to access transactional data in real time and to analyze large volumes of data quickly. A few SAP HANA–based solutions are available for the real estate industry. SAP HANA's adoption is growing in the real estate segment as more and more organizations are planning to move to HANA to get the benefits of real-time information, faster processing, and the predictive capabilities of the solution to stay competitive in the business.

Mobility

The real estate industry is highly human dependent, and organizations are challenged to meet the multiple and ever-growing requirements of various stakeholders. Real estate managers who are required to lease properties need to deal with various stakeholders like vendors, tenants, buyers, and banks. Real estate agents who are buying and selling properties for their customers need to have a solution that can be accessed on the fly and is device supported. Gone are the days where agents used to capture information on personal computers and need to go to the office to access it. If an agent is showing any property to a customer, he needs to have real-time information about the property to conclude the deal successfully. Integration with enterprise CRM systems provides quick and easy access to the information required for capturing and tracking lead status. As real estate is a people-centered business, real estate professionals must keep up with the demands of their consumers. Mobile technologies integrated with SAP can address most of these challenges. Mobile devices in the field can capture real estate data and share them with a central server on which an SAP REFX platform is installed. The information can thus be made available ahead of time for planning. Information on the vacancy of objects, lease term expiration, rent outstanding, utility payment due dates and other relevant data can be easily populated in the system and used internally or sent to customers and vendors. Thus, you can enhance productivity and customer service at a reduced operational cost. Mobile technologies that can be deployed are the Global Positioning System (GPS) for tracking assets and location-based services; radio frequency identification (RFID) for locating real estate assets; RFID readers and scanners for faster scans; and mobile phones with business applications for inquiries, updates, and two-way communication.

Consumers want instant information, but fulfilling that expectation of an immediate response time is difficult for real estate companies who don't have mobile-enabled technology and won't be able to compete with other real estate companies who continue to make information available online in order to approach their consumers.

Mobile solutions that are integrated with Google Maps help agents and real estate managers provide complete information access. A 3D view of the property with improved images enables the viewing of property on tablet devices, and you need not physically visit the site to view the property.

Social Media Integration

Given the increased use of social networks worldwide, social media is opening up new business opportunities by creating two-way communication, enabling customer feedback and response in real time. It is important for the real estate industry to tap the potential of social media to drive efficiencies and connect with customers and business partners. Information and feedback on social media is vital information for sales and support functions. Analysis and interpretation of it is often a challenge, as information is not in a structured format. Social media allows the sharing of information relevant to the industry, such as updates on real estate prices, market trends, vacant space availability, and new compliance requirements relating to property, complaints, feedback, and views. Modern businesses are proactively handling customer issues and complaints through Facebook and Twitter. Many real estate players are posting property details on Twitter to help find customers, and visual presentations are shared on social media to attract them. Recorded videos and demonstrations showing unique differentiators of services can have a positive impact on customers. Social media is complementary to the real estate business. Integration with social media is important for making full use of SAP. Leading real estate players have portals that provide data access to all partners and customers. SAP can share its data, such as the availability of real estate properties, buildings, or assets, on social networks. A real estate company using social media to offer real estate assets to customers along with SAP can have much wider options for penetrating the market.

Analytics

Analytics has been used as a tool for reporting historical data to analyze so as to take corrective action for the future. However, with technology advancement, it has moved to being a real-time provider of data. The next step forward is to analyze trends based on data and predict for the future in order to take proactive steps. However, the major challenge is data residing in disparate systems. The availability of integrated data can lead to improved efficiency, reduced costs, and enhanced customer satisfaction. Organizations implementing SAP REFX have this data residing in a single system, saving the time required to obtain data and retaining the sanctity of the data.

In the Flexible Real Estate Management module, there are reports for the following objects, providing key performance indicators, and analytics can be based on these KPIs:

- Master data

- Real estate contract

- Measurements

- Conditions

- Business partners

- Service charge settlements

- Controlling

SAP REFX is a data-intensive solution that will generate a wealth of data. It is recommended you review its analytics requirements and build a strategy to archive non-critical data and move relevant data, which will enable the monitoring of key performance indicators and the creation of dashboards for decision makers at every level of the organization.

Internet of Things and Real Estate

The concept of the Internet of Things (IoT) presents unprecedented possibilities for the management and operation of real estate. Sensors, a tiny chip, can register changes in temperature, light, pressure, sound, and motion. These sensors have been used by city planners and transportation specialists to measure vehicular traffic, and data produced helps in determining the capacity for roads and other planning tasks. Sensor technology is being applied to commercial real estate and other types of businesses, and the benefits are considerable. In terms of property evaluation and market analysis, the information that's obtained from sensors can be tremendously valuable. We can put sensors on the equipment in a building, and every ten seconds we get a read on the air temperature, which is helpful in determining if the air conditioning system is working efficiently or needs maintenance, and we can generate a work order to fix it.

With the emergence of IoT, any part of a real estate object, like a building, can become a point to capture and send data for analysis and action. The speed of data transmission and processing time has increased tremendously. A scanner can provide basic temperature monitoring and support a building automation system that uses IoT, and we can look for an integrated solution that senses and adjusts heat and humidity based on the number of people that have entered the building. Advanced analytics combined with IOT can change the way real estate operators are managing their business.

Cloud Computing

More and more businesses are looking for cost-efficient operating solutions, which has led them to the adoption of the Cloud. Cloud for real estate will help you keep your agents one step ahead of the competition at all times. Your employees will be able to access listings, contracts, and business applications in the office or in the field, and it can keep your business up to date with the latest and best technology on the market, providing the most efficient collaboration and security for your agents and clients.

Commercial real estate businesses are typically operated in the traditional way with hundreds of spreadsheets and lot of paper work. The Cloud has made its way in the construction and commercial real estate business, changing the way we rent, buy, and sell. With the Cloud at its back end, technology is witnessing heights in the real estate sector, helping collect data and collaborating and sharing it on the move. Real estate agents and buyers can now carry on cleaner and faster transactions, which ultimately lead to time savings and valuable customers' satisfaction. A number of businesses in real estate are enjoying the advantages of cloud computing.

Organizations adopting the Cloud will be able to reduce their costs by accessing systems at an affordable rate. You can save space used for systems and infrastructure, and smooth and seamless remote access allows a greater number of employees to be in the field and operating efficiently. One can be relived from IT maintenance duties and focus on the core business once moved to the Cloud. The real estate business can extract relevant information and better target customers with ease and simplicity.

Now, think of the real estate professional at the airport showing some vacant duty-free shops to a potential customer, who requests the details of the operating expenses of the duty-free shops for previous years and operating expenses for all shops in the building. The real estate professional can get all this information on a mobile device by accessing the company's database on the Cloud. He or she need not go back to the office to get the required details.

Business Case Justification for Investment

A strong business case is a prerequisite for committing any information technology investment. A proper business case has to be prepared and put up for senior management's approval before the start of the project. This helps in sanctioning funds for the project and also acts as a yardstick to measure the progress of the project at each stage. The business case justifies the investment of time, money, and resources into a project by outlining the larger benefits that the organization will get by implementing said project. Including the necessity of the project, cost, timelines, various options available for addressing the painful area, and how the selected option is the best one to meet the overall objective will strengthen the business case. Every possible benefit, tangible and intangible, supported by estimated financial workings needs to be hashed out. Risks and costs associated with the project need to be clearly mentioned. A calculation of projected costs, with justifications for each line of expenditure, is required when requesting approval, and also projected timelines for each activity need to be provided.

Summary

Businesses can get really powerful when technology meets up with the right strategy. The commendable era we are in gives us a chance to build the future. The time has come for a change. Real estate is one major industry that is becoming complacent with time. Owing to the spectacular technology adoptions, consumer acceptance has grown and is rapidly leaving the conventional methods of trading far behind. Accessibility has increased. Information can now be reached from anywhere. Customers are enjoying a feeling of control and hence are more comfortable trading real estate. For quite a long time, this industry has struggled to keep up with the transforming innovations. Now, the time is ripe. Taking the right decisions in the right direction will change your business and turn it toward ultimate growth. The SAP REFX platform integrated with HANA, a mobility platform, a social media platform, and business intelligence (BI) can give you access to real-time information while providing you with analytical capabilities for structured and unstructured data. After evaluating the capabilities and features of SAP REFX, we strongly believe that it can help you obtain an early return on investment.

CHAPTER 10

Step-by-Step Guide for Configuring and Implementing SAP REFX

In this chapter we will provide a complete business scenario for REFX, with a step-by-step guide for configuring the system. We will also cover the master data creation process in detail. The objective is to enable the reader to configure REFX with the help of detailed screenshots and provided explanations.

Basic Settings in REFX

We need to carry out the following steps to configure the SAP REFX system.

Activate Real Estate Extension

To be able to use the functions of Flexible Real Estate Management in the SAP ECC Extension, the activation checkbox has to be checked (Figure 10-1).

Transaction Code

SPRO

Menu Path

IMG ➤ Flexible Real Estate Management (RE-FX) ➤ Basic Settings ➤ Activate Real Estate Extension

J. Daithankar, *SAP Flexible Real Estate Management*, DOI 10.1007/978-1-4842-1482-4_10

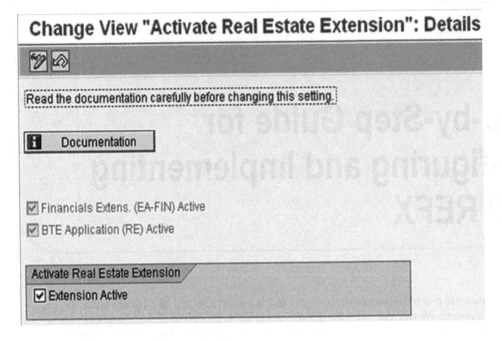

Figure 10-1. *Activate real estate extension*

Create Basic Settings in Company Code

Here, you create basic settings for company codes that are used in Flexible Real Estate Management (Figure 10-2).

We need to create settings for each company code in which we want to manage real estate objects (Figure 10-3). Financial Assets Management has to be active in each company code you use.

Transaction Code

SPRO

Menu Path

IMG ➤ Flexible Real Estate Management (RE-FX) ➤ Basic Settings ➤ Make Basic Settings in Company Code

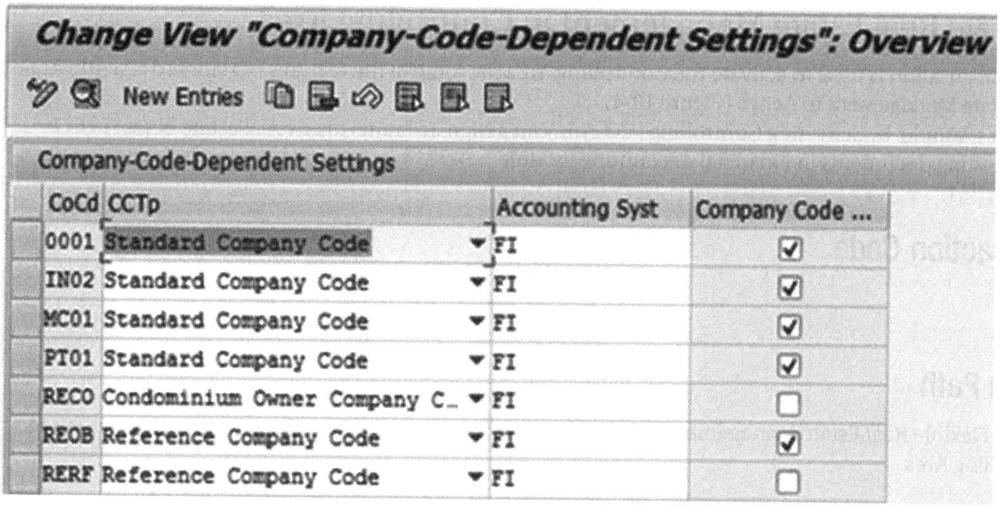

Figure 10-2. *"Company-Code-Dependent Settings": Overview*

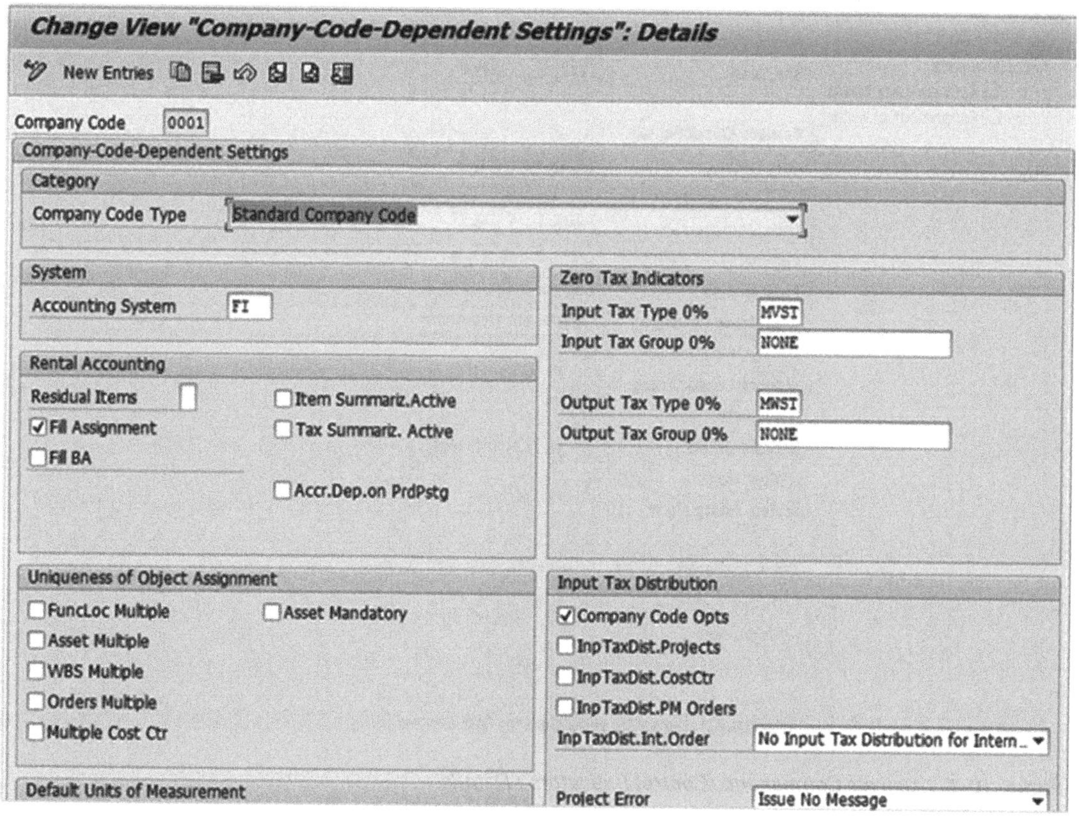

Figure 10-3. *"Company-Code-Dependent Settings": Details*

Activate Real Estate Management in Controlling Area

This configuration is used to activate the Controlling Area for some of the features of standard SAP REFX. Set Real Estate Management to Active (Figure 10-4).

For example, by activating Controlling (CO) you can assign accounts to any real estate object in CO when posting documents in Financial Accounting module.

Transaction Code

SPRO

Menu Path

IMG ➤ Flexible Real Estate Management (RE-FX) ➤ Basic Settings ➤ Activate Real Estate Management in Controlling Area

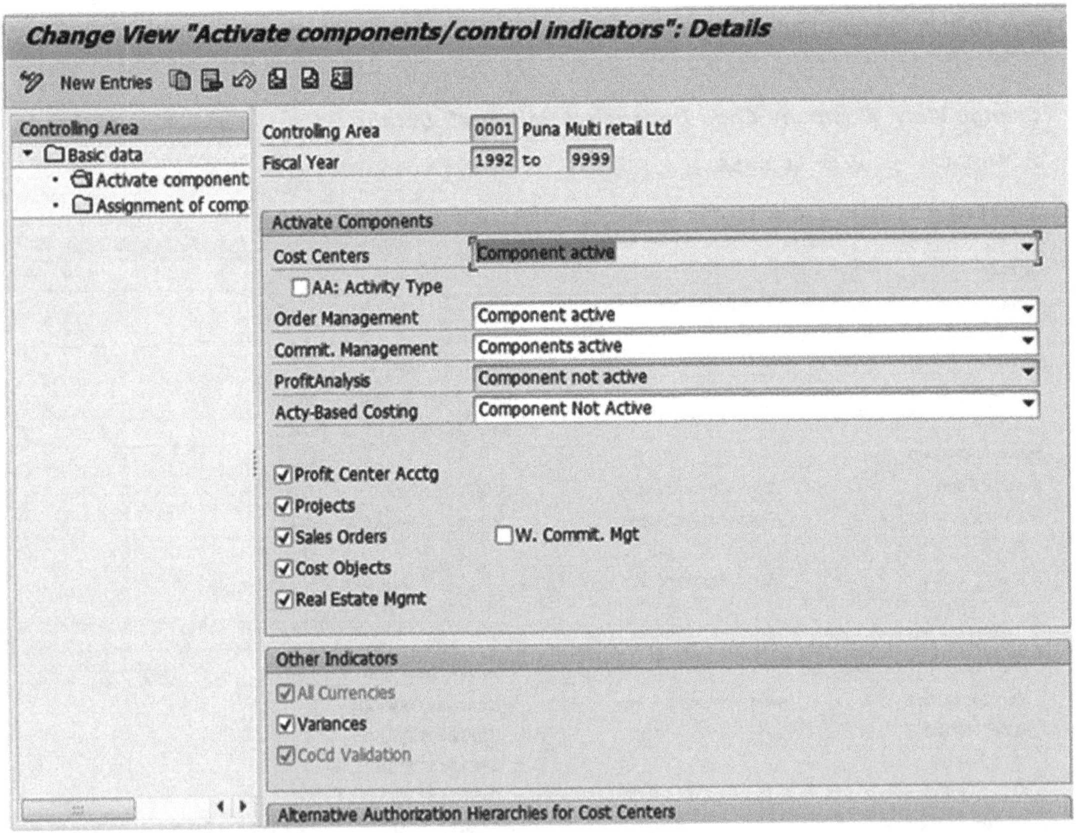

Figure 10-4. *"Activate Components/Control Indicators": Details*

Once the Controlling Area is activated, you can assign the company code to it (Figure 10-5).

Transaction Code

SPRO

Menu Path

IMG ➤ Flexible Real Estate Management (RE-FX) ➤ Basic Settings ➤ Assignment of Company Code in Controlling Area

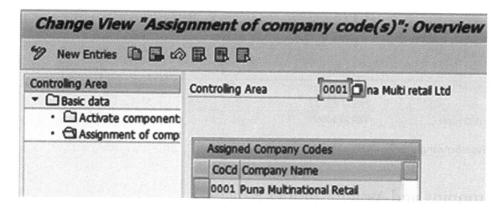

Figure 10-5. *Assignment of company code*

Business Partner Settings in REFX

Most real estate processes require the maintenance of data regarding business partners or contacts. Some require financial information, such as payable or receivable processing. SAP Real Estate utilizes the central SAP Business Partner (BP) to track information on individuals and entities for financial, contact, and other purposes. The BP is linked to the relevant RE data record via business partner roles. Business partner roles identify the relationship of the BP to the RE object and its processes. Based on the role, SAP may require critical vendor or customer information. Vendor and customer master data will be maintained within Finance, with the business partner records being automatically created through business partner synchronization. If a customer or vendor is created automatically while creating a business partner, then whenever we make any changes in BP, automatically changes get reflected in the customer/vendor via synchronization.

Maintain Number Ranges for Business Partner

In this activity, you will define number ranges for business partners (Figure 10-6). Business partners are synchronized with FI vendors based on Vendor group. It is possible that the same number range is assigned in both the vendor and business partner.

Transaction Code

SPRO

Menu Path

IMG ➤ Flexible Real Estate Management (RE-FX) ➤ Business Partner ➤ Relevant Settings for Business Partner in RE Context ➤ Number Range ➤ Business Partner Number Range

Display Number Range Intervals

NR Object	Business partner			

Intervals

No.	From number	To number	Current number	Ext
01	0000000001	0999999999	0	☐
AB	A	ZZZZZZZZZZ		☑
MD	9000000000	9999999999		☑

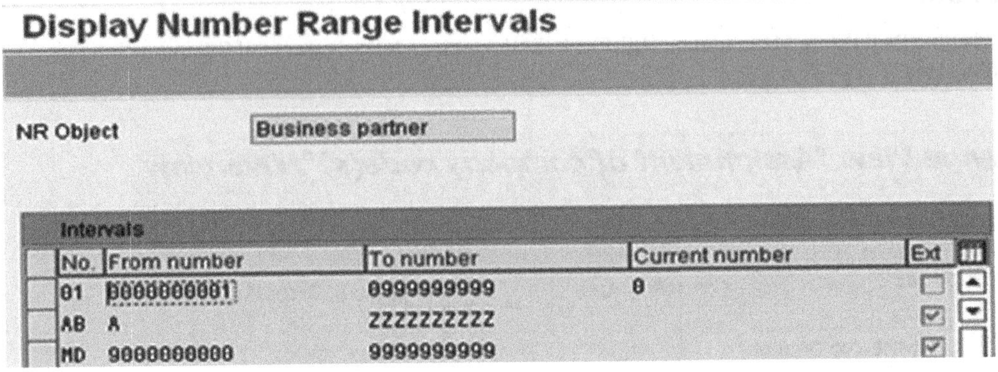

Figure 10-6. Number ranges for business partner

Define Grouping and Assign Number Ranges

In this activity, you will define groupings of business partners (Figure 10-7).

Transaction Code

SPRO

Menu Path

IMG ➤ Flexible Real Estate Management (RE-FX) ➤ Business Partner ➤ Relevant Settings for Business Partner in RE Context ➤ Number Range ➤ Business Partner Number Range

Change View "BP groupings": Overview

Grouping	Short name	Description	Number ra	External	Int.Std.Grping	Ext.Std.Grpi
0001	Int.No.Assgnmnt	Internal Number Assignment	01	☐	⦿	
0002	Ext.No.Assgnmnt	External Number Assignment	AB	☑		⦿
IMMO	Real Estate	Real Estate Partner (I)	01	☐	○	

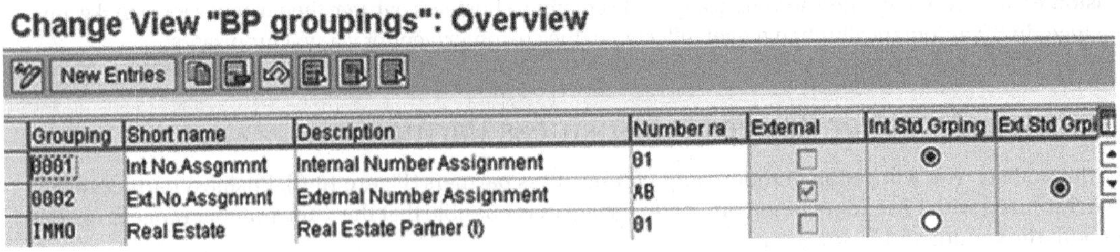

Figure 10-7. Grouping screen to assign number ranges

Define Business Partner Roles

In this IMG activity you will define the business partner roles and their attributes (Figure 10-8). You will also define the role categories with other relevant data (Figure 10-9).

Transaction Code

SPRO

Menu Path

IMG ➤ Flexible Real Estate Management (RE-FX) ➤ Business Partner ➤ Relevant Settings for Business Partner in RE Context ➤ Business Partner Roles ➤ Define Business Partner Roles

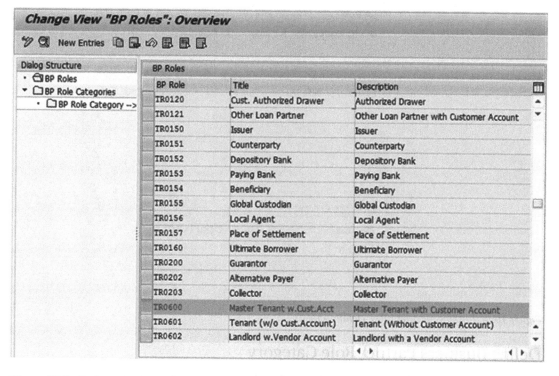

Figure 10-8. Business partner roles

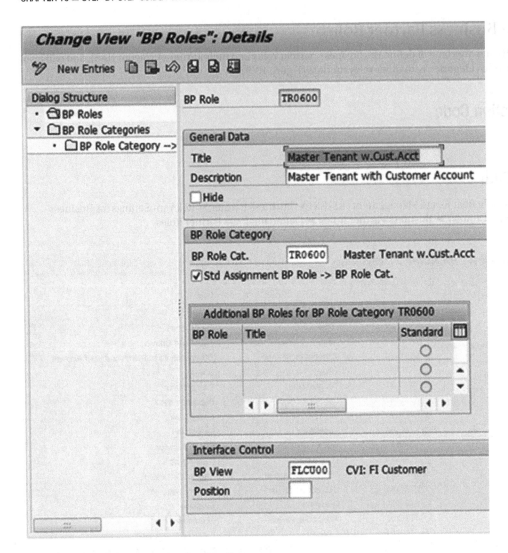

Figure 10-9. Business partner roles, Details screen

Define Business Partner Role Category

For each of the business partner roles that you defined in the previous step, you have to create role categories (Figure 10-10) and assign a business transaction to the role categories (Figure 10-11).

Transaction Code

SPRO

Menu Path

IMG ➤ Flexible Real Estate Management (RE-FX) ➤ Business Partner ➤ Relevant Settings for Business Partner in RE Context ➤ Business Partner Roles ➤ Define Business Partner Roles ➤ Define Business Partner Role Categories

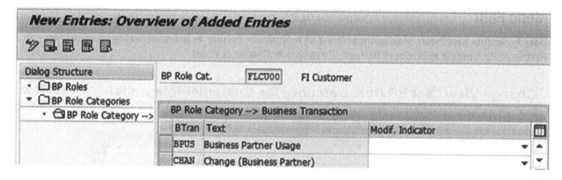

Change View "BP Role Categories": Overview

Role Cat.	Title	Description
BBP000	Vendor	Vendor
BBP001	Bidder	Bidder
BBP002	Portal Provider	Portal Provider
BBP003	Plant	Plant
BBP004	Purchasing Firm	Purchasing Firm
BBP005	Service Provider	Service Provider
BBP006	Invoicing Party	Invoicing Party
BKK010	Account Holder	Account Holder (FS: BCA)
BKK020	Authorized Drawer	Authorized Drawer (FS: BCA)
BKK030	Correspondence Recipient	Correspondence Recipient (FS: BCA)
BKK200	Acct Maintenance Officer	Account Maintenance Officer (FS: BCA)
BUP001	Contact Person	Contact Person
BUP002	Prospect	Prospect
BUP003	Employee	Employee
BUP004	Organizational Unit	Organizational Unit
BUP005	Internet User	Internet User
CACSA1	Commission Contract Part.	Commission Contract Partner
CACSA2	Commission Clerk	Commission Clerk
CACSA3	Agents	Agents
CBIH10	External Person	External Person
CBIH20	Authority	Authority
CMS001	Security Partner	Security Partner (FS: CMS)

Figure 10-10. Business partner role categories

Figure 10-11. Business partner role categories to business transaction

Maintain Number Assignment for Direction BP to Customer

In this activity, you will assign an account group from FI to each business partner grouping (Figure 10-12).

Transaction Code

SPRO

Menu Path

IMG ➤ Flexible Real Estate Management (RE-FX) ➤ Business Partner ➤ Relevant Settings for Business Partner in RE Context ➤ Business Partner - Customer ➤ Number Assignment: Assign Account Group to Customers

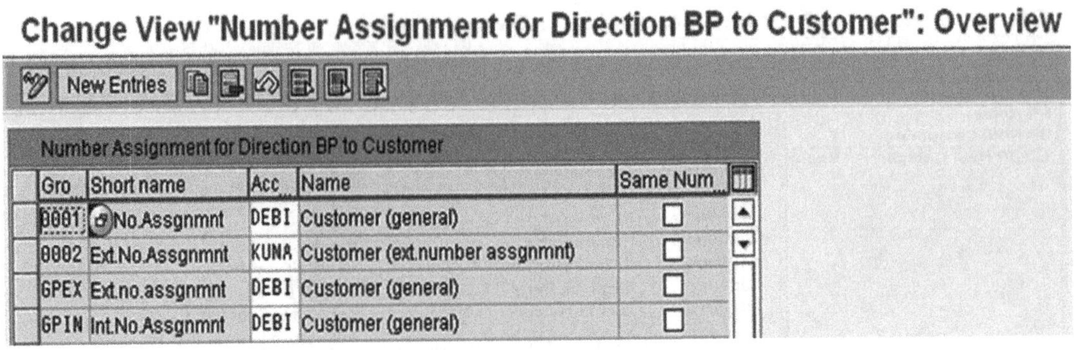

Figure 10-12. *Number Assignment for Direction BP to Customer screen*

Set BP Role Category for Customer Integration

In this activity, we will create settings for the role categories that need to have a customer account in Financial Accounting (for example, master tenant with customer account; Figure 10-13).

Transaction Code

SPRO

Menu Path

IMG ➤ Flexible Real Estate Management (RE-FX) ➤ Business Partner ➤ Relevant Settings for Business Partner in RE Context ➤ Business Partner - Customer ➤ Customer Roles

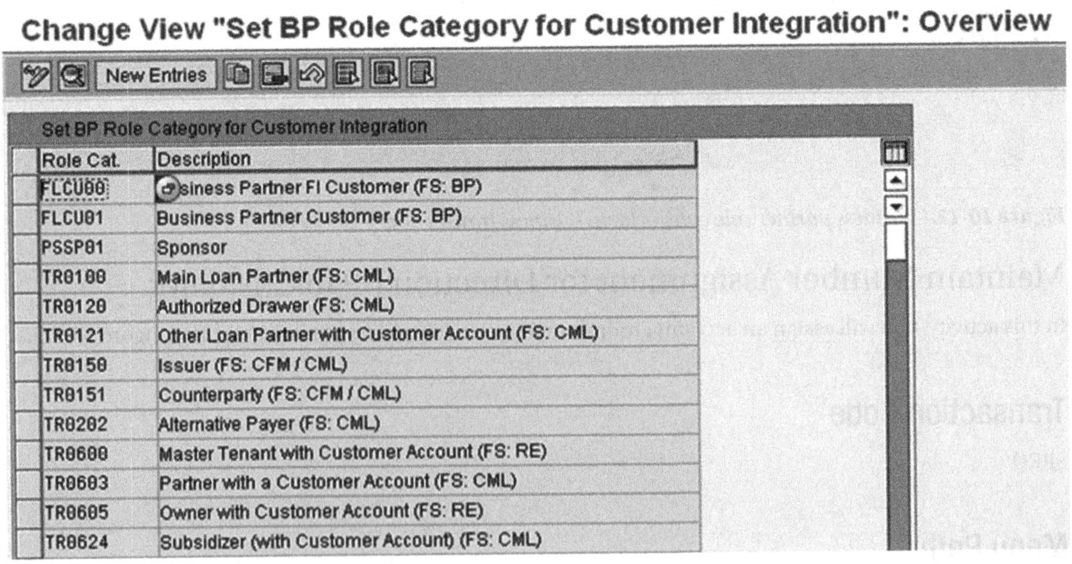

Figure 10-13. *Set BP Role Category for Customer Integration screen*

Define Standard Values for Automatic Creation of Customers (Company-Code Dependent)

In this section you will fill in pre-settings for creating company-code-dependent customer data (Figure 10-14). These pre-settings are used when you process a business partner in the customer role of the respective company code for the first time and access the processing screen in contract management (Figure 10-15).

Transaction Code

SPRO

Menu Path

IMG ➤ Flexible Real Estate Management (RE-FX) ➤ Business Partner ➤ Relevant Settings for Business Partner in RE Context ➤ Business Partner - Customer ➤ Standard Values for Automatic Creation of Customers (Company-Code Dependent)

Display View "Standard Values for Automatic Creation of Customers": Ov
PTyp
Text
Authorization group
Alternat.payer in B
IMV
Rental agreement (Real Estate)

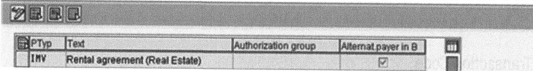

Figure 10-14. Standard Values for Automatic Creation of Customers screen

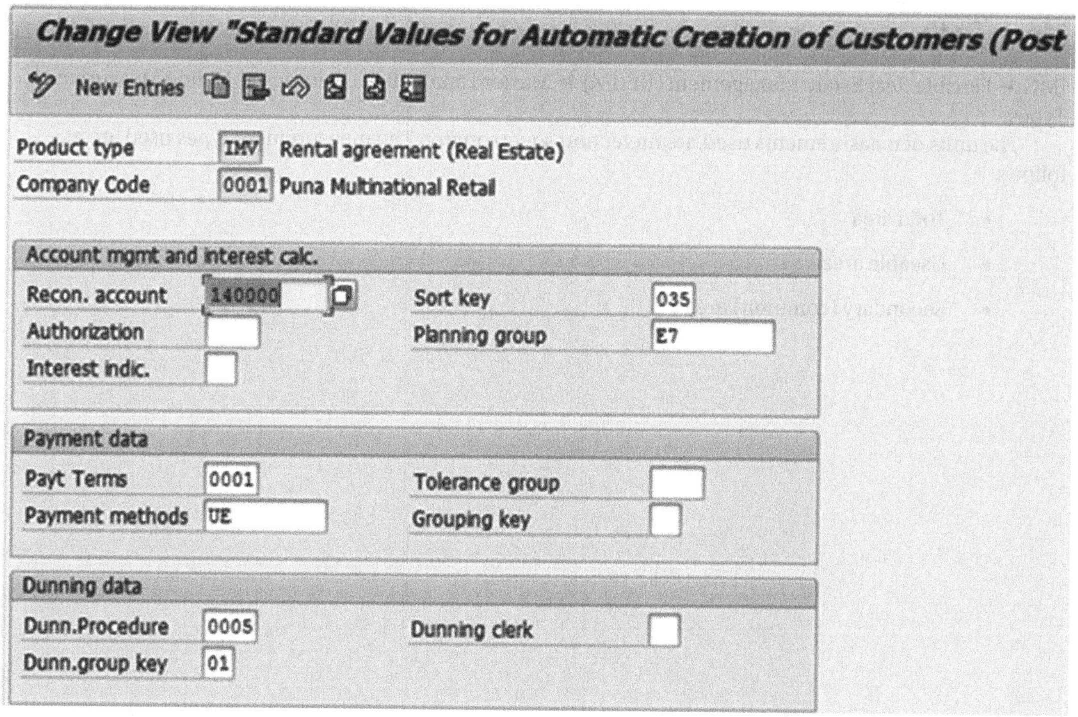

Change View "Standard Values for Automatic Creation of Customers (Post
New Entries
Product type
IMV
Rental agreement (Real Estate)
Company Code
0001
Puna Multinational Retail
Account mgmt and interest calc.
Recon. account
140000
Sort key
035
Authorization
Planning group
E7
Interest indic.
Payment data
Payt Terms
0001
Tolerance group
Payment methods
UE
Grouping key
Dunning data
Dunn.Procedure
0005
Dunning clerk
Dunn.group key
01

Figure 10-15. Standard values for automatic creation of customers, company-code dependent

Master Data in REFX

The following are the master data in the SAP REFX system.

Define Measurement Types

In this section, you will define measurement types for business entity, building, rental objects, and contracts (Figure 10-16). Measurements are used to record measurable traits of objects. The measurement type indicates the type of trait that is being measured. Area measurements are also recorded as measurements. Measurement types represent all quantifiable attributes, such as space (ft^2, m^2, acres, and hectares), dimensions (height, linear feet/length), volume (m^3 or ft^3), or number (desks, internet connections). Measurements can be used to calculate rent (both payable and receivable); to define available, rentable, and occupied space; to distribute costs (in service charge settlements or transferring contract costs to RE objects); and for cost or revenue-controlling analysis (so-called statistical key figures, such as cost per ft^2). Measurements will reflect what is currently available within the AutoCAD drawings. These measurements will be available on all master data levels when appropriate, and will be the basis for space management cost allocations. Due to the nature of customers' international presence, multiple measurement types will be created, reflecting the type utilized within that locality as well as a conversion to other standard measurements.

Measurements are also the basis for the calculation of condition amounts in lease rentals.

Transaction Code

SPRO

Menu Path

IMG ➤ Flexible Real Estate Management (RE-FX) ➤ Master Data ➤ Basic Settings ➤ Define Measurement Types

The units of measurements used are meter and square meter. The measurement types used are as follows:

- Total area

- Useable area

- Secondary (common) area

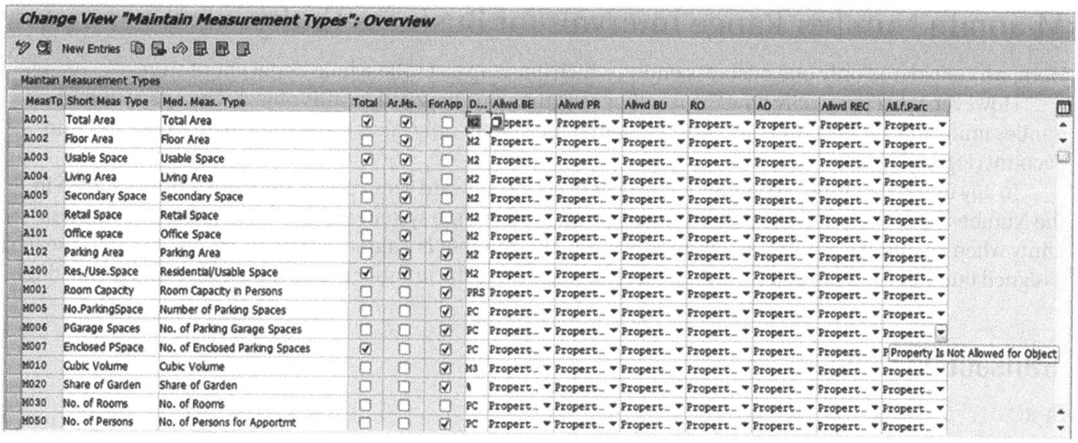

Change View "Maintain Measurement Types": Overview

New Entries

Maintain Measurement Types

MeasTp	Short Meas Type	Med. Meas. Type	Total	Ar.Ms.	ForApp	D...	Allwd BE	Allwd PR	Allwd BU	RO	AO	Allwd REC	All.f.Parc
A001	Total Area	Total Area	☑	☑	☐	M2	Propert..	Propert..	Propert..	Propert..	Propert..	Propert..	Propert..
A002	Floor Area	Floor Area	☐	☑	☐	M2	Propert..	Propert..	Propert..	Propert..	Propert..	Propert..	Propert..
A003	Usable Space	Usable Space	☑	☑	☐	M2	Propert..	Propert..	Propert..	Propert..	Propert..	Propert..	Propert..
A004	Living Area	Living Area	☐	☑	☐	M2	Propert..	Propert..	Propert..	Propert..	Propert..	Propert..	Propert..
A005	Secondary Space	Secondary Space	☐	☑	☐	M2	Propert..	Propert..	Propert..	Propert..	Propert..	Propert..	Propert..
A100	Retail Space	Retail Space	☐	☑	☐	M2	Propert..	Propert..	Propert..	Propert..	Propert..	Propert..	Propert..
A101	Office space	Office Space	☐	☑	☐	M2	Propert..	Propert..	Propert..	Propert..	Propert..	Propert..	Propert..
A102	Parking Area	Parking Area	☐	☑	☑	M2	Propert..	Propert..	Propert..	Propert..	Propert..	Propert..	Propert..
A200	Res./Use.Space	Residential/Usable Space	☑	☑	☑	M2	Propert..	Propert..	Propert..	Propert..	Propert..	Propert..	Propert..
M001	Room Capacity	Room Capacity in Persons	☐	☐	☑	PRS	Propert..	Propert..	Propert..	Propert..	Propert..	Propert..	Propert..
M005	No.ParkingSpace	Number of Parking Spaces	☐	☐	☑	PC	Propert..	Propert..	Propert..	Propert..	Propert..	Propert..	Propert..
M006	PGarage Spaces	No. of Parking Garage Spaces	☐	☐	☑	PC	Propert..	Propert..	Propert..	Propert..	Propert..	Propert..	Propert..
M007	Enclosed PSpace	No. of Enclosed Parking Spaces	☑	☐	☑	PC	Propert..	Propert..	Propert..	Propert..	Propert..	Propert..	Property Is Not Allowed for Object
M010	Cubic Volume	Cubic Volume	☐	☐	☑	M3	Propert..	Propert..	Propert..	Propert..	Propert..	Propert..	Propert..
M020	Share of Garden	Share of Garden	☐	☐	☑	%	Propert..	Propert..	Propert..	Propert..	Propert..	Propert..	Propert..
M030	No. of Rooms	No. of Rooms	☐	☐	☐	PC	Propert..	Propert..	Propert..	Propert..	Propert..	Propert..	Propert..
M050	No. of Persons	No. of Persons for Apportmt	☐	☐	☑	PC	Propert..	Propert..	Propert..	Propert..	Propert..	Propert..	Propert..

Figure 10-16. *Measurement types*

Define Tenancy Law

You will specify here which tenancy laws you want to use in the system (Figure 10-17). You can specify for the business entity in the contract which tenancy law covers the relevant object (in the case of the business entity, the dependent objects are also covered).

Transaction Code

SPRO

Menu Path

IMG ➤ Flexible Real Estate Management (RE-FX) ➤ Master Data ➤ Basic Settings ➤ Define Tenancy Law

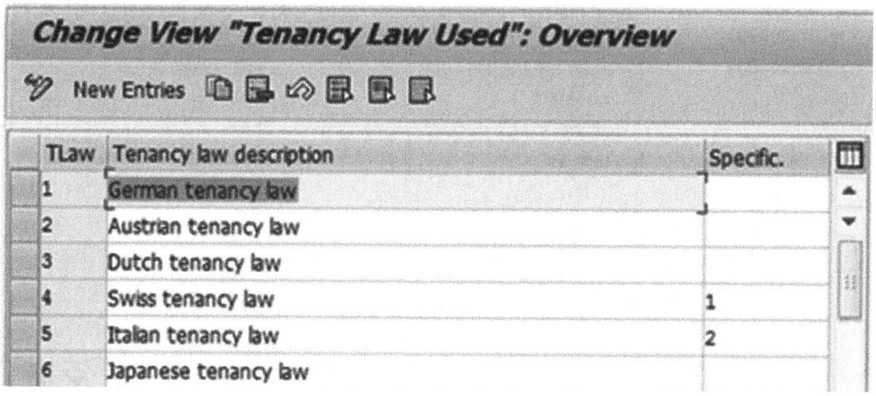

Change View "Tenancy Law Used": Overview

New Entries

TLaw	Tenancy law description	Specific.
1	German tenancy law	
2	Austrian tenancy law	
3	Dutch tenancy law	
4	Swiss tenancy law	1
5	Italian tenancy law	2
6	Japanese tenancy law	

Figure 10-17. *Tenancy law*

Maintain Number Range Intervals for Business Entity

Here, we considered only one business entity, which encompasses the whole department store.

However, you can specify how the number assignment is handled for this object. The specification applies uniformly for the company code. Note that the system only takes the setting for interval "01" into account (Figure 10-18).

In any internal number assignment, the system counts upward sequentially from the number shown in the Number field. For buildings, properties, and rental objects, the system assigns the number per business entity when an internal number assignment is used. This number is unique within the company code. The next assigned number for these objects is therefore not identical to the number that is shown here in Customizing.

Transaction Code

SPRO

Menu Path

IMG ➤ Flexible Real Estate Management (RE-FX) ➤ Master Data ➤ Usage View Business Entity ➤ Maintain Number Range Intervals for Business Entity

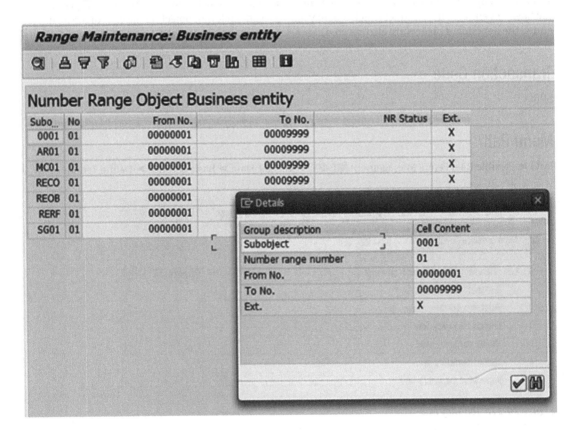

Figure 10-18. Number range intervals for business entity

Maintain Number Range Intervals for Buildings

Here, you can specify how number assignment is handled for this object. The specification applies uniformly for the company code. Note that the system only takes the setting for interval "01" into account (Figure 10-19).

For internal number assignments, the system counts upward sequentially from the number shown in the Number field. For buildings, properties, and rental objects, the system assigns the number per business entity when an internal number assignment is used. This number is unique within the business entity. The next assigned number for these objects is therefore not identical with the number shown here.

Transaction Code

SPRO

Menu Path

IMG ➤ Flexible Real Estate Management (RE-FX) ➤ Master Data ➤ Usage View ➤ Building ➤ Building Number Range

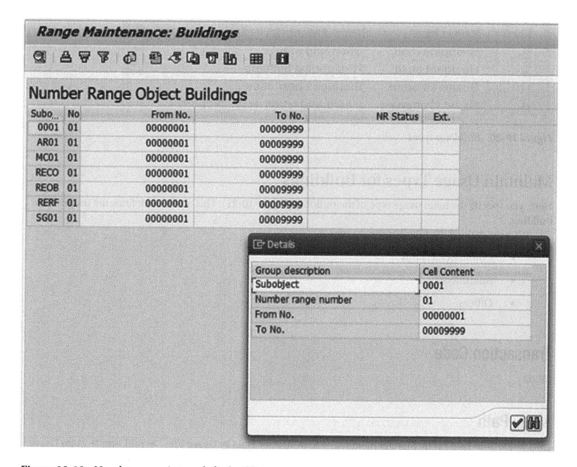

Figure 10-19. *Number range intervals for buildings*

Maintain Buildings Types

Here, you define the types of buildings, like shopping mall, residential building, and so on, you are managing (Figure 10-20).

Transaction Code

SPRO

Menu Path

IMG ➤ Flexible Real Estate Management (RE-FX) ➤ Master Data ➤ Usage View ➤ Building ➤ Building Types

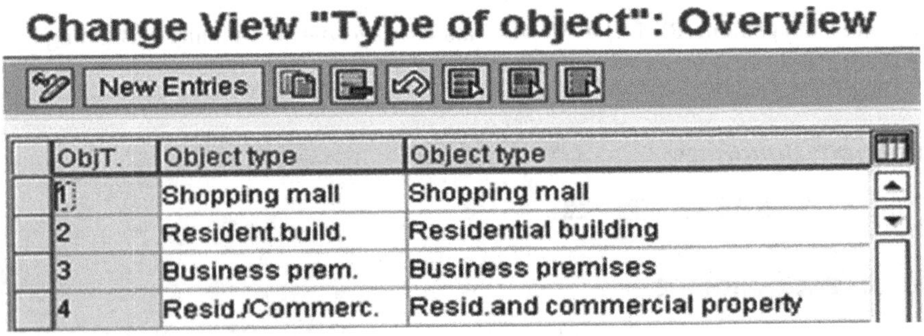

Change View "Type of object": Overview

ObjT.	Object type	Object type
1	Shopping mall	Shopping mall
2	Resident.build.	Residential building
3	Business prem.	Business premises
4	Resid./Commerc.	Resid.and commercial property

Figure 10-20. Buildings types

Maintain Usage Types for Buildings

Here, you specify the main usage type of the building (Figure 10-21). This attribute defines the usage of the building.

We have defined the following usage types:

- Commercial shops
- Apartments
- Offices

Transaction Code

SPRO

Menu Path

IMG ➤ Flexible Real Estate Management (RE-FX) ➤ Master Data ➤ Usage View ➤ Building ➤ Main Usage Types

Change View "Main usage types (properties, buildings)": Overview

New Entries

MUsagTyp	Main usage type
00000001	Apartments
00000002	Office shops
00000003	commercial shops

Figure 10-21. *Main usage types*

Maintain Number Range Intervals for Rental Objects

Here, you can specify how the number assignment is handled for this usage object. The specification applies uniformly for the company code. Note that the system only takes the setting for interval "01" into account (Figure 10-22).

For the internal number assignment, the system counts upward sequentially from the number shown in the Number field. For buildings, properties, and rental objects, the system assigns the number per business entity when an internal number assignment is used. This number is unique within the business entity. The next assigned number for these objects is therefore not identical to the number that is shown here.

Transaction Code

SPRO

Menu Path

IMG ➤ Flexible Real Estate Management (RE-FX) ➤ Master Data ➤ Usage View ➤ Rental Object ➤ Number Range for Rental Objects

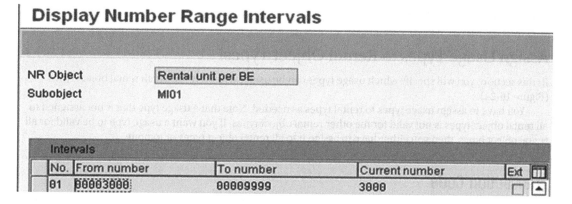

Display Number Range Intervals

NR Object   Rental unit per BE

Subobject   MI01

Intervals

No.	From number	To number	Current number	Ext
01	00003000	00009999	3000	☐

Figure 10-22. *Number range intervals for rental objects*

Maintain External Usage Types for Rental Objects

In this section, you will specify the external usage types for rental objects (Figure 10-23) and assign an internal usage type to them. In addition, you can specify here if a usage type should participate in settlements or not.

The usage type specifies:

- Which screen sequence is used for master data maintenance of the rental object

- Which rental object types (rental unit or pooled space/rental space) are allowed

- Which condition types are allowed for the rental object (by assigning a condition group per usage type)

Although assigning an internal usage type is mandatory, the assignment is informational only.

Transaction Code

SPRO

Menu Path

IMG ➤ Flexible Real Estate Management (RE-FX) ➤ Master Data ➤ Usage View ➤ Rental Object ➤ Usage Type ➤ Usage Types

Change View "External Usage Types": Overview

	New Entries							

External Usage Types

UT	Usage Type Medium Name	Short Name	Sett.	IUT	IntUsageTypeNa	Cat	
1	Commercial shops	Commercial shop	☐	3	Commerc.ten.law	2 Commercial	
2	Apartments	Apartments	☐	1	Priv.fin.accomm	1 Non-commercial	
3	Office purposes	Office purposes	☐	3	Commerc.ten.law	2 Commercial	

Figure 10-23. External usage types for rental objects

Assign Usage Types to Rental Object Types

In this section, you will specify which usage types can be used exclusively for which rental object types (Figure 10-24).

You have to assign usage types to rental types as needed. Note that a usage type that is not assigned to all rental object types is not valid for the other rental object types. If you want a usage type to be valid for all rental object types, then you either have to assign it to all rental object types or to none.

Transaction Code

SPRO

Menu Path

IMG ➤ Flexible Real Estate Management (RE-FX) ➤ Master Data ➤ Usage View ➤ Rental Object ➤ Usage Type ➤ Usage Types per Rental Object Types

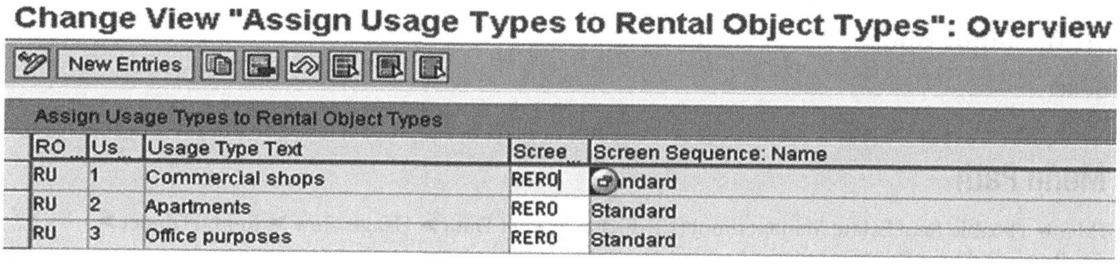

Change View "Assign Usage Types to Rental Object Types": Overview

RO	Us	Usage Type Text	Scree	Screen Sequence: Name
RU	1	Commercial shops	RERO	Standard
RU	2	Apartments	RERO	Standard
RU	3	Office purposes	RERO	Standard

Figure 10-24. Assign Usage Types to Rental Object Types screen

Maintain Measurement Types per Usage Types

In this step, you can create specifications for measurement types for rental objects that apply for individual usage types (Figure 10-25).

You have defined which measurement types are allowed in general for rental objects in the Measurement Types IMG activity.

You assigned external usage types to the rental object types in the Usage Type per Rental Object Type IMG activity.

Transaction Code

SPRO

Menu Path

IMG ➤ Flexible Real Estate Management (RE-FX) ➤ Master Data ➤ Usage View ➤ Rental Object ➤ Usage Type ➤ Measurement Types per Usage Type

Change View "Measurements for Rental Objects": Overview

MeasTp	Short Meas Type	Us...	Usage Type	MainMeas.	Measurement Type Use	DefUnit
A004	Living Area	1	Priv.fin.accomm	☑	Property Is Default for Object (on Sc... ▾	M2
A100	Retail Space	4	Store	☑	Property Is Default for Object (on Sc... ▾	M2
A101	Office space	5	Office	☑	Property Is Default for Object (on Sc... ▾	M2
M020	Share of Garden	1	Priv.fin.accomm	☐	Property Is Allowed for Object ▾	%

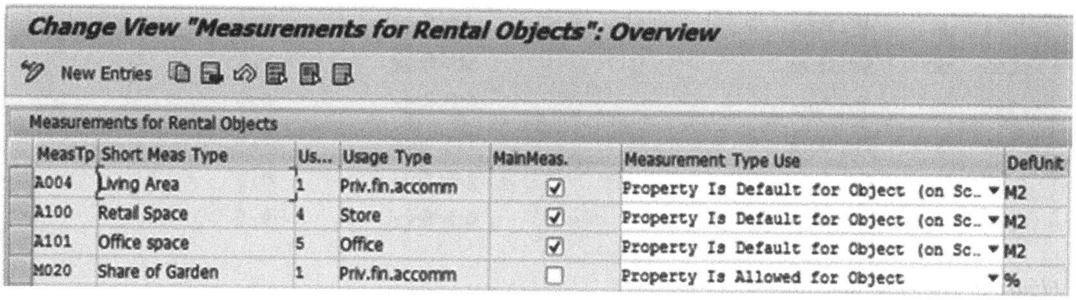

Figure 10-25. Measurement types per usage types

Maintain Floor Descriptions

In this section, you will create the storeys' names for buildings and define a number for each storey (Figure 10-26).

Transaction Code

SPRO

Menu Path

IMG ➤ Flexible Real Estate Management (RE-FX) ➤ Master Data ➤ Usage View ➤ Rental Object ➤ Attributes ➤ Floor Descriptions

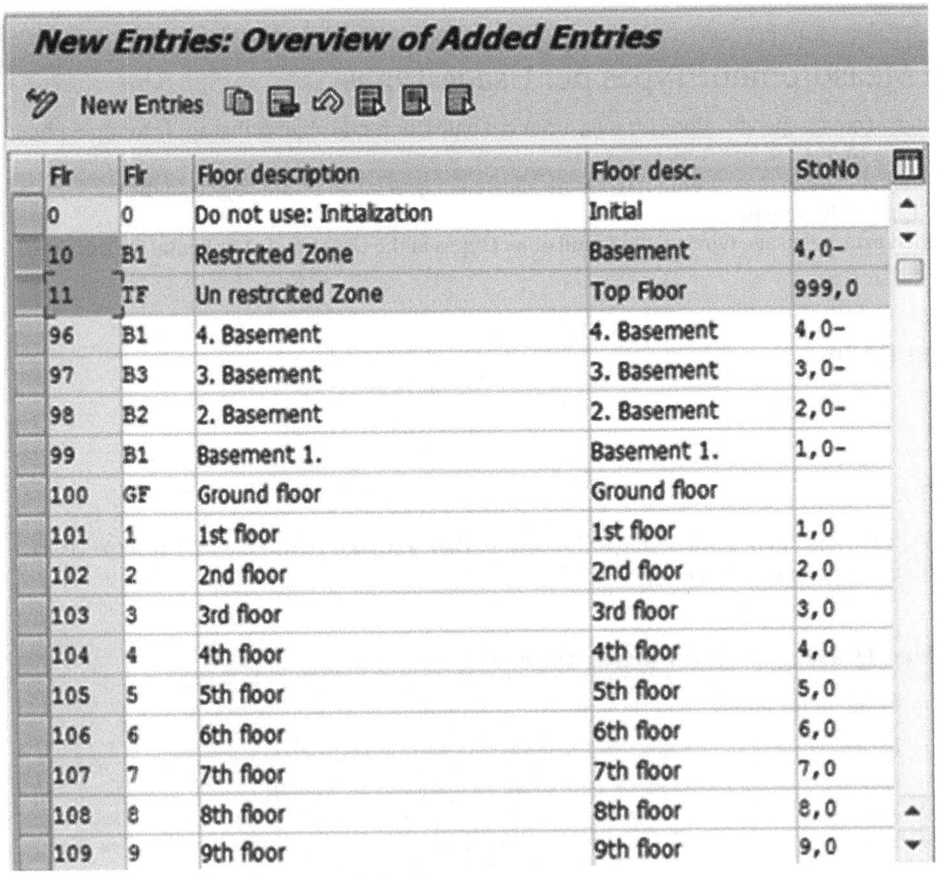

New Entries: Overview of Added Entries

Flr	Flr	Floor description	Floor desc.	StoNo
0	0	Do not use: Initialization	Initial	
10	B1	Restrcited Zone	Basement	4,0-
11	TF	Un restrcited Zone	Top Floor	999,0
96	B1	4. Basement	4. Basement	4,0-
97	B3	3. Basement	3. Basement	3,0-
98	B2	2. Basement	2. Basement	2,0-
99	B1	Basement 1.	Basement 1.	1,0-
100	GF	Ground floor	Ground floor	
101	1	1st floor	1st floor	1,0
102	2	2nd floor	2nd floor	2,0
103	3	3rd floor	3rd floor	3,0
104	4	4th floor	4th floor	4,0
105	5	5th floor	5th floor	5,0
106	6	6th floor	6th floor	6,0
107	7	7th floor	7th floor	7,0
108	8	8th floor	8th floor	8,0
109	9	9th floor	9th floor	9,0

Figure 10-26. Floor descriptions

Contracts in REFX

Maintain Number Range Intervals for Contracts

In this activity, you will specify how number assignment is handled for your contracts (Figure 10-27). The specification applies for the company code entered. You can assign number range intervals to individual contract types.

For an external number assignment, you can specify the number range for the contract.

For an internal number assignment, the system counts upward sequentially from the number shown in the Number field.

Transaction Code

SPRO

Menu Path

IMG ➤ Flexible Real Estate Management (RE-FX) ➤ Contract ➤ Number Assignment ➤ Number Range for Contracts

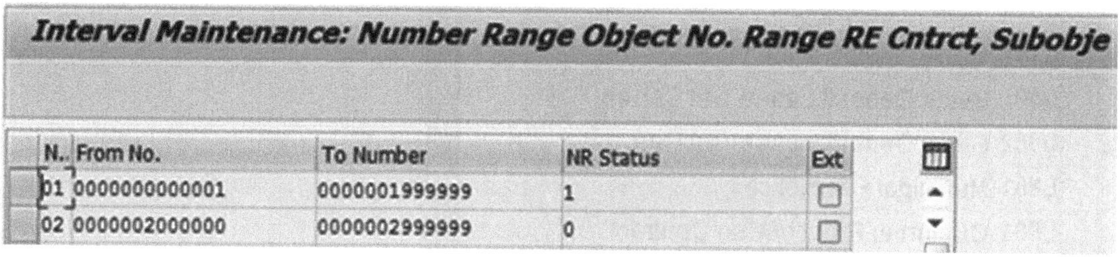

Interval Maintenance: Number Range Object No. Range RE Cntrct, Subobje

N..	From No.	To Number	NR Status	Ext	
01	0000000000001	0000001999999	1	☐	▲
02	0000002000000	0000002999999	0	☐	▼

Figure 10-27. *Number range intervals for contracts*

Define Contract Types

In this section, you will specify contract types (Figure 10-28). The contract type controls the purpose of the contract (Figure 10-29).

The contract types used here are commercial lease-out.

Transaction Code

SPRO

Menu Path

IMG ➤ Flexible Real Estate Management (RE-FX) ➤ Contract ➤ Contract Type ➤ Define Contract Types

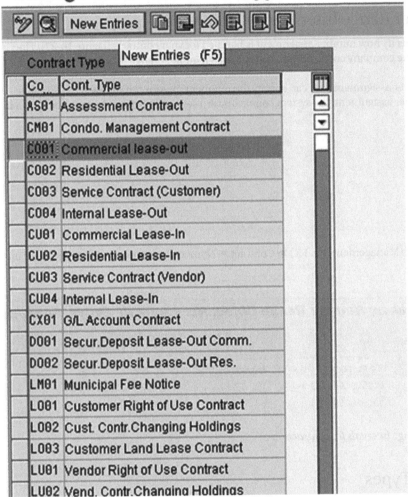

Figure 10-28. Contract types

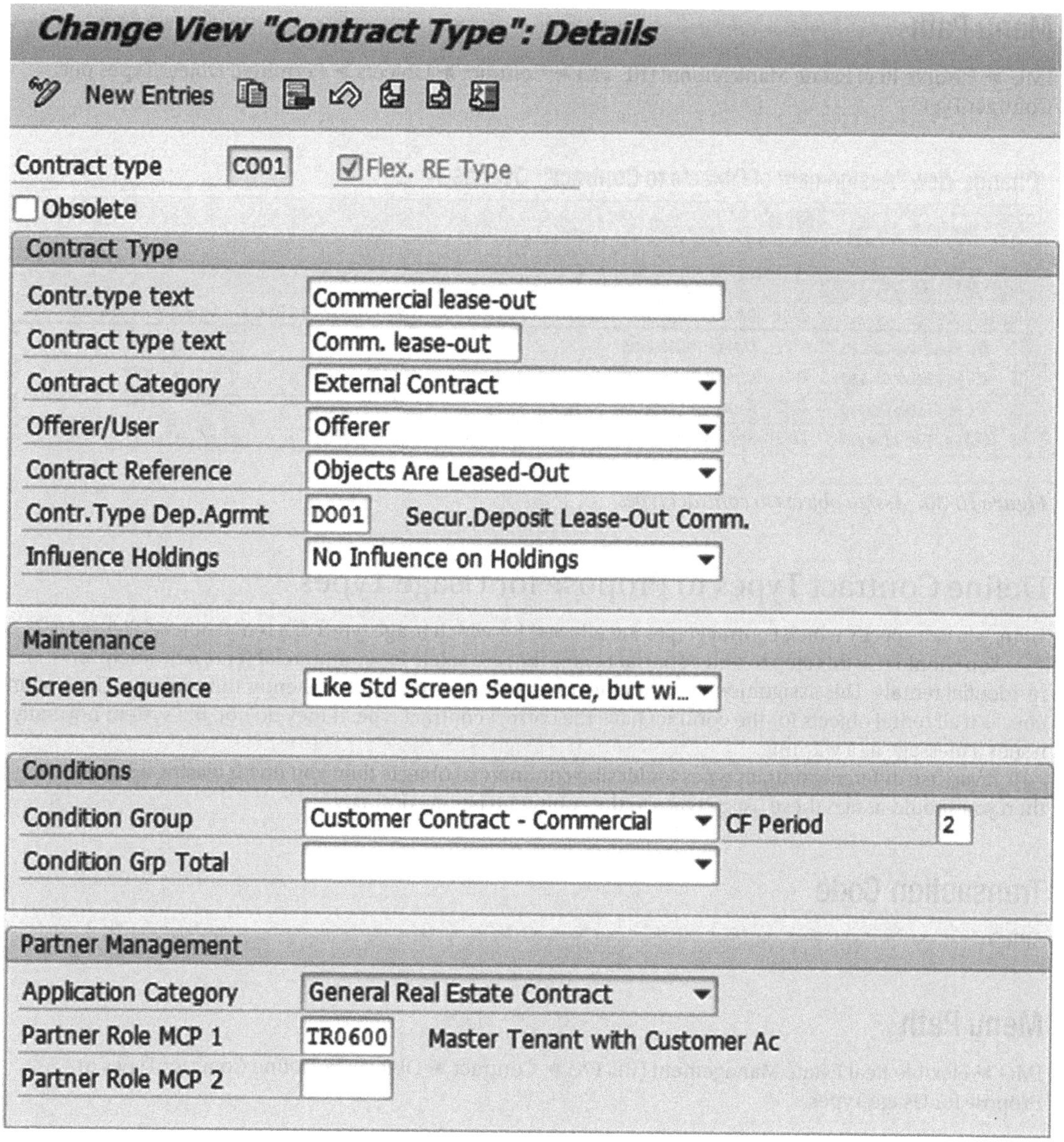

Change View "Contract Type": Details

New Entries

Contract type	CO01	☑ Flex. RE Type
☐ Obsolete	

Contract Type

Contr.type text	Commercial lease-out
Contract type text	Comm. lease-out
Contract Category	External Contract ▼
Offerer/User	Offerer ▼
Contract Reference	Objects Are Leased-Out ▼
Contr.Type Dep.Agrmt	DO01 Secur.Deposit Lease-Out Comm.
Influence Holdings	No Influence on Holdings ▼

Maintenance

Screen Sequence	Like Std Screen Sequence, but wi... ▼

Conditions

Condition Group	Customer Contract - Commercial ▼ CF Period 2
Condition Grp Total	▼

Partner Management

Application Category	General Real Estate Contract ▼
Partner Role MCP 1	TR0600 Master Tenant with Customer Ac
Partner Role MCP 2	

Figure 10-29. Contract Types screen: Details

Assign Objects to Contract Types

Here, you will specify for each contract type (differentiation criterion) which objects can be assigned to it (Figure 10-30). You can also assign real estate objects (in contrast with master data objects) as assignment objects. In addition, you can specify that these objects can be grouped together into object groups.

Transaction Code

SPRO

Menu Path

IMG ➤ Flexible Real Estate Management (RE-FX) ➤ Contract ➤ Objects ➤ Permitted Object Types per Contract Type

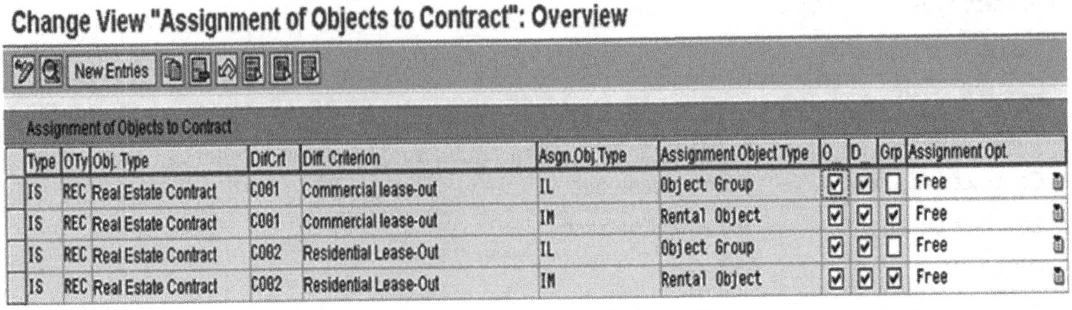
Change View "Assignment of Objects to Contract": Overview

New Entries

Assignment of Objects to Contract

Type	OTy	Obj. Type	DifCrt	Diff. Criterion	Asgn.Obj.Type	Assignment Object Type	O	D	Grp	Assignment Opt.
IS	REC	Real Estate Contract	C001	Commercial lease-out	IL	Object Group	☑	☑	☐	Free
IS	REC	Real Estate Contract	C001	Commercial lease-out	IM	Rental Object	☑	☑	☑	Free
IS	REC	Real Estate Contract	C002	Residential Lease-Out	IL	Object Group	☑	☑	☐	Free
IS	REC	Real Estate Contract	C002	Residential Lease-Out	IM	Rental Object	☑	☑	☑	Free

Figure 10-30. *Assign objects to contract types*

Define Contract Types to Propose for Usage Types

Here, you can specify which contract types are allowed for which usage types of a rental object (Figure 10-31).

You should use this step to enter contract types that are solely for commercial rentals or solely for residential rentals. This assignment is only a means of assisting you when you enter the contract. The system checks if all rental objects for the contract have the correct contract type. If they do not, the system normally issues a message as a warning.

If you use different contract types for leasing commercial objects than you do for leasing apartments, then you should assign these usage types to the contract types accordingly.

Transaction Code

SPRO

Menu Path

IMG ➤ Flexible Real Estate Management (RE-FX) ➤ Contract ➤ Objects ➤ Define Contract Types to Propose for Usage Types

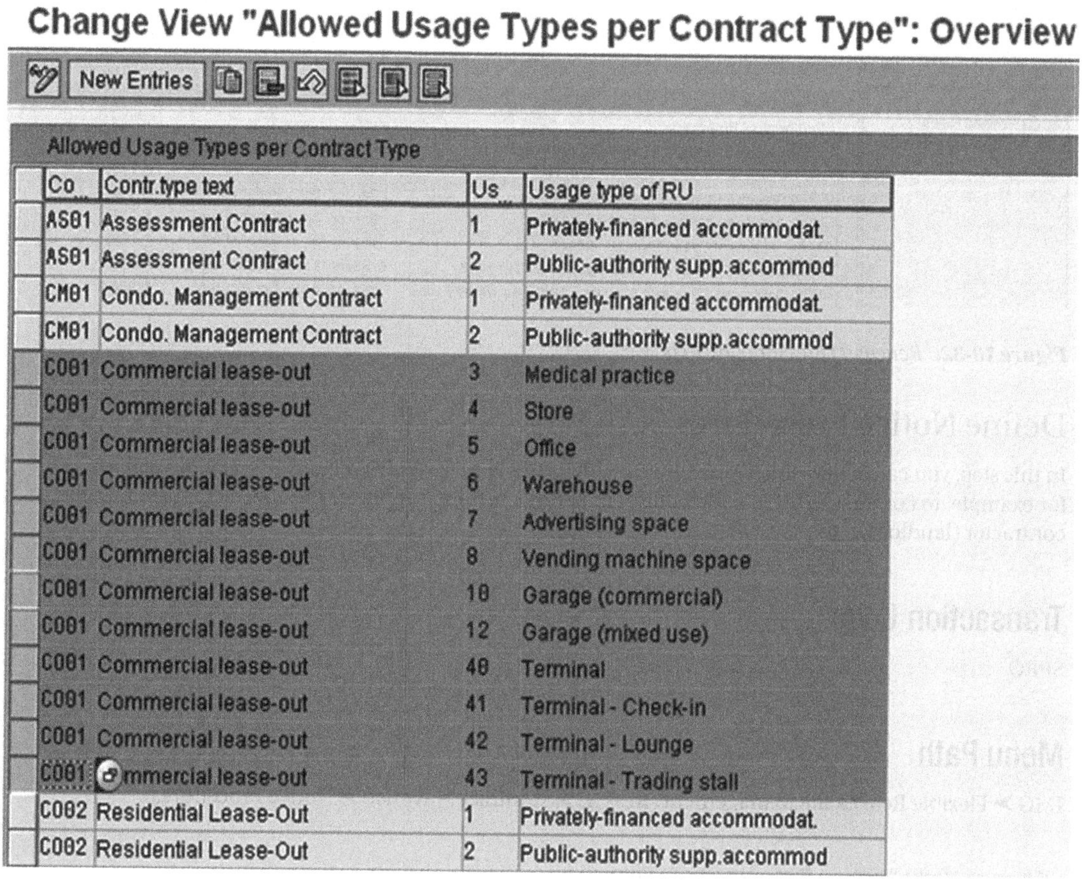

Change View "Allowed Usage Types per Contract Type": Overview

Co	Contr.type text	Us	Usage type of RU
AS01	Assessment Contract	1	Privately-financed accommodat.
AS01	Assessment Contract	2	Public-authority supp.accommod
CM01	Condo. Management Contract	1	Privately-financed accommodat.
CM01	Condo. Management Contract	2	Public-authority supp.accommod
C001	Commercial lease-out	3	Medical practice
C001	Commercial lease-out	4	Store
C001	Commercial lease-out	5	Office
C001	Commercial lease-out	6	Warehouse
C001	Commercial lease-out	7	Advertising space
C001	Commercial lease-out	8	Vending machine space
C001	Commercial lease-out	10	Garage (commercial)
C001	Commercial lease-out	12	Garage (mixed use)
C001	Commercial lease-out	40	Terminal
C001	Commercial lease-out	41	Terminal - Check-in
C001	Commercial lease-out	42	Terminal - Lounge
C001	Commercial lease-out	43	Terminal - Trading stall
C002	Residential Lease-Out	1	Privately-financed accommodat.
C002	Residential Lease-Out	2	Public-authority supp.accommod

Figure 10-31. *Contract types to propose for usage types*

Define Renewal Rules for Contracts

In this step, you will specify the rules for the renewal of real estate contracts (Figure 10-32). There are two types of contracts:

- Without fixed term (no renewals, since there is no defined contract end)
- With fixed term (renewal rules used)

Transaction Code

SPRO

Menu Path

IMG ➤ Flexible Real Estate Management (RE-FX) ➤ Contract ➤ Renewal ➤ Renewal Rules

Change View "Renewal Rules": Overview

𝒱 𝒬 New Entries 🗋 🗐 🖉 🗉 🗐 🗐			

Dialog Structure	Renewal Rules		
▽ 🗃 Renewal Rules	RRul	Renewal Rule Name	Autom. Renewal Type	Text Module Name
📁 Extension Periods	1000	2 Options for 3 Years; 3 months Notice Period	One or More Repetitions ☐ 1000	
	1100	1 Option for 5 Years; 1 Year Notice Period	One or More Repetitions ☐ 1100	
	1200	2 Options for 1 Year; 6 Months Notice Period	One or More Repetitions ☐ 1200	
	1300	2 Options for 5 Years; 1 Year Notice Period	One or More Repetitions ☐ 1300	
	2000	1 Renewal of 1 Year; 3 Months Notice Period	One or More Repetitions ☐ 2000	
	2100	Recurring Renewal of 1 Year; 3 Months Notice Period	R Repetition of Last Rule ☐ 2100	
	3000	1 Option and 1 Renewal, Each for 1 Year; 3 Mo. Notice Period	One or More Repetitions ☐ 3000	

Figure 10-32. Renewal rules for contracts

Define Notice Procedures

In this step, you can create notice procedures with multiple notice rules (Figure 10-33). This applies, for example, to contract terms in which different periods of notice apply for the contractee (tenant) and contractor (landlord).

Transaction Code

SPRO

Menu Path

IMG ➤ Flexible Real Estate Management (RE-FX) ➤ Contract ➤ Notice ➤ Notice Procedures

Change View "Notice Procedures": Overview

𝒱 𝒬 New Entries 🗋 🗐 🖉 🗉 🗐 🗐		

Dialog Structure	Notice Procedures	
▽ 🗃 Notice Procedures	Noti	Notice Procedure Name	Text Module Name
📁 Cancellation Rules	1000	For Both Parties: 3 Months for End of Month (3rd Bus.Day)	1000
	1100	For Both Parties: 3 Months for End of Quarter (3rd Bus.Day)	1100
	2000	Standard Residential (DE)	2000

Figure 10-33. Notice Procedures screen

Conditions and Flows in REFX

Define Calculation Formulas

Calculation formulas are used to calculate the condition amount. The calculation formula may be based on a number of predefined formulas, or an enhancement may be developed to meet specific customer requirements. The calculation formulas, as shown in Table 10-1 and Figures 10-34 and 10-35, will be configured for use on real estate contracts.

Table 10-1. *Calculation Formulas*

Ext Rule	Calculation Formula Name
A	Fixed Amount

Transaction Code

SPRO

Menu Path

IMG ➤ Flexible Real Estate Management (RE-FX) ➤ Conditions and Flows ➤ Calculation and Distribution Formulas ➤ Calculation Formulas

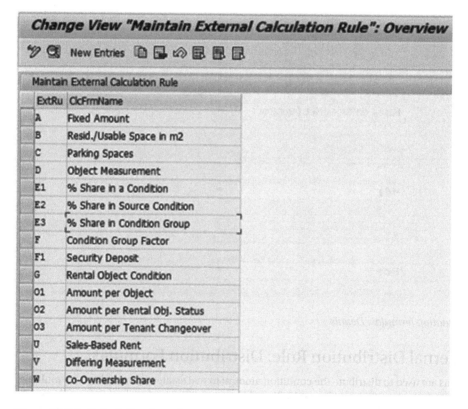

Figure 10-34. *Calculation formulas*

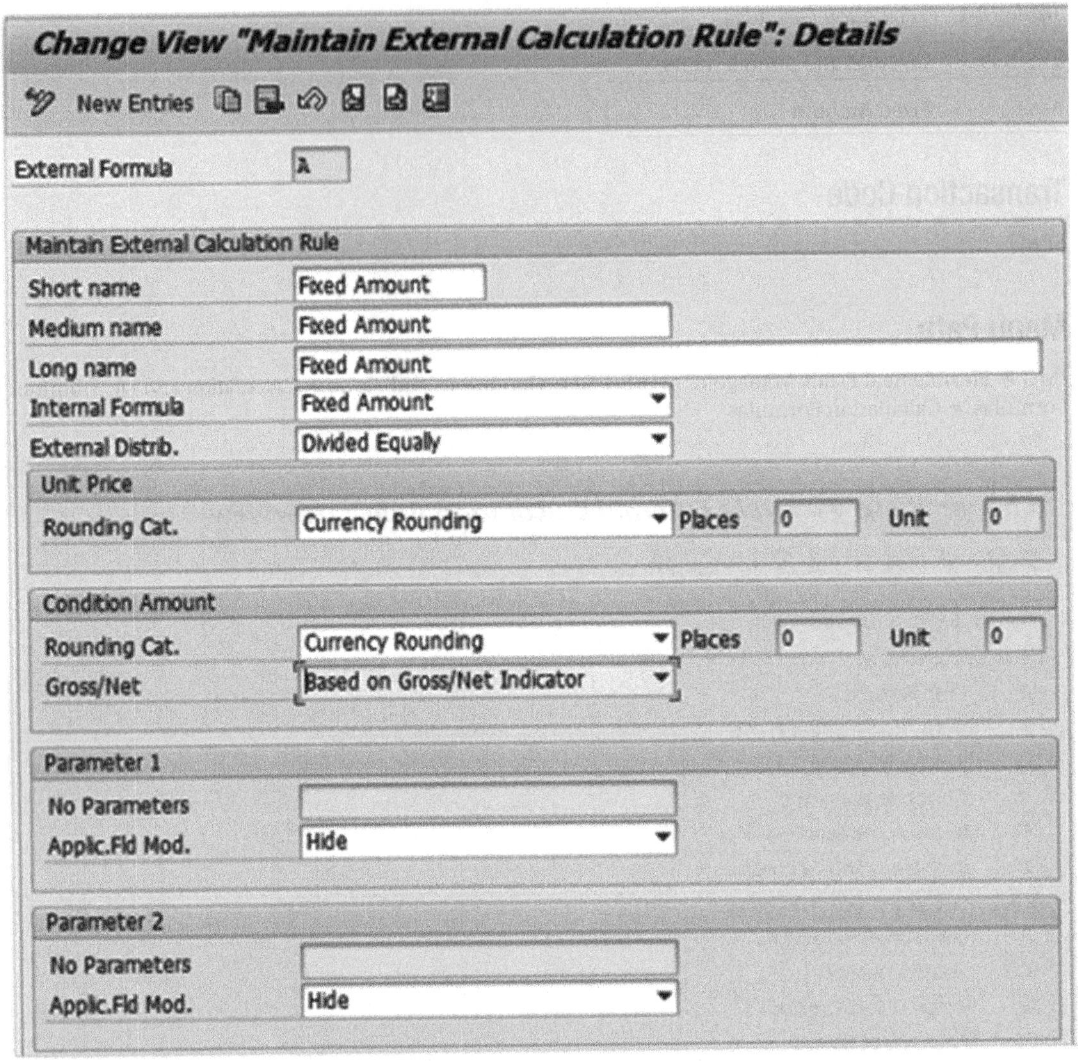

Figure 10-35. Calculation formulas: Details

Maintain External Distribution Rule: Distribution Formulas

Distribution formulas are used to distribute the condition amount to real estate objects if there are multiple objects assigned to the real estate contract (Figure 10-36 and Figure 10-37). The distribution formula may be based on a number of predefined formulas, or an enhancement may be developed to meet specific customer requirements. The following distribution formulas will be configured for use on real estate contracts.

Transaction Code

SPRO

Menu Path

IMG ➤ Flexible Real Estate Management (RE-FX) ➤ Conditions and Flows ➤ Calculation and Distribution Formulas ➤ Distribution Formulas

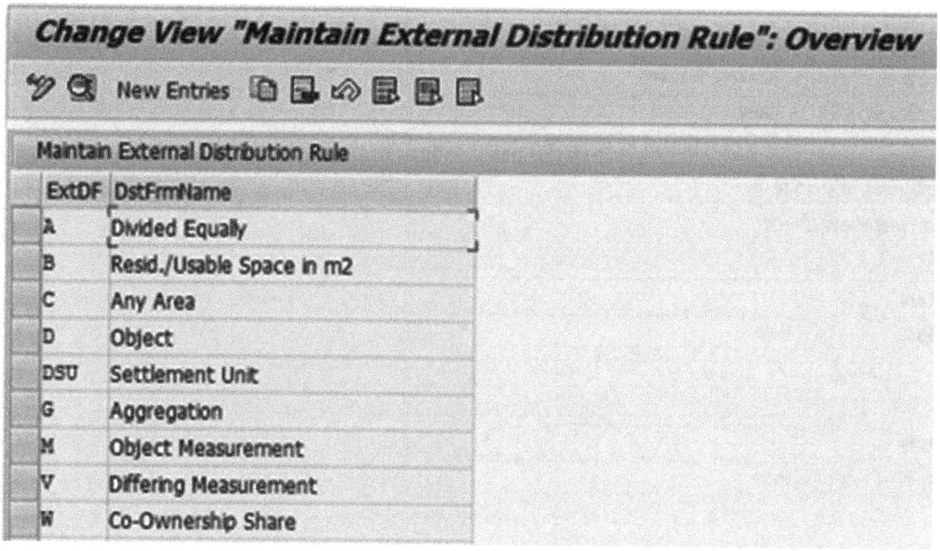

Change View "Maintain External Distribution Rule": Overview

Maintain External Distribution Rule

ExtDF	DstFrmName
A	Divided Equally
B	Resid./Usable Space in m2
C	Any Area
D	Object
DSU	Settlement Unit
G	Aggregation
M	Object Measurement
V	Differing Measurement
W	Co-Ownership Share

Figure 10-36. Maintain external distribution rule, distribution formulas

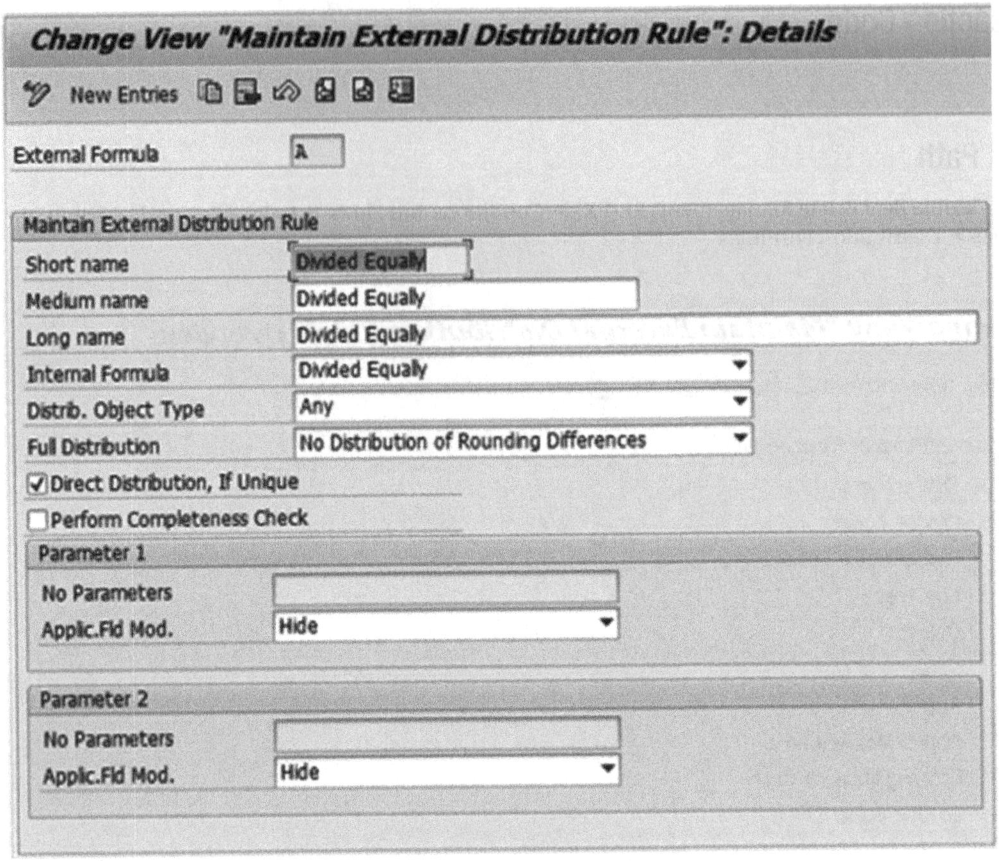

Figure 10-37. Maintain external distribution rule, distribution formulas: Details

Define Condition Types

In this section, you will specify condition types for your real estate contracts (Figure 10-38 and Figure 10-39). Condition types are the most visible component of lease accounting to the user. The selection of a condition type on the real estate contract drives the account assignment and the accounting treatment in the case of FAS13 straight-lining. Condition types are assigned to condition groups, which are assigned to contract types.

It is recommended that the condition type name indicates what kind of process it will be used for— payable or receivable. Since condition types are assigned to contract types via condition groups, the distinction is not mandatory, but it may aid the user in reporting and analysis.

This relationship ensures that only condition types that are applicable for a contract type are available for use by the user.

Transaction Code

SPRO

Menu Path

IMG ➤ Flexible Real Estate Management (RE-FX) ➤ Conditions & Flows ➤ Condition Types and Condition Groups ➤ Define Condition Types

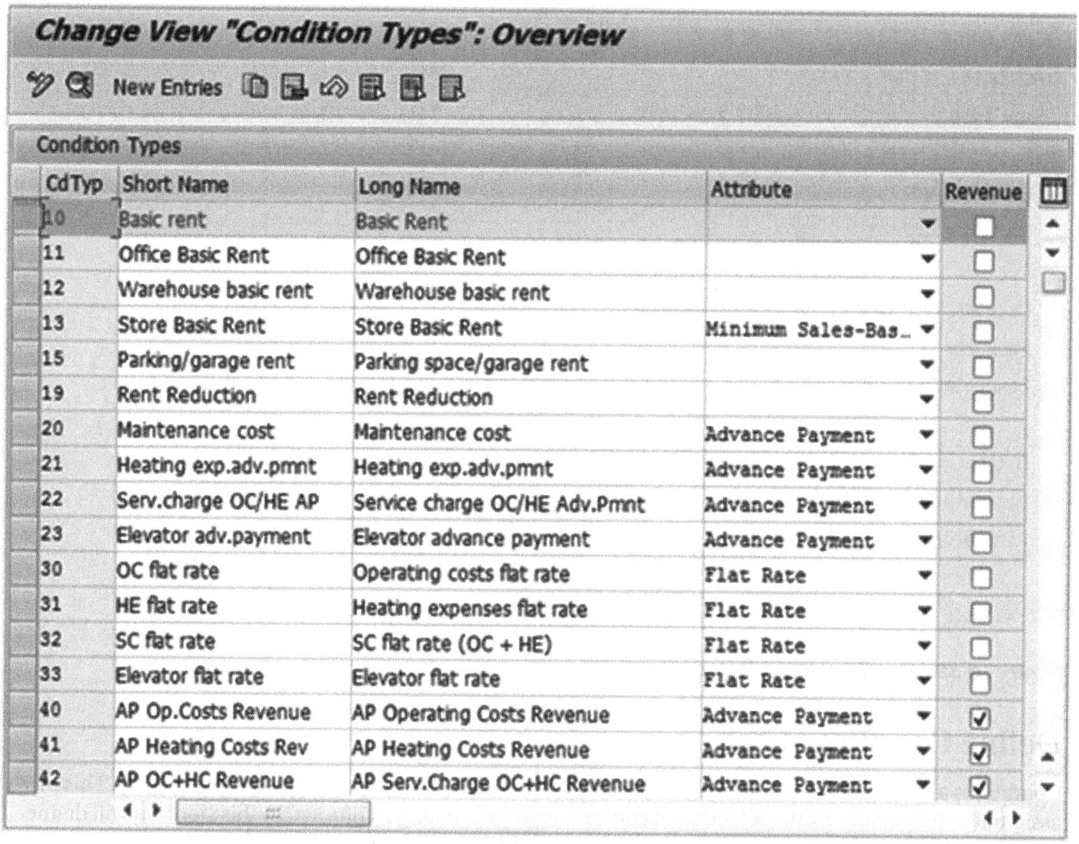

Change View "Condition Types": Overview

New Entries

Condition Types

CdTyp	Short Name	Long Name	Attribute	Revenue
10	Basic rent	Basic Rent		☐
11	Office Basic Rent	Office Basic Rent		☐
12	Warehouse basic rent	Warehouse basic rent		☐
13	Store Basic Rent	Store Basic Rent	Minimum Sales-Bas...	☐
15	Parking/garage rent	Parking space/garage rent		☐
19	Rent Reduction	Rent Reduction		☐
20	Maintenance cost	Maintenance cost	Advance Payment	☐
21	Heating exp.adv.pmnt	Heating exp.adv.pmnt	Advance Payment	☐
22	Serv.charge OC/HE AP	Service charge OC/HE Adv.Pmnt	Advance Payment	☐
23	Elevator adv.payment	Elevator advance payment	Advance Payment	☐
30	OC flat rate	Operating costs flat rate	Flat Rate	☐
31	HE flat rate	Heating expenses flat rate	Flat Rate	☐
32	SC flat rate	SC flat rate (OC + HE)	Flat Rate	☐
33	Elevator flat rate	Elevator flat rate	Flat Rate	☐
40	AP Op.Costs Revenue	AP Operating Costs Revenue	Advance Payment	☑
41	AP Heating Costs Rev	AP Heating Costs Revenue	Advance Payment	☑
42	AP OC+HC Revenue	AP Serv.Charge OC+HC Revenue	Advance Payment	☑

Figure 10-38. Condition types

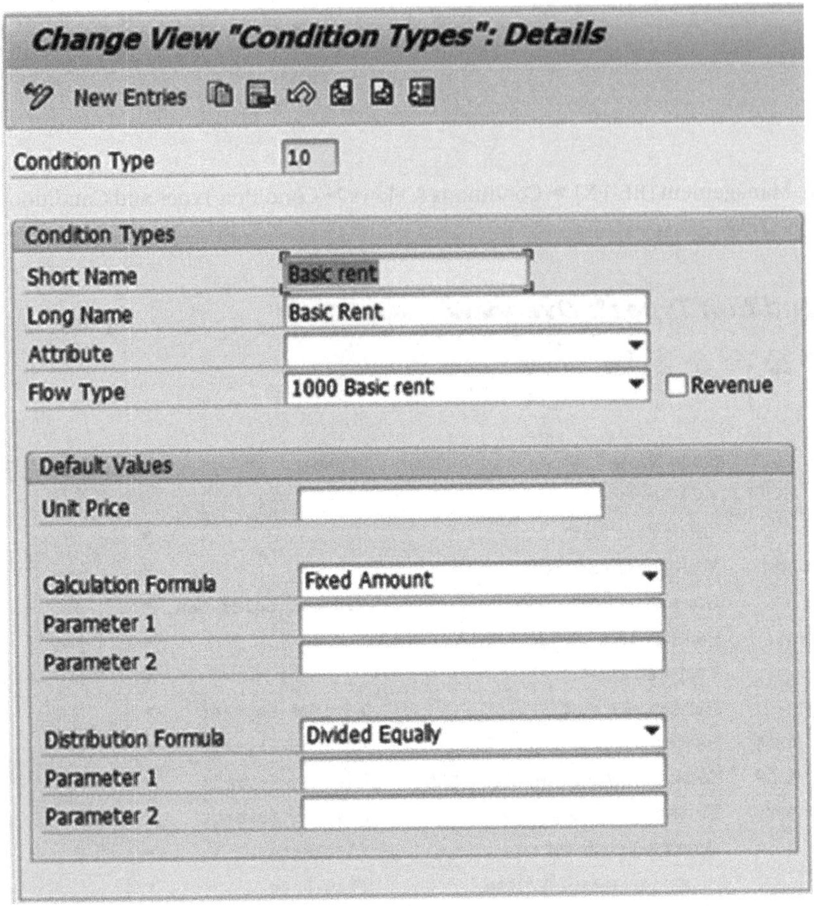

Figure 10-39. Condition types: Details

Define Condition Groups

Conditions are assigned to condition groups, which are assigned to contract types (Figure 10-40). This assignment helps simplify the selection of conditions when creating a contract. In this step you will define condition groups and assign condition types to them, which are as follows:

- Per contract type (customer, vendor, and so on)

- Per usage type of the rental object (commercial, residential, and so on)

Condition groups are mandatory. The only conditions available in the contract or rental object are those that you have assigned to the given condition group for that contract or object.

Transaction Code

SPRO

Menu Path

IMG ➤ Flexible Real Estate Management (RE-FX) ➤ Conditions & Flows ➤ Condition Types and Condition Groups

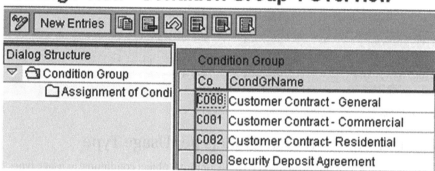

Figure 10-40. *Condition groups*

Assign Condition Types to Condition Groups

Here, you will assign the condition types to the condition groups defined earlier (Figure 10-41).

Transaction Code

SPRO

Menu Path

IMG ➤ Flexible Real Estate Management (RE-FX) ➤ Conditions & Flows ➤ Condition Types and Condition Groups ➤ Condition Groups ➤ Define Condition Groups & Assign Condition Types

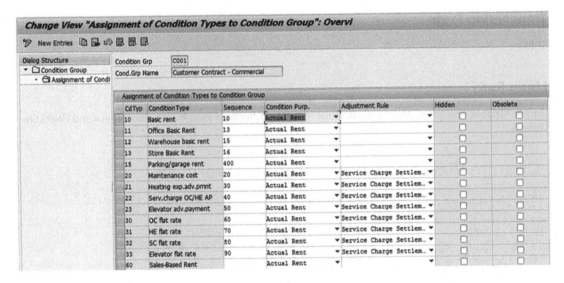

Figure 10-41. *Assign condition types to condition groups*

Assign Condition Groups to Rental Objects per Usage Type

In this step, you will assign condition groups, which you created for rental object conditions, to usage types of rental objects (Figure 10-42).

Transaction Code

SPRO

Menu Path

IMG ➤ Flexible Real Estate Management (RE-FX) ➤ Conditions & Flows ➤ Condition Types and Condition Groups ➤ Condition Groups ➤ Assign Condition Group to Rental Object per Usage Type

Change View "Condition Group for Rental Object per Usage Type": Overvi

Us	RU UseType	Co	CondGrName	
1	Commercial shops	C001	Customer Contract - Commercial	
2	Apartments	C002	Customer Contract- Residential	
3	Office purposes	C001	Customer Contract - Commercial	

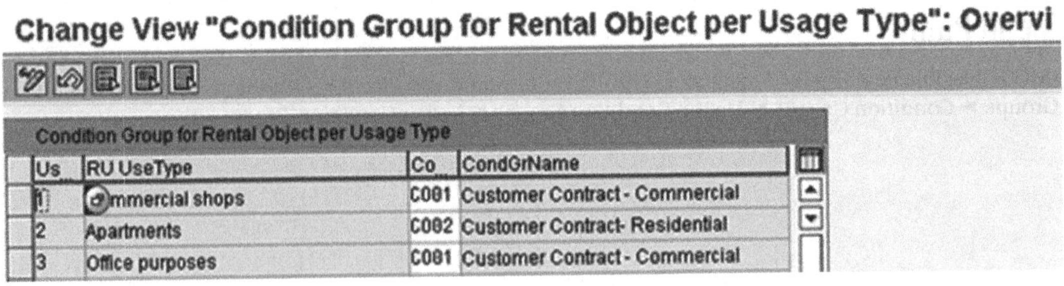

Figure 10-42. *Assign condition groups to rental object per usage type*

Assign Condition Groups to Contract per Contract Type

In this step, you will assign the condition groups, which you created for contract conditions, to contract types (Figure 10-43).

198

Transaction Code

SPRO

Menu Path

IMG ➤ Flexible Real Estate Management (RE-FX) ➤ Conditions & Flows ➤ Condition Types and Condition Groups ➤ Condition Groups ➤ Assign Condition Group to Contract per Contract Type

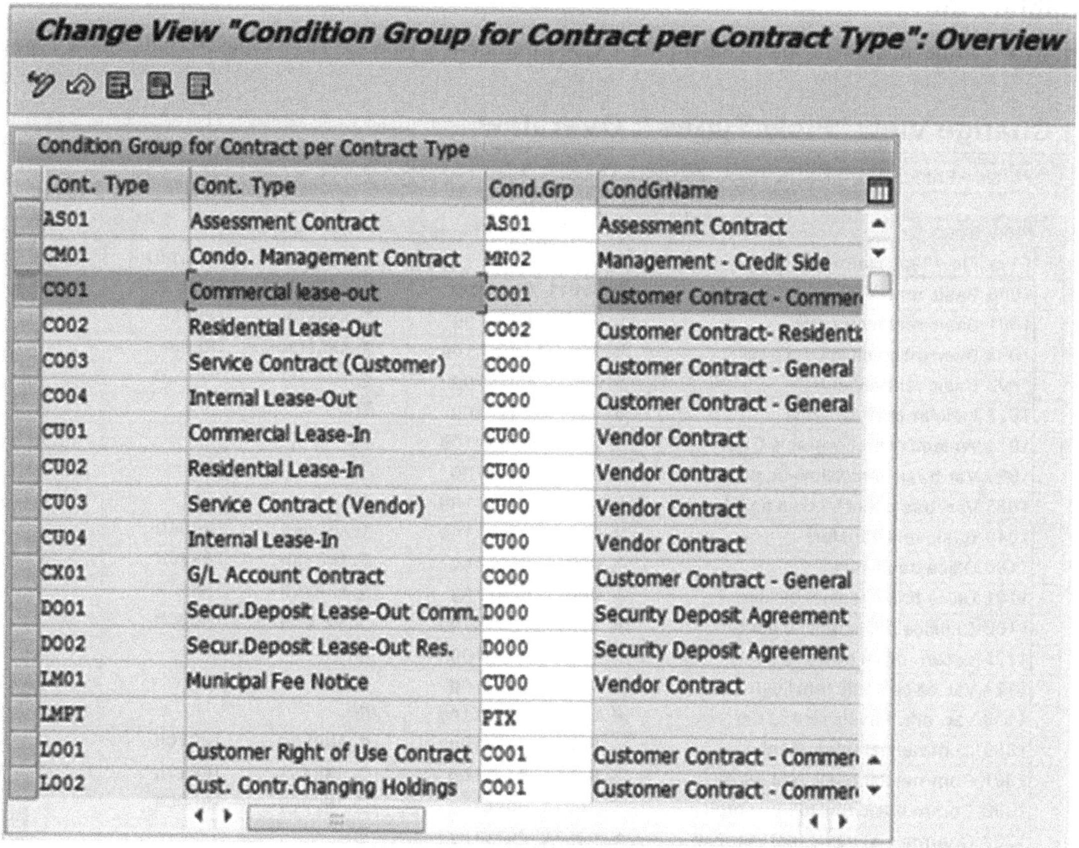

Cont. Type	Cont. Type	Cond.Grp	CondGrName
AS01	Assessment Contract	AS01	Assessment Contract
CM01	Condo. Management Contract	MN02	Management - Credit Side
CO01	Commercial lease-out	CO01	Customer Contract - Commen
CO02	Residential Lease-Out	CO02	Customer Contract- Residentk
CO03	Service Contract (Customer)	CO00	Customer Contract - General
CO04	Internal Lease-Out	CO00	Customer Contract - General
CU01	Commercial Lease-In	CU00	Vendor Contract
CU02	Residential Lease-In	CU00	Vendor Contract
CU03	Service Contract (Vendor)	CU00	Vendor Contract
CU04	Internal Lease-In	CU00	Vendor Contract
CX01	G/L Account Contract	CO00	Customer Contract - General
DO01	Secur.Deposit Lease-Out Comm.	DO00	Security Deposit Agreement
DO02	Secur.Deposit Lease-Out Res.	DO00	Security Deposit Agreement
LM01	Municipal Fee Notice	CU00	Vendor Contract
LMPT		PTX	
LO01	Customer Right of Use Contract	CO01	Customer Contract - Commen
LO02	Cust. Contr.Changing Holdings	CO01	Customer Contract - Commen

Figure 10-43. *Assign condition groups to contract per contract type*

Define Flow Types

In this step, you will define flow types (Figure 10-44). This is a prerequisite for creating condition types and for account determination. Flow types classify flows in the following:

- Cash flow
- Accounting

The conditions are assigned to flow types, which are tied to the account determination. Flow types specify how conditions will be treated within the cash flow and account determination. It is through the flow type that a condition is specified as either a debit or a credit posting. Accrual and deferral types may also be defined at this point.

For some transactions, it is not possible to post using the flow type originally assigned (that is derived from the condition type). For these transactions, you have to assign a reference flow type. You make this assignment using a relationship key in the Assign Reference Flow Types IMG activity in the next section.

Transaction Code

SPRO

Menu Path

IMG ➤ Flexible Real Estate Management (RE-FX) ➤ Conditions & Flows ➤ Flow Types ➤ Define Flow Types

Change View "Flow Types": Overview

FTyp	Flow Type Name	D/C		AcrType(Ac	AcrTyp(Def	FTyp
1000	Basic rent	S Debit Posting		ANRVCN	TRRVCN	
1001	Basic rent receivable	S Debit Posting		ANRVCN	TRRVCN	
1002	Basc rnt credit foll.-up post.	H Credit Posting		ANCOCN	TRCOCN	
1003	Basic rent vacancy	S Debit Posting				
1013	Installment Payments	S Debit Posting				
1014	Writeoff of Irrecoverable Debt	H Credit Posting				
1023	Vac.basic rent follow-up post.	S Debit Posting				
1033	Vac. basic rent f.u.cred.post.	H Credit Posting				
1040	Basic rent transfer	H Credit Posting		ANCORO	TRCORO	
1100	Office basic rent	S Debit Posting		ANRVCN	TRRVCN	
1101	Office basic rent receivable	S Debit Posting		ANRVCN	TRRVCN	
1102	Cr.office basic rent f.u.post.	H Credit Posting		ANCOCN	TRCOCN	
1103	Vacany office basic rent	S Debit Posting				
1123	Vac.office basic rent f.u.post	S Debit Posting				
1133	Vac. office basic rent c.f.u.p	H Credit Posting				
1300	Commercial Basic Rent	S Debit Posting		ANRVCN	TRRVCN	
1301	Commercial basic rent recvbl.	S Debit Posting		ANRVCN	TRRVCN	
1302	Comm.basic rent foll-up credit	S Debit Posting		ANCOCN	TRCOCN	
1303	Commercial basic rent vacancy	S Debit Posting				
1323	Comm. basic rent vac. foll-up	S Debit Posting				
1333	Comm. basic rent vac. f.u.cred	H Credit Posting				
1340	Commercial basic rent transfer	H Credit Posting		ANCORO	TRCORO	

Figure 10-44. Flow types

Assign Reference Flow Types

In this step, you will assign reference flow types to flow types (Figure 10-45).

With certain business transactions, postings cannot be made using the flow type that was originally assigned (the flow type derived from the condition type). For such transactions, reference flow types must be assigned. You will create these assignments in this activity using a relationship key. As an example, if a condition was increased after the periodic processing run, a follow-up posting is required to post the incremental condition increase. In this case, a reference flow type 10—"Follow-Up Posting Due to Condition Increase"—is used to record the entry. If the condition was decreased after the periodic processing run, a follow-up posting is also required to post the incremental condition decrease. In this case, a reference flow type 20—"Follow-Up Posting Due to Condition Decrease"—is used to record the entry. The flexibility of using different flow types allows for posting adjustments to different GL accounts if required.

The periodic processing program also generates the transfer postings. The transfer posting reverses the posting on the contract and posts the transaction amount to the building/property real estate object. A reference flow type of 30—"Distribution Transfer Posting"—is also assigned to a flow type.

Transaction Code

SPRO

Menu Path

IMG ➤ Flexible Real Estate Management (RE-FX) ➤ Conditions & Flows ➤ Flow Types ➤ Assign Reference Flow Types

Change View "Assignment of Reference Flow Types": Overview

New Entries

Assignment of Reference Flow Types

Relation	Flo	Flow Type Name	Ref	Flow Type Name
10 Follow-Up Postings Du	1000	Basic rent	1001	Basic rent receivable
10 Follow-Up Postings Du	1100	Office basic rent	1101	Office basic rent receivable
10 Follow-Up Postings Du	3000	Maintenance Costs	3001	Maint Cost flat rate recbl
10 Follow-Up Postings Du	5500	Management Costs	5501	Receivable Management Costs
20 Follow-Up Postings Du	1000	Basic rent	1002	Basc rnt credit foll.-up post.
20 Follow-Up Postings Du	1100	Office basic rent	1102	Cr.office basic rent f.u.post.
20 Follow-Up Postings Du	3000	Maintenance Costs	3002	Maint Costs f.u. credit
20 Follow-Up Postings Du	5500	Management Costs	5502	FollPost. Mgmt Costs Credit
30 Distribution Postings	1000	Basic rent	1040	Basic rent transfer
30 Distribution Postings	3000	Maintenance Costs	3040	Maint Costs transfer
30 Distribution Postings	3001	Maint Cost flat rate recbl	3041	Main Costs transfer f.u.p.
30 Distribution Postings	3002	Maint Costs f.u. credit	3042	Maint Costs trsfr f.u. credit
30 Distribution Postings	5500	Management Costs	5540	Transfer Management Costs
30 Distribution Postings	5501	Receivable Management Costs	5541	Trsfr Recvbl Management Costs
30 Distribution Postings	5502	FollPost. Mgmt Costs Credit	5542	Trsfr FollPost. Mgmt Costs Cr.
60 Vacancy		1000	Basic rent	1003	Basic rent vacancy
60 Vacancy		1001	Basic rent receivable	1023	Vac.basic rent follow-up post.
60 Vacancy		1002	Basc rnt credit foll.-up post.	1033	Vac. basic rent f.u.cred.post.
60 Vacancy		1100	Office basic rent	1103	Vacany office basic rent
60 Vacancy		1101	Office basic rent receivable	1123	Vac.office basic rent f.u.post
60 Vacancy		1102	Cr.office basic rent f.u.post.	1133	Vac. office basic rent c.f.u.p
60 Vacancy		3000	Maintenance Costs	3003	Vacancy Maint Costs flat rate

Figure 10-45. Assign reference flow types

Assign Flow Types to Condition Types

You can assign defined flow types to the condition type (Figure 10-46). Assign the flow types that you want to be used for the periodic posting for external contracts. The system derives all other flow types from the reference flow types.

Transaction Code

SPRO

Menu Path

IMG ➤ Flexible Real Estate Management (RE-FX) ➤ Conditions & Flows ➤ Flow Types ➤ Assign Flow Type to Condition Type

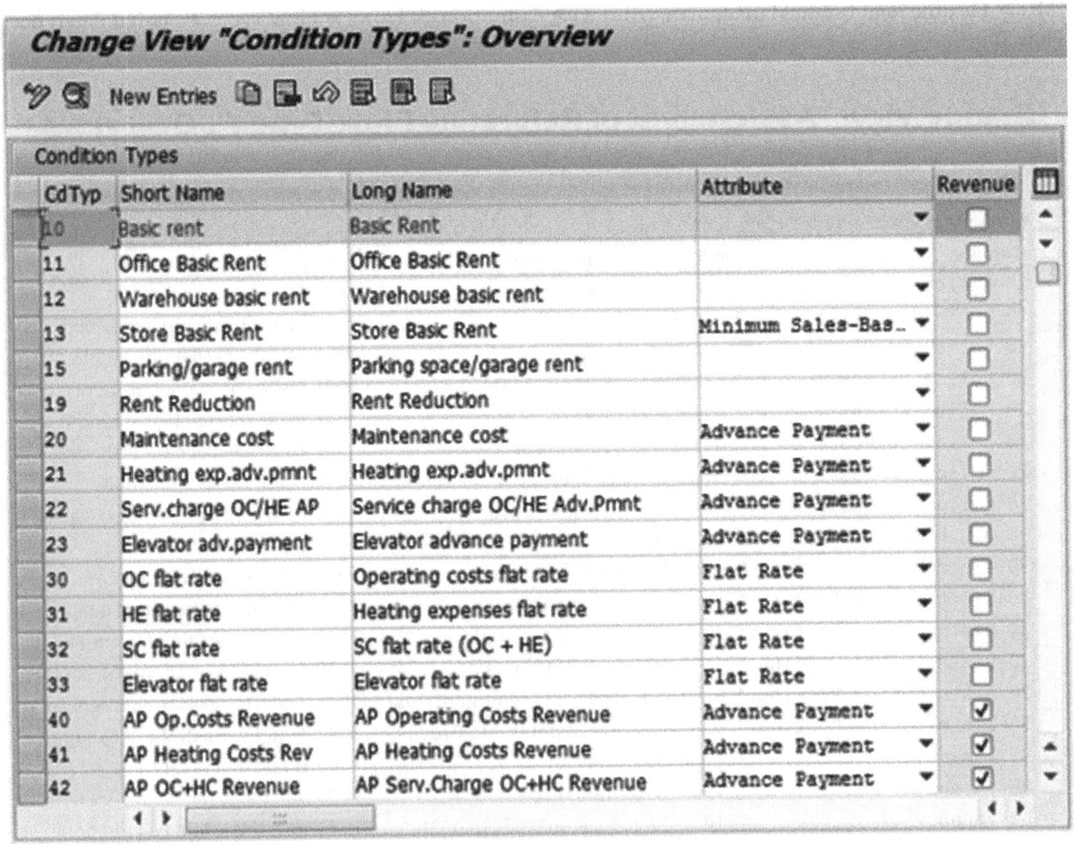

CdTyp	Short Name	Long Name	Attribute	Revenue
10	Basic rent	Basic Rent		☐
11	Office Basic Rent	Office Basic Rent		☐
12	Warehouse basic rent	Warehouse basic rent		☐
13	Store Basic Rent	Store Basic Rent	Minimum Sales-Bas...	☐
15	Parking/garage rent	Parking space/garage rent		☐
19	Rent Reduction	Rent Reduction		☐
20	Maintenance cost	Maintenance cost	Advance Payment	☐
21	Heating exp.adv.pmnt	Heating exp.adv.pmnt	Advance Payment	☐
22	Serv.charge OC/HE AP	Service charge OC/HE Adv.Pmnt	Advance Payment	☐
23	Elevator adv.payment	Elevator advance payment	Advance Payment	☐
30	OC flat rate	Operating costs flat rate	Flat Rate	☐
31	HE flat rate	Heating expenses flat rate	Flat Rate	☐
32	SC flat rate	SC flat rate (OC + HE)	Flat Rate	☐
33	Elevator flat rate	Elevator flat rate	Flat Rate	☐
40	AP Op.Costs Revenue	AP Operating Costs Revenue	Advance Payment	☑
41	AP Heating Costs Rev	AP Heating Costs Revenue	Advance Payment	☑
42	AP OC+HC Revenue	AP Serv.Charge OC+HC Revenue	Advance Payment	☑

Figure 10-46. Assign flow types to condition types

Accounting in REFX

We need to carry out the following activities to configure accounting in the SAP REFX system.

Define Tax Types

In this activity you will enter the necessary tax types (Figure 10-47). Specifying tax types is mandatory. Tax types are country dependent. You can define multiple tax types for each country.

Transaction Code

SPRO

Menu Path

IMG ➤ Flexible Real Estate Management (RE-FX) ➤ Accounting ➤ Automatically Generated Accounting Documents ➤ Taxes ➤ Define Tax Types

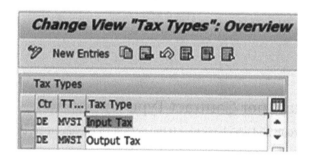

Figure 10-47. Tax types

Create Tax Groups

Specifying tax groups is mandatory. The tax group determines the tax rate for a transaction. The tax group, together with the country, the tax type, and possibly the region, determines the tax percentage rate.

The following tax groups, as shown in Table 10-2 and Figure 10-48, have been defined.

Table 10-2. Tax Groups

Tax Group	Meaning
Full	Full tax rate
Half	Half tax rate
None	No taxation

Transaction Code

SPRO

Menu Path

IMG ➤ Flexible Real Estate Management (RE-FX) ➤ Accounting ➤ Automatically Generated Accounting Documents ➤ Taxes ➤ Create Tax Groups

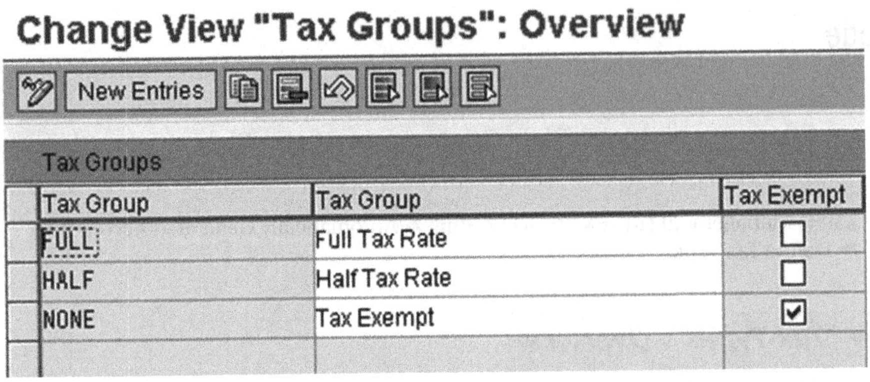

Change View "Tax Groups": Overview

Tax Group	Tax Group	Tax Exempt
FULL	Full Tax Rate	☐
HALF	Half Tax Rate	☐
NONE	Tax Exempt	☑

Figure 10-48. *Tax groups*

Maintain Default Values for Tax Rate per Contract Type

Here you will specify, per contract type, which tax group and which tax type is the default when you create a contract (Figure 10-49).

Transaction Code

SPRO

Menu Path

IMG ➤ Flexible Real Estate Management (RE-FX) ➤ Accounting ➤ Automatically Generated Accounting Documents ➤ Taxes ➤ Default Values for Tax Rate per Contract Type

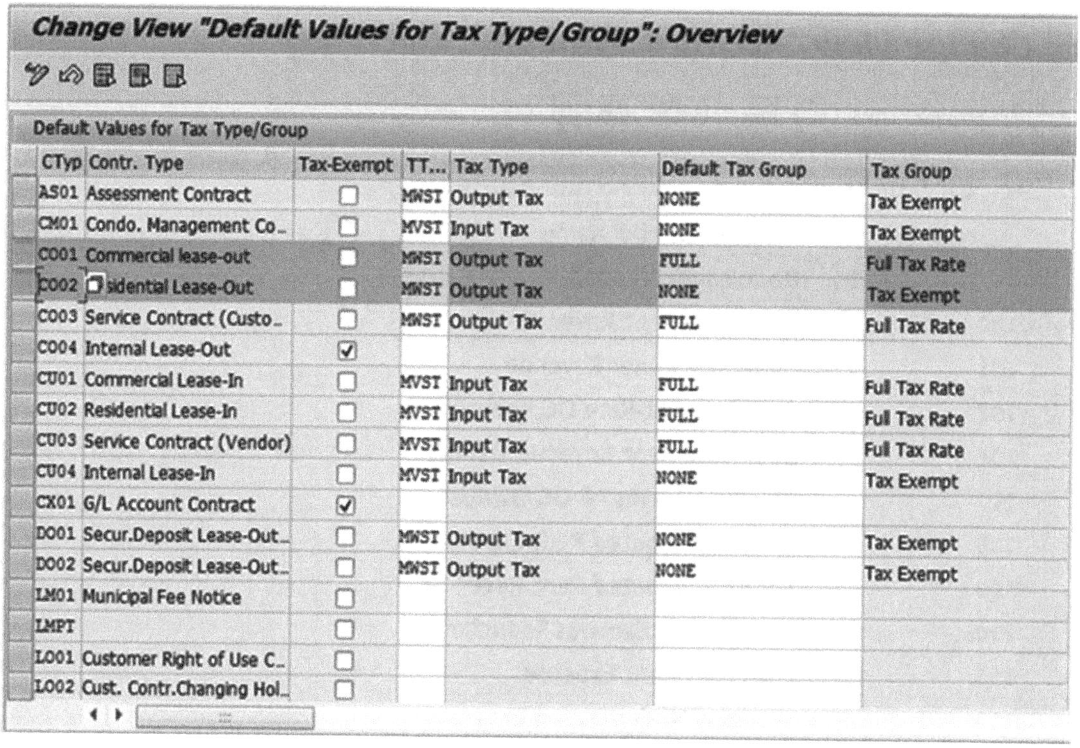

Change View "Default Values for Tax Type/Group": Overview

Default Values for Tax Type/Group

CTyp	Contr. Type	Tax-Exempt	TT...	Tax Type	Default Tax Group	Tax Group
AS01	Assessment Contract	☐	MWST	Output Tax	NONE	Tax Exempt
CM01	Condo. Management Co...	☐	MVST	Input Tax	NONE	Tax Exempt
CO01	Commercial lease-out	☐	MWST	Output Tax	FULL	Full Tax Rate
CO02	☐ sidential Lease-Out	☐	MWST	Output Tax	NONE	Tax Exempt
CO03	Service Contract (Custo...	☐	MWST	Output Tax	FULL	Full Tax Rate
CO04	Internal Lease-Out	☑				
CU01	Commercial Lease-In	☐	MVST	Input Tax	FULL	Full Tax Rate
CU02	Residential Lease-In	☐	MVST	Input Tax	FULL	Full Tax Rate
CU03	Service Contract (Vendor)	☐	MVST	Input Tax	FULL	Full Tax Rate
CU04	Internal Lease-In	☐	MVST	Input Tax	NONE	Tax Exempt
CX01	G/L Account Contract	☑				
DO01	Secur.Deposit Lease-Out...	☐	MWST	Output Tax	NONE	Tax Exempt
DO02	Secur.Deposit Lease-Out...	☐	MWST	Output Tax	NONE	Tax Exempt
LM01	Municipal Fee Notice	☐				
LMPT		☐				
LO01	Customer Right of Use C...	☐				
LO02	Cust. Contr.Changing Hol...	☐				

Figure 10-49. *Default values for tax rate per contract type*

Account Symbols

Here you will specify the account symbols (Figure 10-50).

Transaction Code

SPRO

Menu Path

IMG ➤ Flexible Real Estate Management (RE-FX) ➤ Accounting ➤ Automatically Generated Accounting Documents ➤ Account Determination ➤ Account Symbol

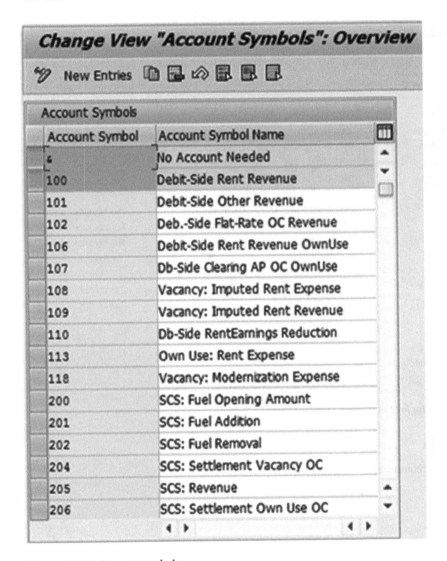

Figure 10-50. *Account symbols*

Assign Account Symbols to Flow Types

Here you will assign account symbols to flow types (Figure 10-51).

Transaction Code

SPRO

Menu Path

IMG ➤ Flexible Real Estate Management (RE-FX) ➤ Accounting ➤ Automatically Generated Accounting Documents ➤ Account Determination ➤ Assign Account Symbol to Flow Type

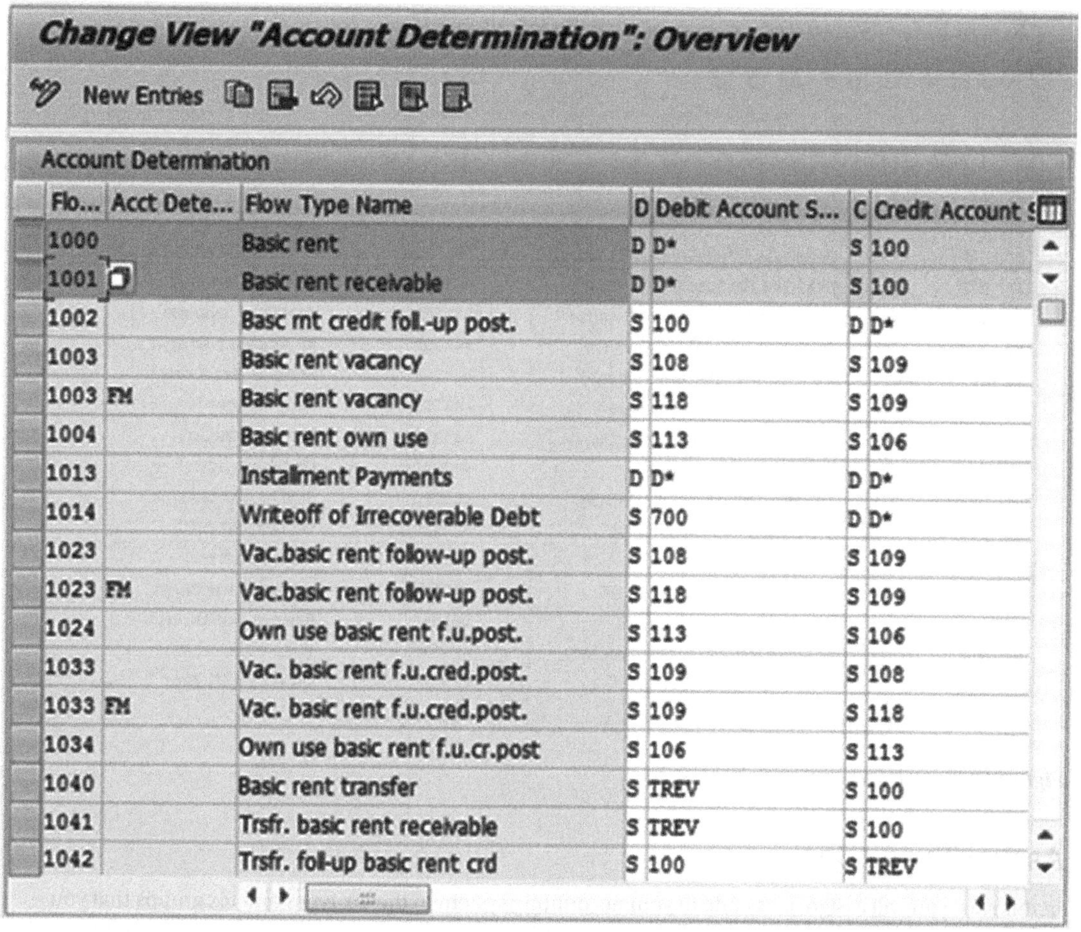

Flo...	Acct Dete...	Flow Type Name	D	Debit Account S...	C	Credit Account S
1000		Basic rent	D	D*	S	100
1001		Basic rent receivable	D	D*	S	100
1002		Basc rnt credit foll.-up post.	S	100	D	D*
1003		Basic rent vacancy	S	108	S	109
1003	FM	Basic rent vacancy	S	118	S	109
1004		Basic rent own use	S	113	S	106
1013		Installment Payments	D	D*	D	D*
1014		Writeoff of Irrecoverable Debt	S	700	D	D*
1023		Vac.basic rent follow-up post.	S	108	S	109
1023	FM	Vac.basic rent follow-up post.	S	118	S	109
1024		Own use basic rent f.u.post.	S	113	S	106
1033		Vac. basic rent f.u.cred.post.	S	109	S	108
1033	FM	Vac. basic rent f.u.cred.post.	S	109	S	118
1034		Own use basic rent f.u.cr.post	S	106	S	113
1040		Basic rent transfer	S	TREV	S	100
1041		Trsfr. basic rent receivable	S	TREV	S	100
1042		Trsfr. foll-up basic rent crd	S	100	S	TREV

Figure 10-51. *Assign account symbols to flow types*

Replace Account Symbol with GL Accounts

The account symbols specified in the Account Symbols IMG activity have to be replaced by GL Accounts in the accounting system, dependent on the chart of accounts (Figure 10-52). Account determination is then able to find these GL accounts.

Transaction Code

SPRO

Menu Path

IMG ➤ Flexible Real Estate Management (RE-FX) ➤ Accounting ➤ Integration FI-GL,FI-AR,FI-AP ➤ Account Determination ➤ Replace Account Symbol with GL Accounts

Change View "Substitute Account Symbols": Overview

⁇ New Entries ▢ ▢ ▢ ⌂ ▢ ▢ ▢

Substitute Account Symbols

Ch...	Account Symbol	Account Symbol Name	Spe...	G/L account	Short Text	AtAltFiscY
INT	ε	No Account Needed				
INT	100	Debit-Side Rent Revenue		841000	Rental rev. 3rd pty	
INT	01	Debit-Side Other Revenue		841050	Other rental rev.	
INT	102	Deb.-Side Flat-Rate OC Revenue		841070	Rev.flat rate o.cost	
INT	106	Debit-Side Rent Revenue OwnUse		841080	Rental rev. own use	
INT	107	Db-Side Clearing AP OC OwnUse		841099	RE Allocate prepymnt	
INT	108	Vacancy: Imputed Rent Expense		470700	Accrued vacancy rent	
INT	109	Vacancy: Imputed Rent Revenue		841700	Accd vac.rent rev.	
INT	110	Db-Side RentEarnings Reduction		888900	Rntl sales deduct.	
INT	113	Own Use: Rent Expense		470000	Occupancy costs	
INT	118	Vacancy: Modernization Expense		451000	Building maintenance	
INT	204	SCS: Settlement Vacancy OC		470520	RE Rent unit settl.	
INT	205	SCS: Revenue		841050	Other rental rev.	
INT	206	SCS: Settlement Own Use OC		470580	Settl.own use op.cst	
INT	207	SCS: Revenue Own Use OC		841580	Rev.own use OC sett.	
INT	208	SCS:Writeoff AP OC Own/Vacancy		470590	Write-off AP op.cost	
INT	209	SCS: Clearing AP Vacancy OC		470750	Clg vcy op.cst adv.p	

◄ ►

Figure 10-52. *GL account mapping*

Assign Tax Codes

In this step, you will assign a tax code in your accounting system to the tax types and tax groups that you defined in Flexible Real Estate Management (Figure 10-53). You define tax codes in Customizing for your accounting system.

The tax code is needed for calculating service tax. The tax code assignment is both country dependent and time dependent. The tax code is needed for calculating tax on sales and purchases.

Transaction Code

SPRO

Menu Path

IMG ➤ Flexible Real Estate Management (RE-FX) ➤ Accounting ➤ Integration FI-GL,FI-AR,FI-AP ➤ Taxes ➤ Assign Tax Codes

Change View "Tax Code Assignment": Overview

New Entries

Tax Code Assignment

C...	Ta...	Tax Group	Valid From	T.	Valid To
DE			01.01.1900		
DE	MVST	FULL	01.01.1900	V1	
DE	MVST	HALF	01.01.1900	V2	
DE	MVST	NONE	01.01.1900	V0	
DE	MWST	FULL	01.01.1900	A1	
DE	MWST	HALF	01.01.1900	A2	
DE	MWST	NONE	01.01.1900	A0	

Figure 10-53. *Assign tax codes*

Assign Tax Transaction Key

In this step you will assign a tax type to the tax transaction key (Figure 10-54). This assignment is both country dependent and time dependent. The tax transaction key specifies which tax account is posted to.

Transaction Code

SPRO

Menu Path

IMG ➤ Flexible Real Estate Management (RE-FX) ➤ Accounting ➤ Integration FI-GL,FI-AR,FI-AP ➤ Taxes ➤ Assign Tax Transaction

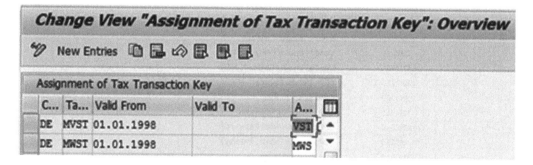

Change View "Assignment of Tax Transaction Key": Overview

New Entries

Assignment of Tax Transaction Key

C...	Ta...	Valid From	Valid To	A...
DE	MVST	01.01.1998		VST
DE	MWST	01.01.1998		MWS

Figure 10-54. *Assign tax transaction key*

Define Posting Activities

Using the one-time postings function, you can post documents in Financial Accounting (FI) with reference to data in Flexible Real Estate Management (REFX; Figure 10-55 and Figure 10-56).

The data entry screens for one-time postings are considerably simplified, as compared to the normal FI interface, and better adapted to the needs of real estate management.

You first enter the posting activity and the company code. Based on the settings made in Customizing for posting activities, the system constructs one or more documents that you can then add to (for example, by entering the invoice amount or the concrete real estate object).

Based on the customization settings you make for the posting activity, the system determines the following (among other information):

- How many documents are to be posted

- How many items the documents being posted have

- Default data for the document header and the line items (especially account symbols, bank details, account assignment objects, and percentage of total amount)

- If and how distribution should be made to objects of the contract

Transaction Code

SPRO

Menu Path

IMG ➤ Flexible Real Estate Management (RE-FX) ➤ Accounting ➤ One-Time Postings ➤ Define Posting Activities

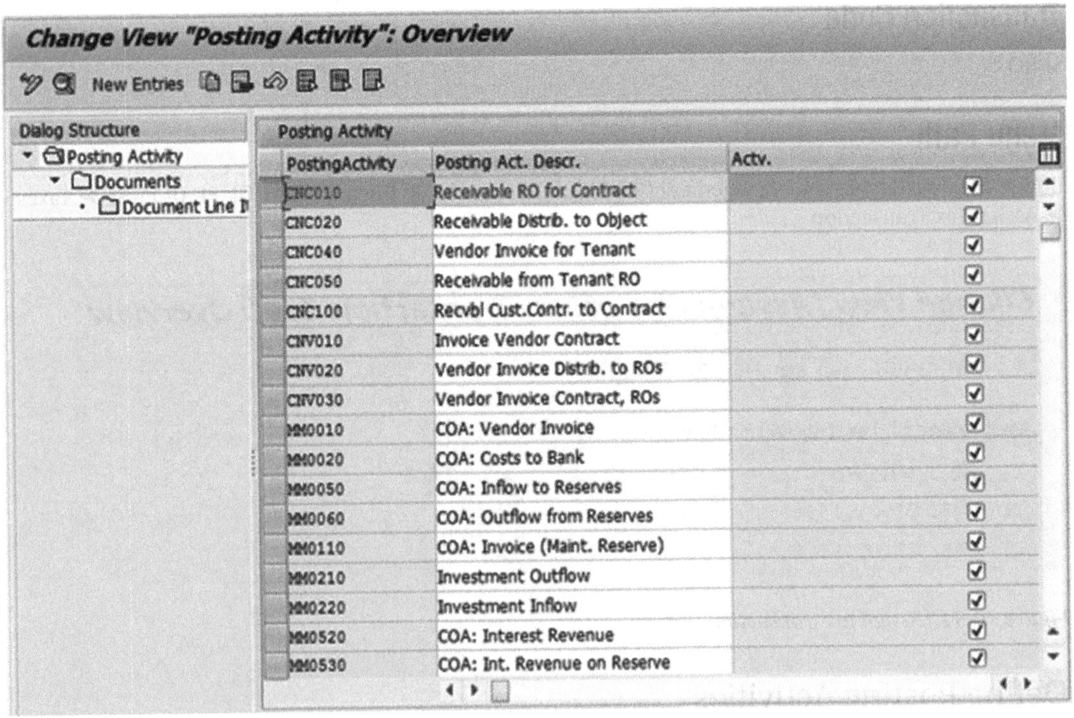

Figure 10-55. *Posting activities*

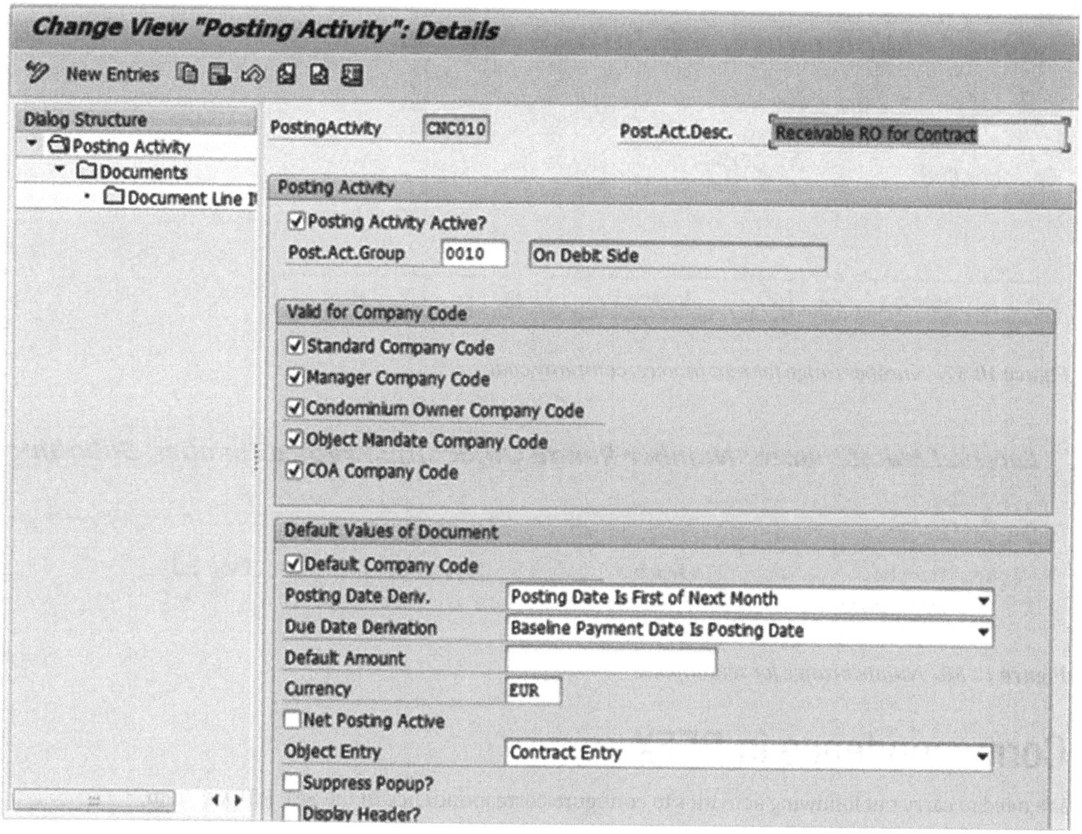

Figure 10-56. *Posting activities: Details*

Maintain Number Range for Rent Invoice

Here, you will specify the number range interval to be used for the invoice number.

Define at least one number range interval for each company code (Figure 10-57) in which invoices are printed, and for each fiscal year for which you want to print invoices (Figure 10-58). If this interval already has the number "01", you do not need to create any number range settings in the IMG activity Company Code-Dependent Settings for Invoice.

Choose "Internal Number Assignment" for all intervals.

Transaction Code

SPRO

Menu Path

IMG ➤ Flexible Real Estate Management (RE-FX) ➤ Accounting ➤ Rent Invoice ➤ Number Range for Rent Invoice

Range Maintenance: RE: Invoice Number
Change documents
Company Code
0001
Intervals
Intervals
NR Status

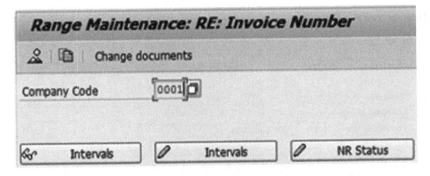

Figure 10-57. *Number range for rent invoice, company code*

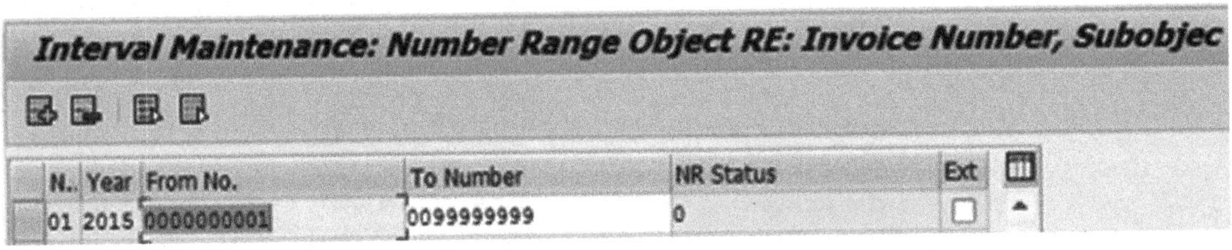

Interval Maintenance: Number Range Object RE: Invoice Number, Subobjec
N..
Year
From No.
To Number
NR Status
Ext
01
2015
0000000001
0099999999
0

Figure 10-58. *Number range for rent invoice*

Correspondence in REFX

We need to carry out following activities to configure correspondence in the SAP REFX system.

Define Forms

In this activity, you will specify the forms you want to use for correspondence activities (Figure 10-59).

Define the forms you need and assign a form object to them (PDF-based form or smart form). We usually use smart forms for generating output forms.

Transaction Code

SPRO

Menu Path

IMG ➤ Flexible Real Estate Management (RE-FX) ➤ Correspondence ➤ PDF-Based Forms (Mass Print and Single Print) ➤ Forms ➤ Define Forms

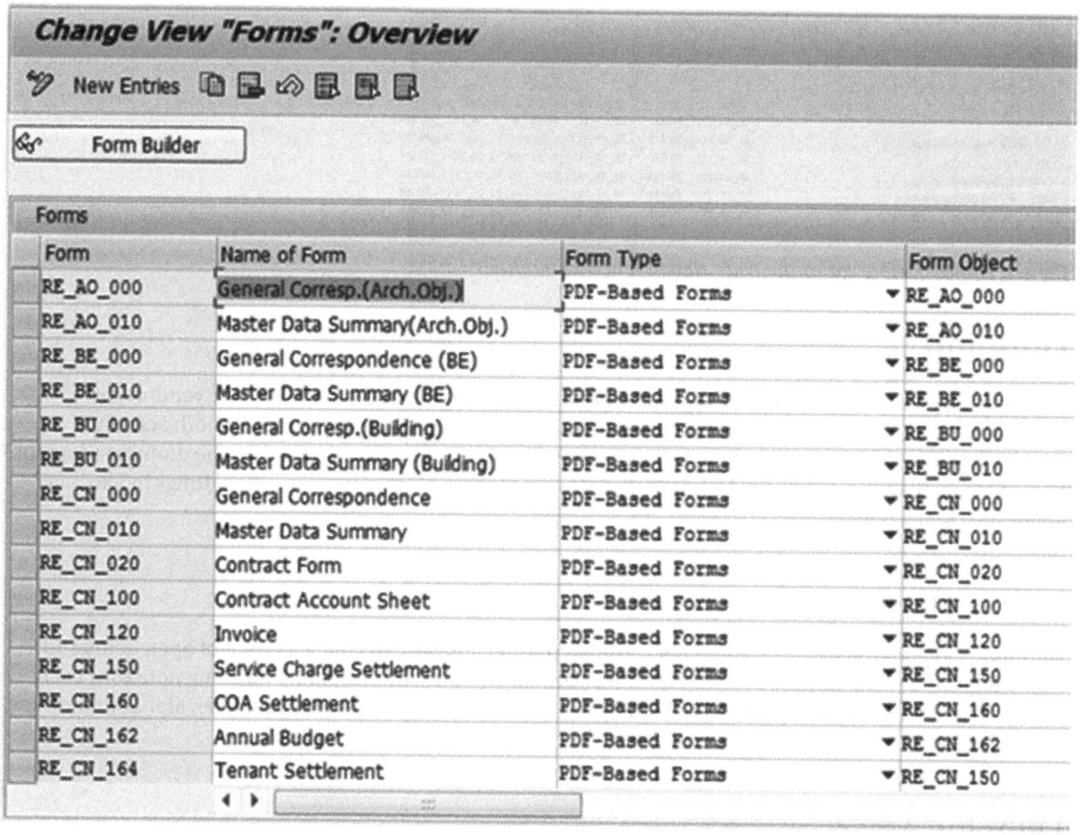

Change View "Forms": Overview

🖉 New Entries 📋 🖫 ⚙ 🖳 🖳 🖳

🖉   Form Builder

Forms

Form	Name of Form	Form Type	Form Object
RE_AO_000	General Corresp.(Arch.Obj.)	PDF-Based Forms	▼ RE_AO_000
RE_AO_010	Master Data Summary(Arch.Obj.)	PDF-Based Forms	▼ RE_AO_010
RE_BE_000	General Correspondence (BE)	PDF-Based Forms	▼ RE_BE_000
RE_BE_010	Master Data Summary (BE)	PDF-Based Forms	▼ RE_BE_010
RE_BU_000	General Corresp.(Building)	PDF-Based Forms	▼ RE_BU_000
RE_BU_010	Master Data Summary (Building)	PDF-Based Forms	▼ RE_BU_010
RE_CN_000	General Correspondence	PDF-Based Forms	▼ RE_CN_000
RE_CN_010	Master Data Summary	PDF-Based Forms	▼ RE_CN_010
RE_CN_020	Contract Form	PDF-Based Forms	▼ RE_CN_020
RE_CN_100	Contract Account Sheet	PDF-Based Forms	▼ RE_CN_100
RE_CN_120	Invoice	PDF-Based Forms	▼ RE_CN_120
RE_CN_150	Service Charge Settlement	PDF-Based Forms	▼ RE_CN_150
RE_CN_160	COA Settlement	PDF-Based Forms	▼ RE_CN_160
RE_CN_162	Annual Budget	PDF-Based Forms	▼ RE_CN_162
RE_CN_164	Tenant Settlement	PDF-Based Forms	▼ RE_CN_150

Figure 10-59.   *Define forms*

Define Company-Code-Dependent Text Modules

In this activity, you will define company-code-dependent text modules (Figure 10-60).

Transaction Code

SPRO

Menu Path

IMG ➤ Flexible Real Estate Management (RE-FX) ➤ Correspondence ➤ PDF-Based Forms (Mass Print and Single Print) ➤ Forms ➤ Define Company-Code-Dependent Text Modules

Change View "Company-Code-Dependent Text Modules": Overview

New Entries

Company-Code-Dependent Text Modules

Co...	Company Name	Header	Footer	Signature	Sender	Further Text 1	Further Text 2	Further Text 3
			RE_CA_TEXT_FOOTER	RE_CA_TEXT_SIGNATURE	RE_CA_TEXT_SENDER			
0001	Puna Multinational Retail		RE_CA_TEXT_FOOTER	RE_CA_TEXT_SIGNATURE	RE_CA_TEXT_SENDER			
MC01	MC01		RE_CA_TEXT_FOOTER	RE_CA_TEXT_SIGNATURE	RE_CA_TEXT_SENDER			
RECO	Sondereigentum (WEG)		RE_CA_TEXT_FOOTER	RE_CA_TEXT_SIGNATURE	RE_CA_TEXT_SENDER			
RECB	Referenz Objektmandate		RE_CA_TEXT_FOOTER	RE_CA_TEXT_SIGNATURE	RE_CA_TEXT_SENDER			
RERF	WEG Referenzbuchungskreis		RE_CA_TEXT_FOOTER	RE_CA_TEXT_SIGNATURE	RE_CA_TEXT_SENDER			

Figure 10-60. Define company-code-dependent text modules

Dunning

Dunning is a process that enables reminder communications to be sent to customers or vendors for outstanding invoices, requesting a payment to be made. Dunning programs are set for both accounts receivable and accounts payable. The dunning procedure for the contract is based on the dunning program of the Financial Accounting module, but we can use it by creating real estate–specific settings in Flexible Real Estate Management.

Define Dunning Groupings

Dunning notices are generally created per business partner, but we can create a group of open items and dun this group to send notices covering the entire group. We can send a separate dunning notice for each rental object to the business partner by defining a grouping key, which is a two-character, alphanumeric key, with the contract number field.

Dunning Areas

Dunning area means the client or company code or sales organization or business area in which we are working on the dunning program (Figure 10-61). Dunning areas are used when more than one organizational unit in a company code is responsible for dunning. We have the option of dunning it at the organization level, like the sales organization, or business area and may not be necessarily be running it at the company-code level. We can specify all dunning areas that we want to consider in REFX. However, the use of a dunning area is optional.

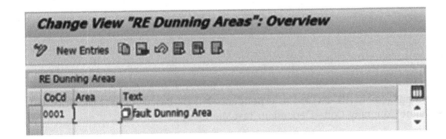

Change View "RE Dunning Areas": Overview

New Entries

RE Dunning Areas

CoCd	Area	Text
0001		Default Dunning Area

Figure 10-61. Dunning areas

Assign Application/Role Category/Dunning Parameter

In this activity, we will specify which additional business partners should be sent dunning notices. We can assign a role category to an application category of a business partner, and we can mention if the role is the dunning recipient, alternative dunning recipient, or not a dunning recipient.

As required, complete and review the following fields, as shown in Table 10-3 and Figure 10-62.

Table 10-3. *Assign Application/Role Category/Dunning Parameter*

Application Category	Role Category	Indicator	Dunning Level
Lease-Out	Master tenant with customer	Dunning recipient	

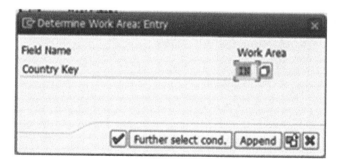

Figure 10-62. *Dunning parameter per BP roles*

Determine Dunnable Payment Methods

We have to determine which incoming payment methods can be dunned and define any payment methods as dunnable if we want them to be dunned in Flexible Real Estate Management (Figure 10-63 and Figure 10-64).

Figure 10-63. *Dunning payment method: Determine Work Area: Entry screen*

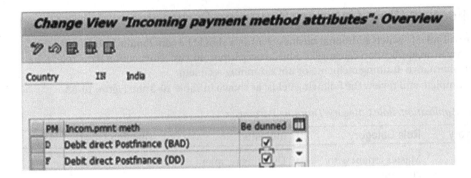

Figure 10-64. *Dunning payment method*

Summary

In this chapter we have seen how REFX standard configuration needs to be carried out with a step-by-step guide. This reviewed basic settings, business partners, master data, contracts, and accounting functions in detail.

Index

Get the eBook for only $5!

Why limit yourself?

Now you can take the weightless companion with you wherever you go and access your content on your PC, phone, tablet, or reader.

Since you've purchased this print book, we're happy to offer you the eBook in all 3 formats for just $5.

Convenient and fully searchable, the PDF version enables you to easily find and copy code—or perform examples by quickly toggling between instructions and applications. The MOBI format is ideal for your Kindle, while the ePUB can be utilized on a variety of mobile devices.

To learn more, go to www.apress.com/companion or contact support@apress.com.

Printed in the United States
By Bookmasters